Twayne's English Authors Series

EDITOR OF THIS VOLUME

Sylvia E. Bowman

Indiana University

George Bernard Shaw

TEAS 236

George Bernard Shaw

GEORGE BERNARD SHAW

By ELDON C. HILL

Miami University

TWAYNE PUBLISHERS

A DIVISION OF G. K. HALL & CO., BOSTON

Library of Congress Cataloging in Publication Data

Hill, Eldon Cleon, 1906 -
George Bernard Shaw.

(Twayne's English authors series ; TEAS 236)
Bibliography: p. 165 - 78
Includes index.
1. Shaw, George Bernard, 1856 - 1950—Criticism and inter-
pretation.
PR5367.H5   1978   822'.9'12   77-26133
ISBN 0-8057-6709-6

For Garland, Sean, and Sara

Contents

About the Author

A graduate of DePauw University, Dr. Eldon C. Hill received his M.A. degree from the University of Wisconsin, and his Ph.D. from the Ohio State University. He has taught at Ohio Wesleyan University, Lake Forest College, and Miami University. He has published articles in encyclopedias and professional journals, including *American Literature* and *Modern Drama*, and has served as book critic on the *Indianapolis News* and the *Capital Times*, Madison, Wisconsin.

More than twenty years of teaching both undergraduate and graduate courses that emphasized Shaw's plays and nonfictional works have helped prepare Dr. Hill for the writing of this book. He has done extensive research in libraries, including the New York Public Library Berg Collection, the Yale and Harvard libraries, the University of North Carolina Henderson Collection, and the British Museum, the chief depository of original Shaw mannuscripts, notebooks, and letters. A highlight of his studies at Chapel Hill was the privilege of several conversations with the late Dr. Archibald Henderson, whom Shaw once designated as his "Biographer-in-Chief."

Preface

This survey and critical study is for the reader who seeks an understanding of Bernard Shaw's life and work. It is not for Shaw specialists, of whom there are an astounding and growing number in the United States, Britain, and other parts of the world. Library shelves are bulging with books and articles written by these specialists year after year. Many of their writings are excellent and illuminating; but others, the works of scholars for scholars, to the general reader are likely to be cumbersome and dull. Some of the best of the new or comparatively recent books are compilations of Shaw's own writings that have been rescued from dusty repositories.

Indeed, no other modern literary figure has written so much or has had so much written about him. Shaw himself asserted, half jokingly, that he had fifteen reputations—"a critic of art, a critic of music, a critic of literature, a critic of the drama, a novelist, a dramatist, an economist, a funny man, a street-corner agitator, a Shelleyan atheist, a Fabian Socialist, a vegetarian, a humanitarian, a preacher, and a philosopher."[1] He might have added "letter-writer," for, in sheer numbers alone, Shaw is probably the greatest epistolary correspondent the world has known. When an American publisher proposed an edition of his collected letters in 1949, Shaw replied with characteristic exaggeration: "Put it out of your head. There are billions of them, and I am adding to them every day." Dan H. Laurence, the authoritative editor of the first two volumes of the correspondence, declares that Shaw, "by conservative estimate," wrote a quarter of a million letters and postcards ("squeezing as many as two hundred cramped but completely legible words on a single card!") in his lifetime.[2]

In addition to the large volumes of letters and the drama and fiction, Shaw wrote a great mass of autobiography, self-criticism, and socioeconomic nonfiction. All in all, Stanley Weintraub, the distinguished scholar and editor of *The Shaw Review*, is undoubtedly correct in terming Shaw "one of the most documented and recorded of human beings."[3]

Moreover, the Niagara of Shaw's purely creative work is unequaled among major dramatists of the past centuries; and, in fiction, he produced five novels and part of another besides a number of short stories. For the theatre, he wrote more than fifty plays—approximately half again more than Shakespeare. To deal with all these works would take us far beyond the limit of this survey and study; judicious selection, therefore, has been my rule in the pages that follow. To show the development of his plays, I have chosen to write about them in the order of their production rather than to present them in purely expository form in essays such as "Shaw on Religion," "Shaw on War and Peace," "Shaw and Socialism," and the like. To follow my narrative thread makes, I trust, for greater readability.

Necessarily, I shall devote attention to the more important dramas of what might be called the Shaw Canon. I shall deal with his novels and early plays mainly for the part they had in his long apprenticeship. I shall concentrate on his major plays for the light they shed on his chief message to the world, his almost incessant preachment in favor of social justice and in opposition to war and all other forms of violence.

From first to last, this message has a deep religious basis, but his style in conveying it is never too solemn or soporific. On the whole, his work has a remarkable relevance to the issues of our day. Anyone interested, for instance, in women's liberation or in the younger generation's revolt or in the never-ending human struggle for peace will find in Shaw an effective advocate. Accordingly, we shall be concerned chiefly with the living ideas in the living drama of Shaw.

The Selected Bibliography lists most of the leading authorities in the field and gives up-to-date information on the subject. The "Correspondence" section is the fullest to be published to date, and the list of Special Bibliographies from the *Shaw Review* and *Modern Drama* are here presented for the first time in book form.

"Knowledge," said Dr. Samuel Johnson, "is of two kinds. We know a subject ourselves, or we know where we can find information upon it." I trust that this book will add to the reader's knowledge and that the extensive bibliography and annotations will help him to find his way through the vast, complex, and fascinating world of Bernard Shaw.

ELDON C. HILL

Miami University
Oxford, Ohio

Acknowledgments

To the Society of Authors, representatives of the Shaw Estate, I am indebted for permission to examine original materials in the British Museum and especially for permission to quote passages from Shaw's writings to illustrate critical points and to illuminate the dramatist, the man, and the thinker. To the writers and publishers of all publications mentioned in the Notes and References I am also grateful.

I wish to thank Miami University for giving me a semester's leave of absence in which to work on this book. To Stanley Weintraub, Dan H. Laurence, Louis Crompton, and the late Archibald Henderson and his wife, Lucile Kelling Henderson, I owe much, not only for permission to quote from their works about Shaw, but also for their words of encouragement in the present survey and study. I am especially obliged to Dr. Sylvia E. Bowman, whose expert editing has greatly enhanced this book. I also thank Walter Havighurst for his heartening interest and helpful suggestions.

Many librarians have been courteous to me and generous with their time. Though I cannot name them all, I should make special salutes to Leland Dutton, Mary Stanton, Peter Flinterman, William Wortman, Mickey Sparkman, and Sarah Barr of the Miami University Library staff. To Helen Adamson and Regina D'Addabbo, typists whose skill is matched only by their graciousness, I express heartfelt thanks. Finally, I owe much to my wife, Mary, for helping in more ways than I could enumerate.

Chronology

1856   George Bernard Shaw born in Dublin, July 26, the only son and third child of George Carr Shaw and Lucinda Elizabeth Shaw.

1867 - Attends the Wesleyan Connexional School, Dublin.
1868

1869   After brief period at a private school, enters Central Model Boys School, Dublin, in February and continues in it till September.

1871   Becomes clerk in Land Agency office.

1875   Writes a letter to the editor of *Public Opinion* protesting against a Moody-Sankey evangelistic revival in Dublin—his debut in print.

1876   Leaves Ireland in March for London, his mother having preceded him there four years earlier.

1879   Joins firm in London arranging for the installation of Edison telephones.

1879 - Writes five unsuccessful novels, to wit: *Immaturity, The*
1883   *Irrational Knot, Love Among the Aritsts, Cashel Byron's Profession,* and *The Unsocial Socialist.*

1882   Hears Henry George, the American Single Tax advocate, lecture in London; an experience, Shaw said, that changed the whole course of his life. Shortly thereafter he reads Karl Marx's *Das Kapital,* which also turns his mind toward economics.

1884   Helps organize the Fabian Socialist Society.

1885   Does book reviews for the *Pall Mall Gazette.* Also begins to write regularly on art for *The World.*

1888 - Writes music criticism for *The Star.*
1890

1889   Edits *Fabian Essays,* to which he contributed the "Economic Basis of Socialism" and "Transition to Social Democracy."

1890   Serves as music critic for *The World* till 1894. Lectures on Henrik Ibsen before the Fabian Society.

1891   *The Quintessence of Ibsenism.*

1892   *Widower's Houses,* his first play.

1893   *The Philanderer* and *Mrs. Warren's Profession.*

1894   Starts writing dramatic criticism for *Saturday Review,* Frank Harris's journal. Writes *Arms and the Man* and *Candida.*

1895   *The Man of Destiny* and *The Sanity of Art.*

1896   *You Never Can Tell* and *The Devil's Disciple.*

1897   Elected to St. Pancras Vestry.

1898   Marries Charlotte Payne-Townshend, a wealthy Irish heiress and fellow Fabian. *Caesar and Cleopatra* and *The Perfect Wagnerite. Plays Pleasant and Unpleasant* published in two volumes, containing his first seven plays.

1899   *Captain Brassbound's Conversion.*

1900   *Fabianism and the Empire, A Manifesto of the Fabian Society.*

1901   *The Admirable Bashville* and *Plays for Puritans.*

1903   *Man and Superman* completed.

1904   *John Bull's Other Island. How He Lied to Her Husband.* Runs as Progressive candidate for London County Council; defeated.

1905   *Major Barbara* and *Passion, Poison, and Petrifaction.*

1906   *The Doctor's Dilemma.* The Shaws move to country house in Ayot St. Lawrence, Hertfordshire; it later comes to be known as "Shaw's Corner," their home for the rest of their lives.

1908   *Getting Married. The Sanity of Art.*

1909   *The Shewing-Up of Blanco Posnet. Press Cuttings.* Presents evidence to Parliamentary Committee on the licensing of plays.

1910   *Misalliance. The Dark Lady of the Sonnets.*

1911   *Fanny's First Play.* Elected to Academic Committee, the Royal Society of Literature.

1912   *Androcles and the Lion* cmpleted; *Overruled* produced.

1913   *Pygmalion. Great Catherine. Heartbreak House* written, but not produced. Shaw's mother dies.

1914   "An Open Letter to President Wilson," published in *The Nation* (London) in November. *Common Sense About the War.*

1915   *O'Flaherty, V.C.,* " a recruiting pamphlet."

1916   *The Inca of Perusalem. Augustus Does His Bit.*

1917   *Annajanska, The Bolshevik Empress* (Also entitled *Annajanska, The Wild Grand Duchess.*) *How to Settle the Irish Question.* Visits Western Front as guest of British army.

1919   *Peace Conference Hints.*

1920   Completes *Back to Methuselah*, his longest play. *Heartbreak House* first produced, the Theatre Guild, New York.

1922   *Jitta's Atonement* (a translation of Siegfried Trebitsch's *Frau Gitta's Suhe* into English). *Back to Methuselah.*

1923   *St. Joan.*

1925   Awarded the Nobel Prize for Literature.

1928   *The Intelligent Woman's Guide to Socialism and Capitalism.*

1929   *The Apple Cart* completed in six weeks; staged in August at the first Malvern Festival for the production of Shaw's plays.

1931   *Too True to be Good.* Visits Russia; interviews Marshal Stalin.

1932   The Shaws sail on *The Empress of Britain* for a voyage around the world.

1933   Stops briefly in California, Florida, and New York in April; his first and only visit to America. Lectures at the Metropolitan Opera House on "The Future of Political Science in the United States." *A Village Wooing. On the Rocks.*

1934   *The Simpleton of the Unexpected Isles. The Six of Calais.*

1935   *The Millionairess.*

1937   *Cymbeline Refinished.* (Shaw's revision of Shakespeare).

1938   *Geneva* produced at Malvern.

1939   *In Good King Charles's Golden Days.*

1943   Death of Mrs. Shaw in London, September 12, at eighty-six.

1944   *Everybody's Political What's What?*

1948   *Buoyant Billions.*

1949   *Shakes Versus Shav. Sixteen Self Sketches.*

1950   Shaw Society of America founded on his birthday, July 26. *Farfetched Fables. Why She Would Not.* Shaw dies at Ayot St. Lawrence, November 2, at the age of ninety-four. His ashes mingled with Charlotte's and scattered in their garden.

CHAPTER 1

Backgrounds and Foregrounds

I G. B. S. and Bernard Shaw

THE first problem that confronts anyone who writes of Shaw is that of his dual identity—Bernard Shaw and G. B. S., his familiar alter ego or persona. Shaw once wrote, "The celebrated G.B.S. is about as real as a pantomime ostrich."[1] Again when asked to state his honest opinion of G.B.S., Shaw replied: "Oh, one of the most successful of my fictions but getting a bit tiresome, I should think. G.B.S. bores me except when he is saying something that needs saying and can best be said in the G.B.S. manner. G.B.S. is a humbug."[2] In fact, Shaw declared that "The critics were the victims of the long course of hypnotic suggestion by which G.B.S. the journalist manufactured an unconventional reputation for Bernard Shaw the author."

He then explained why he used his self-created publicity agent: "In England as elsewhere the spontaneous recognition of really original work begins with a mere handful of people, and propagates itself so slowly that it has become a commonplace to say that genius, demanding bread, is given a stone after its possessor's death. The remedy for this is sedulous advertisement. Accordingly, I have advertised myself, whilst still in middle life, [he was forty-four] almost as legendary a person as the Flying Dutchman."[3] What the real Shaw was like he spent hundreds of pages trying to explain; but, for the moment, his statement to Arthur Bingham Walkley will serve: "You must take me as I am, a reasonable, patient, consistent, apologetic, laborious person, with the temperament of a schoolmaster and the pursuits of a vestryman. No doubt that literary knack of mine which happens to amuse the British public distracts attention from my character; but the character is there none the less, solid as bricks."[4] The student of Shaw must be ever alert to determine whether the G.B.S. or the real side of him is speaking in a particular context. For example, in "The Revolutionist's Handbook" in *Man and Superman* John Tanner says, "He who can, does. He who cannot, teaches."

This oft-quoted slur on a profession many readers attributed to Shaw—not to Tanner. Confronted with this statement, Shaw added in his unmistakable handwriting: "What is more they are the only available teachers, because those who can are mostly quite incapable of teaching, even if they had time for it."[5] As this incident indicates, Shaw's meaning is often misconstrued through the practice of ascribing to the author the opinions of his characters. This form of literary fallacy causes not only Shaw but also many other writers to be misrepresented before the world. Shaw's prefaces to his plays and his voluminous nonfiction writings that set forth his opinions make misunderstanding less excusable.

Still another difficulty which Shaw presents to whoever would understand him lies in the immense range of his knowledge. What Robert G. Ingersoll said of Shakespeare applies equally well to Shaw: he "was an intellectual ocean, and the waves of his mind touched all the shores of thought."[6] Art, music, history, religion, philosophy, political thought, and, to a limited extent, science were fields which Shaw explored during his long career. Curiosity was one of the chief traits of his personality; nothing human was alien to him. In 1944 Shaw wrote: "I am in my eighty-eighth year and have still much to learn even within my own very limited capacity."[7] He did not cease hungering and thirsting after knowledge until he was near death.

II   *Early Life and Schooling*

Shaw was born July 26, 1856, at No. 3, later renumbered 33, Synge Street, Dublin. He was the youngest child and only son of George Carr Shaw and Lucinda Gurly Shaw; for the other two children were sisters whose names were Lucinda Frances Carr and Elinor Agnes (familiarly they were Lucy and Agnes). Archibald Henderson's thoroughgoing study of the genealogy led him to comment: "The Shaws in Ireland were an excellent upper-middle-class family. They were gentry with small estates, agriculturists, lawyers, sportsmen, living pleasantly and in comparatively easy circumstances. For two centuries prior to George Bernard Shaw's birth there emerged no conspicuously eminent figures." There was a legend in the family which led G.B.S. to boast: "But I go back to

Shaigh, the third son of Shakespear's [sic] Macduff. Hence my talent for playwrighting."[8] Soberly considered, nothing in Shaw's paternal ancestry helps to explain his genius; and, on the maternal side, even a lesser claim to distinguished blood or social rank existed, though his mother came of good yeoman stock.

George Carr Shaw was unsuccessful as a breadwinner and as a father. Through most of his adult life he was an alcoholic, a fact that deeply affected his son, who wrote with mixed amusement and sadness of his father's weakness. "If you cannot get rid of the family skeleton," said the son, "you may as well make it dance."[9] The chief inheritance of Bernard Shaw from his unfortunate father was a sense of humor that had a strong tinge of irony,[10] but his father's pitiable plight helped to make his son a lifelong teetotaler.

The entire Shaw family was musical; every member could play an instrument; even George Carr Shaw could perform on the trombone between drinks. Inspired by his mother, Bernard acquired before the age of fifteen, according to his testimony, a sound education in Handel, Mozart, Beethoven, Mendelssohn, Rossini, Donizetti, Verdi, and Gounod. This knowledge was the basis of a passion for music which, besides later affording him a livelihood as a music critic in London, deeply affected his work as a dramatist.[11]

Lucinda Gurly Shaw was a singer with a mezzo-soprano voice. This talent, coupled with the giving of private lessons, made it possible for her to become the financial mainstay of the family. She formed a strange relationship with a voice teacher named George John Vandaleur Lee, who became a part of the Shaw *ménage* and left his mark on Bernard, who insisted that Lee was "in his way" a musical genius.[12] Recalling in 1949 how Lee disparaged his professional rivals as "voice wreckers," Shaw added that "He extended this criticism to doctors, and amazed us by eating brown bread instead of white, and sleeping with the window open, both of which habits I acquired and have practised ever since."[13] Suspicion of physicians and the adoption of health fads were not the only things Shaw acquired from Lee, for he also acquired part of his knowledge of music from his mother's teacher, friend, and associate.

The Shaws' social life, because of the father's drinking habits, became practically nonexistent. "After my early childhood," Bernard recalled, "I cannot remember ever paying a visit to a relative's house. If my father and mother had dined out, or gone to a party, their children would have been much more astonished than if the house had caught fire."[14] About this permissive home Shaw observed: "My parents took no moral responsibility for me. I was just something that happened to them and had to be put up with and supported." He could not recall a word of ethical or religious instruction from his mother, and his father only pointed to his own vices and warned the son against imitating them. On the whole, Bernard Shaw felt that his undisciplined upbringing was a fortunate preparation for his free, self-reliant career.[15]

His formal schooling was sketchy, haphazard, and brief. After such private instruction as the family could afford, Shaw in 1867 entered the Wesleyan Connexional School in Dublin, a university preparatory institution which was later called Wesley College, though it did not offer higher learning in the American sense. He remained in this school only a little more than a year, until the summer of 1868. He hated the place, a fact which may explain why he "seems to have been generally near or at the bottom of his classes."[16] After another siege of private instruction, he was next sent to the Central Model Boys School in Marlborough Street, mainly because the fees were low. Parents who could afford it sent five shillings to the school periodically. Ostensibly, this institution was "undenominational and classless," but it was actually supported and conducted by Roman Catholics.

Under the heading "Shame and Wounded Snobbery" Shaw wrote of the Central Model Boys School experience as one of the most traumatic of his life: it was to him what the blacking warehouse was to Dickens.[17] What Shaw calls his "snob tragedy" began with his memory of the school and its grounds: "It was an enormous place, with huge unscaleable railings and gates on which for me might have been inscribed 'All hope abandon, ye who enter here'; for that the son of a Protestant merchant-gentleman and feudal downstart should pass those bars or associate in any way with its hosts of lower middle class Catholic children, sons of petty shopkeepers and tradesmen, was inconceivable from the Shaw point of view."[18] Although Shaw was only in his thirteenth year at the time—an impressionable age—while within the railings of the Model School he snubbed his fellows: "There I was a superior being, and in play hour did not play, but walked up and down with the teachers in their promenade." Outside, he was shunned by the Protestant young gentlemen of his acquaintance. The significance of this experience is that it gave him a permanent, poignant sense of the inequalities in human society.

When his father supported him in his refusal to return to Marlborough Street, Shaw was, as he put it, "duly restored to genteel Protestantism" in the Dublin English Scientific and Commercial Day School, conducted by the Incorporated Society for Promoting Protestant School in Ireland. Shaw referred to it as his "last school prison,"[19] for he later became one of its most famous drop-outs. Quitting school, however, did not end Shaw's education; it began the long road to his becoming one of the most learned men of his day. He could not remember a time when he could not read; and, recalling his boyhood and youth, he said: "Unwittingly I developed a sixth sense of appreciation of great books, such as the Bible, Shakespear, Bunyan, and Dickens, which were full of stories, pulsing exciting incidents, always dratatically told."[20] The King James Version of the Scriptures and these three authors influenced Shaw deeply both in his style and in his subject-matter.

In 1871, Shaw became at the age of fifteen a junior clerk in the real-estate office of C. Uniacke Townshend and Company. He filled the post so well that he was promoted to the position of cashier after a year's service. Though he remained in the office four and a half years, he for the most part hated it; he valued only the opportunity it afforded him to associate with university men who could talk with him—or, better, listen to him—about opera and other cultural topics.[21] Meanwhile, Vandeleur Lee, feeling that he had exhausted his possibilities for fame as a musician in Dublin, decided to try his fortune in London. Not long after Lee had departed for London, Lucinda Gurly Shaw with her two daughters followed him in the spring of 1873, leaving her son and erring husband behind."[22] Bernard and his father shared quarters in Dublin, though they did not see much of each other. The young clerk-cashier continued at his desk till 1876, when he too decided to seek opportunities in London.

Looking back on his years in Dublin, he could not recall them as pleasant, except for his memories of music and literature. To an elderly former neighbor Shaw wrote late in life that, except for his secret self, he was not happy in Dublin, "and when ghosts rise up from that period I want to lay them again with a poker."[23] But one joy he could not forget: the removal of the family when he was ten to Torca Cottage, "high on Dalkey Hill, commanding views of Dublin Bay from Dalkey Island to Howth Head and of Killiney Bay from the island to Bray Head, with a vast and ever-changing expanse of sea and sky." As Shaw reminisced at ninety-one, "I had only to open my eyes there to see such pictures as no painter could make for me. I could not believe such skies existed anywhere else in the world until I read Shakespear's 'This majestical roof fretted with golden fire,' and wondered where he could have seen it if not from Torca Cottage.

"The joy of it has remained with me all my life."[24]

III *Apprenticeship in London*

In the early spring of 1876 Bernard joined his mother and his sister Lucy at No. 13 Victoria Grove, now called Netherton Gardens, London. Shortly before his arrival, the younger sister, Elinor Agnes, had died on the Isle of Wight, a victim of tuberculosis. Only twenty years of age, she had been, according to Shaw, her mother's favorite, though she was the least musical of the family.[25] Whether or not Lucy Gurly Shaw welcomed her son into the household we cannot be sure, for she did not carry her feelings on her sleeve. Some of Shaw's biographers and G.B.S. himself have contributed to what I believe to be the myth of Shaw's parasitism, for the truth probably is that he was no great financial burden to his mother. He ate sparingly, and his clothes were neither fashionable nor expensive since he wore the same suit years on end.

Furthermore, the family, though never affluent, had a few sources of income. Mrs. Shaw took charge of an inheritance of four thousand pounds from her grandfather Gurly, to which her son held partial claim; also she continued to earn money as an assistant to Vandeleur Lee and as an independent music teacher. Out of his meager earnings Shaw's father contributed a pound a week till his death. Bernard, who may have brought to London some savings from his four and a half years of work in the Dublin real-estate office, earned a small amount of money occasionally as an accompanist on the piano; and his elder sister Lucy received remuneration as a singer while under the tutelage of her mother, who had decided to go to London partly to prepare her talented daughter for a career in opera. Lucy, like her mother a mezzo-soprano, did not reach the heights; but for a number of years she achieved professional status as a singer. Bernard himself took many voice lessons from his mother; and, though he was never to sing in public for pay, the training was beneficial to him as a public speaker.[26]

In 1879 Shaw joined a London firm that sold and installed telephones manufactured by the Edison Company. He did not remain long in this employment, for he came to the conclusion that, as a genius, he had to prepare himself for the profession of authorship.[27] This apprenticeship would demand all his brain power, all his time. Since he had to continue his self-education, the reading room of the British Museum became his university.

One September evening in 1882 Shaw heard by chance the American orator, economist, and reformer Henry George speak on the Land Question; and this experience changed Shaw's life. Before leaving the meeting, he bought from one of the stewards a copy of *Progress and Poverty*, the book which made Henry George famous on both sides of the Atlantic.[28] In it George sets forth his doctrine of the Single Tax, a proposal that governments impose only one assessment on the people, a levy on the value of the land. With such a tax, society could eliminate poverty, which was the result, as George believed, of too many taxes. The reformer's views strongly appealed to Shaw, though he did not join the Single Taxers, whose clubs sprang up like mushrooms in America and in Britain. The main point is that for the first time in his life Bernard Shaw became interested in economic questions.

Soon afterward, he went to the British Museum and read Karl Marx's *Das Kapital* in a French translation—an English version had not yet been published.[29] In this devastating attack on the Establishment, Marx—like George—wrote of poverty, but with a difference. He saw the solution of the problem not in a panacea like the Single Tax, but in a class struggle that would lead to violent revolution. The violence in Marxism repelled young Shaw, but he accepted the Marxist principle of nationalization of all forms of capital including the land.

In 1884 Shaw joined a little group of radical thinkers, including Beatrice Potter and Sidney Webb (later husband and wife), Graham Wallas, and Sydney Olivier in organizing a Socialist group to be known as the Fabian Society. The name came from a Roman statesman, Quintus Fabius Maximus, known as the Cunctator, "the delayer," because of his reluctance to fight in the war against Carthage. The Fabians believed in the equal distribution of wealth and in equality of income from birth to death, a revolution that would come about by gradual change through the use of ballots, not bullets. Shaw, who threw himself wholeheartedly into the Fabian cause, wrote pamphlets, tracts, articles in newspapers and magazines, and became a street and platform orator. He estimated that he "delivered upwards of two thousand speeches" from street corners and places like Hyde Park, the City Temple, and Albert

Hall.[30] Also he edited and contributed chapters to *Fabian Essays in Socialism* (1889). All through the years he continued to write nonfiction books about socialism, but the two most important ones are *The Intelligent Woman's Guide to Capitalism and Socialism* (1928) and *Everybody's Political What's What?* (1944). Shaw was one of the first writers to advocate the eight-hour-day for labor. With William Morris, Henry W. Macosty, and others he spoke in favor of the proposal at a time in the early 1890s when it was looked upon as utopian, if not insane.[31]

Edward Bellamy's principle of Nationalism that he first expressed in *Looking Backward* Shaw did not at first accept, but he later regarded it as basic to socialism. In an introduction to the American edition of *Socialism: The Fabian Essays* (1891), Bellamy declared: "Nationalists are socialists who, holding all that socialists agree on, go further, and hold also that the distribution of the cooperative product among the members of the community must not merely be equitable, whatever that term may mean, but must be always and absolutely equal." Bellamy praised the Fabian Society highly, saying, "While the more revolutionary socialists make a show of deriding as too merely academic the propaganda of the Fabians, it may be doubted if work more valuable has ever been done by any socialist organization."[32] Shaw came to accept Bellamy's views, particularly those of nationalism and "equalitarian Distribution," so that "in his social philosophy Shaw began with an American, George, and ended with an American, Bellamy."[33] He did not, however, give Bellamy credit.[34]

Shaw's horizons were by no means limited to economic issues, for the London he came to know in his early twenties was "strongly individualistic, atheistic, Malthusian, evolutionary, Ingersollian, Darwinian, Herbert Spencerian."[35] All these streams of thought flowed through Shaw's mind, especially in meetings of the Zetetical Society, which was formed in 1878 to "furnish opportunities for the unrestricted discussion of Social, Political, and Philosophical subjects." Among the topics the society discussed in one winter were: "The Malthusian State Remedy for Poverty and Dear Food," "Was Shakespeare a Democrat?," "Shelley," "The Irish Land League," and "The Political Freedom of Women, A Necessity for the Nation." Shaw spoke on "On What Is Called 'The Sacredness of Human Life, and Its Bearing on the Question of Capital Punishment.'"[36]

Shaw became, in Dr. Johnson's phrase, "a clubbable man." He

joined the Dialectical Society, the Browning Club, the Royal Society of Literature, the New Shakespeare Society, the Shelley Society,
and others. Throughout his life, he joined clubs, societies, and
organizations that fell within his spheres of interest. But he attended meetings not for social entertainment but for mental stimulation.
Above all, he valued the organizations for the opportunities they afforded him to speak about economic and social issues.

Shaw's writing and speaking as a Socialist were an important part
of his literary apprenticeship; he learned to write with the clarity
and grace which Jonathan Swift and Joseph Addison exemplified in
their day. To put it another way, Shaw mastered the style which
Bonamy Dobrée defines as "the new way of writing."[37] After con-
trasting a passage from Shaw and one from Dean Inge on the same
subject, Dobrée praises Shaw for avoiding clichés and "ready-
made" language; for in the passage cited Shaw "spoke with a lively
voice; there is no fatigue there; it is all vigor. The prose is swift; you
naturally raise and drop your voice as you read it; there is no sense
of solemnity, though it is serious enough. . . ." Yet Shaw's
remarkable style did not happen; it developed. He forged it
through hard work and the determination to communicate his
message to the world. But his first efforts as a creative writer ended
in failure.

IV *Five Unsuccessful Novels*

During all these activities as a Fabian, Shaw made an attempt
from 1879 to 1883 to establish himself as a novelist. That he failed is
now so well known to everyone versed in modern literary and
theatrical history that we do not need to belabor the point.
Although failure to find a publisher cannot always be equated with
lack of merit, whatever merit Shaw's novels possess does not entitle
them to a place in the history of the nineteenth-century novel
alongside Dickens, William Makepeace Thackeray, George Eliot,
Samuel Butler, and Thomas Hardy. To be succinct, we have to
recognize that Shaw's fiction, overshadowed by his dramas, is of
limited interest today.[38]

The first of his novels, which was written at odd times but mainly
at night while he was still holding a position with the Edison
Telephone Company, was entitled (as he said, "with merciless
fitness") *Immaturity*. The chief character in the novel is Robert
Smith, who has some attributes resembling those of Bernard Shaw.

When he describes Smith as "a youth of eighteen with closely cropped yellow hair [Shaw was redheaded], small gray eyes and a slender lathy figure," it seems like self-portraiture. Since Shaw tells us of his diffidence in meeting people in London in the first years after his migration, this description of Smith could fit his creator also: "His delicately cut features and nervous manner indicated some refinement; but his shyness, though fairly well covered up, showed that his experience of society was limited and his disposition sensitive."[39] Like Shaw, Smith also was a clerk who found his job irksome.

The other chief characters are Harriet Russell, a seamstress, who lives in the same Islington lodging-house as Smith; Cyril Scott, an Impressionist painter; Isabella Woodward, daughter of a well-to-do Irish Member of Parliament; Mr. Woodward, her father; Hawkshan, a poet; and Lady Geraldine Porter, who represents high society.

Book I has mainly to do with the affair that develops between Robert Smith and Harriet Russell and with the ways of lower-middle-class people around them. Book II takes us from the lodging-house to more aristocratic circles in Perspective Park, Richmond; and Shaw presents in this section another romantic pair: Cyril Scott, the painter, and Isabella Woodward, the socialite, who associate with an interesting little group of Bohemian artists and musicians. Miss Woodward, Shaw's first female huntress, is in earnest pursuit of Scott. The artist, however, falls in love with Harriet Russell, who has come to Perspective Park to see an aunt who is a housekeeper there. Scott and Harriet, meeting by chance in a picture gallery, are attracted to each other. When she adversely criticizes a painting and does not know it is his work, he is impressed and feels, paradoxically, closer to her than before. Their courtship progresses, and in due course they get married.

Robert Smith, in the meantime, has a strange affair with Isabella Woodward, the daughter of his employer. When Isabella tries to bring Smith to propose or at least to compromise himself, he, being "a monster of propriety," eludes her. When her father casually informs him in a letter that Isabella has married "a Mr. Saunders, who has lately returned from India," Smith gives three cheers—under his breath, so as not to disturb the other lodgers. He is relieved to be no longer obliged to a woman. Some time later when Harriet sees Smith, who has settled into confirmed bachelorhood, they discuss marriage and children. She declares: "You are just a bad case of immaturity!"[40]

Smith answers: "I could never feel grown up; and I believe you were born grown-up. I am afraid I am incurable."

"Time will cure you," she rejoins. "I am curious to see what you will be at forty."

"Married, perhaps. But I can't feel marriageable."

Curiously, Smith was expressing Shaw's own feeling in his twenties and thirties.

Of all the five novels, *Immaturity* was the slowest to be published; for it did not appear until 1931, more than half a century after Shaw wrote it. The most amateurish of his novels, this work is too long and too loosely constructed; and the characters are not well drawn. As a work of art, hardly more need be said about it than that it was part of Shaw's apprenticeship.

His next novel he entitled *The Irrational Knot*. Writing in 1905 Shaw said: "I seriously suggest the *The Irrational Knot* may be regarded as an early attempt on the part of the Life Force to write *A Doll's House* in English by the instrumentality of a very immature writer aged 24." This statement reveals the central meaning of the novel, "a morally original study of a marriage."[41] The relations of men and women often occupied the thinking of important nineteenth-century and earlier writers. Mary Wollstonecraft's *Vindication of the Rights of Women* (1792) and John Stuart Mill's *The Subjection of Women* (1869) had interested Shaw, and Mill's essay was a direct influence on Ibsen's *A Doll's House*. *The Irrational Knot* was the first of Shaw's many studies of sex and matrimony.

The protagonist in this novel, Edward Conolly, an Irish-American electrical engineer, was drawn from Shaw's association with men of Conolly's profession and nationality in the Edison Telephone Company. The kind of man who fascinated Shaw, he was the type that Shaw developed later in Henry Shraker of *Man and Superman*. Not only was Conolly the practical handyman, but he, unlike Shraker, knew music, could play the piano expertly, and possessed a rich baritone voice. When he meets Marian Lind, an aristocratic young woman, at a concert, they are strongly attracted to each other; but she has already formed a close attachment to Sholto Douglas. After the concert, Conolly goes to a theatre with Marian's cousin Marmaduke Lind to see Lalage Virtue, a burlesque actress, with whom Lind is in love. Marmaduke is surprised to learn that Conolly knows Miss Virtue, and he is astonished when he finds she actually is Conolly's sister Susanna.

Marmaduke's family, it turns out, expects him to marry in his own class. On learning this fact, Susanna quarrels with him. He offers to marry her secretly, but she rejects this idea in favor of a liaison. They take quarters together, and Susanna insists on paying the rent. Meanwhile, Marian becomes more and more interested in Conolly when she learns that he is ambitious to become an inventor; he tells her he is in need of money to finance his investigations, and she offers to provide it. Taking a fancy to Conolly as a man of mechanical skill, Reginald Lind, Marian's father, employs him. When Sholto Douglas, Marian's aristocratic suitor, proposes, she rejects him and somewhat later marries Edward Conolly.

Their marriage, however, proves to be unhappy; Edward is so much absorbed in himself and his inventions that he does not give his wife the attention she needs. In fact, when he has the leisure, he prefers to flirt with other women. Feeling neglected, Marian accepts the renewed attentions of Douglas; and they become lovers and elope to New York. On learning of his wife's infidelity, Conolly, the rationalist, is not deeply disturbed. He thinks only of obtaining a divorce, as much for Marian's freedom as his own.

In the meantime, Lalage Virtue, after having a child by Marmaduke out of wedlock, falls victim to alcoholism. She goes to New York, where she has a theatrical engagement in which she fails miserably because of her drinking. As time passes, Marian and Douglas grow tired of each other and quarrel violently. "I despise you more than I do anyone on earth," she tells him as he departs for England, leaving her with only a twenty-pound note and a few dollars. But, as Shaw puts it, she "faced poverty without fear, never having experienced it." She comes to know shame and disgrace as she moves into poor quarters, a place where Susanna Conolly also lives in distress. Learning of his sister's plight, Conolly goes to New York to find Susanna has died. He sees Marian and offers to take her back along with the child she has born to Sholto Douglas. When she declines his offer, he sees her refusal as making "an end of the irrational knot."[42]

Shaw gave his third novel a catchpenny title, which evinces his interest in trying to reach readers. *Immaturity* and *The Irrational Knot* would not attract attention, but *Love Among the Artists*! Anyone looking for juicy situations, however, is courting disappointment. For, as Shaw warns us, "The parties are married in the middle of the book; and they do not elope with or divorce one another, or do anything unusual or improper".[43]

If you find yourself displeased with my story, remember that it is not I, but the generous and appreciative publisher of the book, who puts it forward as worth reading. . . . And I can guarantee you against any plot. You will be candidly dealt with. None of the characters will turn out to be somebody else in the last chapter: no violent accidents or strokes of pure luck will divert events from their normal course: forger, long-lost heir, detective, nor any commonplace of the police court or of the realm of romance shall insult your understanding, or tempt you to read on when you might better be in bed or attending your business.[44]

In Owen Jack, the protagonist of this novel, we encounter a much more complex person than either Robert Smith or Edward Conolly. Jack is a musician, a composer, and a genius; he is moody, proud, egotistical, and rebellious; he is immune to love, in the conventional sense. He affects a wicked, Mephistophelean look to gain attention and at times to frighten persons around him. Like Henry Higgins—and indeed like young Shaw himself—Owen Jack put art above love and marriage; he taught Magdalen Brailsford the art of elocution so well that she succeeded on the stage, but he rejected her proposal of marriage. Arthur Nethercot rightly refers to Jack as a diabolical character.[45]

An important fact to bear in mind about *Cashel Byron's Profession*, Shaw's fourth novel, is that prizefighting was held in the lowest esteem at the time; in fact, it was outlawed in England. The young author, who disagreed with this attitude, asserted of his novel that "on its prizefighting side it is an attempt to take the reader behind the scenes without unfairly confusing professional pugilism with the blackguardly environment which is no more essential to it than to professional cricket." Actually the sport interested Shaw to the extent that he participated as a middleweight and, daringly, as a heavyweight in the Amateur Boxing Championships (England's "Golden Gloves") in March 1883. Unfortunately—or perhaps fortunately—he did not reach the semifinals.[46] Nevertheless, he continued to show an interest in boxing and boxers throughout most of his life.

This novel is in the age-old tradition of story-telling, for the heart of it seems to be the well-worn plot: Boy meets Girl and Obstacle; Boy overcomes Obstacle and wins Girl; Poor Boy turns out to be heir to a Large Fortune. But the narrative is not really that simple, for the hero and heroine have minds as well as bodies. Cashel, though not analytical or brilliant, is capable; and his enamorata, Lydia Carew, is aristocratic, sensitive, and cultured. Like Shaw, Cashel is a school drop-out; and he runs away to Australia, where he finds a job with Ned Skene, former English prizefighting champion. Skene trains Byron, who becomes champion of Australia and the United States. When in England, he trains for a fight near the estate of Lydia Carew. By chance, she sees him and thinks he is a sylvan god; he falls in love with her and tries to conceal the fact he is a pugilist; but she learns the truth. Bashville, Lydia's butler, who is in love with her, tries unsuccessfully to prevent Cashel's seeing Lydia. But she and her boxer marry, and in a short time Cashel inherits a fortune and becomes a Member of Parliament.

Dr. Archibald Henderson is correct in his comment: "This is a romance after the heart of the subscribers to Mudie's and Smith's circulating libraries—bloodthirstily realistic as to the pugilism, frankest of melodramas as to the rest."[47] When William Archer sent a copy of *Cashel Byron* to Robert Louis Stevenson, he replied, "What am I to say? I have read your friend's book with singular relish. If he has written any other, I beg you will let me see it; and if he has not, I beg him to lose no time in supplying the deficiency. . . . It is *horrid fun*. All I ask is more of it. Thank you for the pleasure you gave us, and tell me more of the inimitable author." Stevenson then commented, "I say, Archer, my God, what women!"[48] This was high praise indeed, but no other important contemporary author added to it.

Cashel Byron's Profession, the most readable of Shaw's novels and the first to be published, appeared serially in a little Socialist magazine, *Today*, in 1884; but Shaw received no remuneration. From the magazine plates the publisher issued a shilling edition of the novel, which gave Shaw the satisfaction of seeing his work in book form, but only a minor reputation, and a negligible amount of money.[49] Several other cheap or pirated editions appeared from time to time, always without reward to the author. Years later, on hearing that a play based on this novel was being produced in America, Shaw hastily put together a comedy in Elizabethan blank verse entitled *The Admirable Bashville* (1901) to protect the copyright. The recognition of this novel, mild as it was, alarmed Shaw. "I never think of *Cashel Byron's Profession*," he remarked in 1901, "without a shudder at the narrowness of my escape from becoming a successful novelist at the age of twenty-six. At that moment an adventurous publisher might have ruined me."[50]

Shaw's last novel did not create much stir compared to its predecessor. He surely was not much surprised at its tepid reception, for he—or again G.B.S.—once commented that "People who will read *An Unsocial Socialist* will read anything." By the time he wrote it, Shaw was deeply involved in the Fabian movement.

Sidney Trefusis, the protagonist and Shaw's voice in *An Unsocial Socialist*, is a disagreeable person, a zealot, and an extremist who does one outlandish thing after another. Independently wealthy, owing to an inheritance from his father, a Manchester cotton merchant, Sidney marries Henrietta Jansenius, a lovely and intelligent young woman. Although they are apparently affectionate and happy, Sidney's zeal for socialism causes him to desert his wife: he feels he cannot fulfill his mission to aid in the liberation of the Manchester laborers, whom he regards as his father's wage slaves, without severing his marital ties. Henrietta is brokenhearted. He finds a hideout at Lyvern, a town near a girls' school, Alton College. Assuming the name of Smilash he finds work at the college.

One day Henrietta, who has accompanied her father to Alton, where he has been called on account of the misconduct of his ward, Agatha Wylie, recognizes her husband. She pleads with him to return to her, but he refuses on the grounds that he cannot as her husband carry forward his socialistic work. Not long after her return home, she receives a letter from Agatha who, not knowing his real identity, confides that she believes Smilash is in love with her and that "He calls me his golden idol." When Henrietta visits the college to upbraid Trefusis, he again persuades her to leave him alone. On the trip back home, on an extremely cold day, she contracts pneumonia, which proves fatal. When Sidney returns to London for the funeral, he behaves scandalously. To the doctor who attended Henrietta in her last illness, Trefusis remarks, "I am a young man and shall not cut a bad figure as a widower."

Soon after his wife's death, he proposes to Agatha Wylie after she ironically pleads with him to marry her.

"Are you in love with me?" Sidney asks.

"Not in the least," Agatha answers. "Not the very smallest bit in the world. I do not know anybody with whom I am less in love or less likely to be in love."

"Then you must marry me. If you were in love with me, I should run away. My sainted Henrietta adored me, and I proved unworthy of adoration—though I was immensely flattered."

She accepts him with a warning: "Very well. But mind, I think you are acting very foolishly, and if you are disappointed afterwards, you must not blame *me*."

The novel stops with an episode on a train ride during which Trefusis strangely persuades Gertrude Lindsay to marry the poet Erskine. I say the novel "stops" because, as a matter of fact, *An Un-*

social Socialist is unfinished; it is two long chapters of a projected longer fiction. In an appendix, Sidney Trefusis writes a letter to Bernard Shaw that protests against the novel as a false portrait. Saying that some critics "have been able plausibly to pretend to take the book as a satire on Socialism," he adds, "Whether or no, I am sorry you made a novel of my story, for the effect has been almost as if you had misrepresented me from beginning to end. . . . In conclusion, allow me to express my regret that you can find no better employment for your talent than the writing of novels."

It is difficult to determine if Shaw meant Trefusis to be a sympathetic or a satirical character, but the G.B.S. persona surely had the upper hand in this comment attributed to Shaw: "In an age when the average man's character is rotted at the core by the lust to be a true gentleman, the moral value of such an example as Trefusis is incalculable."[51] As in all his novels, Shaw makes a great many comments about the state of the world, the plight of genius, the need for reform, and other topics. Some of these points are interesting; but, on the whole, *An Unsocial Socialist* is a tiresome novel, as are all the others, with the exception of *Cashel Byron's Profession*.

Although Shaw undertook a sixth novel, he gave it up after writing a few pages and ended forever his efforts as a novelist.[52] In summary, the value of the novels is largely extrinsic. For one thing, as Stanley Weintraub has ably demonstrated, they afforded Shaw a storehouse of situations and characters which he later transmitted into the plays that made him famous.[53] For example, Vivie Warren leaves her mother at the end of *Mrs. Warren's Profession* for the same reason Conolly abandons Marian in *The Irrational Knot*—because she is at heart a "conventional woman." As another instance, the discussions in the second part of *An Unsocial Socialist* presage such disquisitory plays as *Getting Married, Misalliance,* and *Heartbreak House.*[54] The best-known of all the parallels that exist in the novels and the dramas is that part near the end of *Candida* in which Marchbanks says, "Out, then, into the night with me!" and the closing scene of *Love Among the Artists* when Owen Jack exclaims, "Back to the holy garret, oh my soul!" Thus, both characters have foresworn marriage.[55] "Shaw, the playwright," declares Dr. Weintraub, "could never divorce himself from Shaw, the novelist. His ideas for his plays often overflowed the form, necessitating long prefaces (sometimes—as with *Androcles*—longer than the play itself), and once a prose-fiction sequel, where we learn what happens to Eliza after the curtain drops on *Pygmalion*."[56] In still another way, Shaw's novel-writing benefited him as the most important part of his literary apprenticeship, for he gained, step by step, his artistic mastery.

CHAPTER 2

Prelude to Success and Fame

BERNARD Shaw bore failure and disappointment with amazing equanimity. Of his novels he wrote, "Fifty or sixty refusals without a single acceptance forced me into a fierce self-sufficiency."[1] He developed a faith that could almost be called Emersonian, but he could not live on self-reliance alone. He felt an ambition to be a great painter like his hero Michelangelo, but he was frustrated by the kind of instruction that was offered at the School of Design in the South Kensington Department of Science and Art.[2] Averse to depending in part on his mother, he sought a means of earning his livelihood. Though Fabian tracts as well as his novels had brought him no appreciable income, they had taught him that he could write. Writing seemed as natural as breathing. So for almost a decade after abandoning fiction, Shaw devoted himself successively to reviewing art, music, and drama.[3]

I Art Criticism

At first, Shaw dabbled in verse-writing but soon abandoned it;[4] and he also did some hack writing and book-reviewing without appreciable remuneration. Never one to waste time, he spent his days in the reading room of the British Museum fortifying his knowledge of the arts and sciences, particularly the social sciences; there he fell one day into conversation with another frequenter of the great library, a young Scotsman by the name of William Archer. A momentous meeting for both men, it began a mutually helpful friendship that endured until Archer's death in 1924. Archer noted that Shaw had Marx's *Das Kapital* (in the French translation) and the score of Wagner's *Tristan und Isolde* on his desk at the same time.[5] A free thinker and an established critic of the arts, Archer recognized Shaw's intellectual acumen and especially his

34

knowledge of painting, gained from studying books on the subject and from haunting the public galleries of Dublin in his youth and, in more recent times, of London.

Archer, as drama critic for *The World,* was also assigned to write art reviews; but, lacking confidence in himself as a judge of paintings, he invited Shaw to accompany him on his rounds. Shaw contributed so many ideas to the criticisms Archer submitted that he offered Shaw half the money they brought. Hard up as he was, Shaw sent back the check; Archer returned it; and, when Shaw refused it a second time, he stated that "No man has a right of property in the ideas of which he is the mouthpiece. . . . If I am to be paid for what I suggested to you, the painters must clearly be paid for what they suggested to me."[6] Archer soon convinced the editor that Shaw should have the position of art critic, which paid five pence a line; and this work, coupled with free-lancing, made it possible for Shaw to earn one hundred and twelve pounds in 1885, his first year of journalism. From that time on, he was able to pay his way and even to help his mother live more comfortably.

In his work as art critic, Shaw was subjective and impressionistic. Since he believed the way to judge pictures was to study them, he attended all the exhibitions. As always, he was frank, honest—often to the point of being cruel—and radical in his opinions.[7] For example, of three contemporary Romanticists, he wrote: "Madox Brown was a man; Watts is at least an artist and poet; Leighton was only a gentleman." Against the current opinion and especially that of Ruskin, Shaw advocated the work of James McNeill Whistler.[8]

Though Shaw was usually vehemently against Romanticism, he was kind to the Pre-Raphaelites and especially to sentimentalist Edward Burne-Jones, perhaps because, as William Irvine believes, of Shaw's allegiance to and admiration for William Morris,[9] a close friend of Burne-Jones and an associate of the Pre-Raphaelites. Toward Dante Gabriel Rossetti, however, Shaw was unfavorable; he spoke slightingly of his "sad, sensuous daydreams."[10] Among earlier painters, he admirred Bellini, Filippo Lippi, and particularly Michelangelo, whom he regarded as a great man and a great artist "because his every subject is a person of genius." "He never had a commonplace subject," Shaw observed. "His models are extraordinary people. . . . Michael Angelo [*sic*], you see, taught me this—always to put people of genius into my works. I am always setting a genius over against a commonplace person."[11] As we read this statement, we think at once of Caesar, Napoleon, Burgoyne, St.

Joan, Isaac Newton, George Fox—not to mention Marchbanks, Tanner, and Undershaft.

Characteristically, Shaw championed the French Impressionist group of painters—Degas, Monet, Manet, Pissaro—who were in general the subjects of controversy and at times of ridicule. He especially admired the Impressionists' preference for outdoor painting and for pictures that substituted "a natural, observant, real style for a conventional, taken-for-granted, ideal one."[12] In this respect, one other view should be mentioned since it marked Shaw as an advanced thinker: he enthusiastically espoused photography when it was "a pariah among the arts."[13] As early as 1901 Shaw predicted the time when color would enhance the art of the camera and make photography a rival of the canvas and the palette.[14] He also foresaw the time when artists would photograph their models instead of drawing them. He predicted that the lensman and his model would develop a relationship not unlike that of the dramatist and the actor.[15] Incidentally, Shaw from his forties on became an enthusiastic amateur photographer.

Shaw resigned as art critic of the *World* because of a change in the ownership which was not to his liking. When the new proprietor, a woman, insisted that Shaw praise pictures that her friends had painted, he refused. When he saw his articles printed with her emendations, he resigned;[16] but partly out of his work as a critic of pictures came his book of theory and forensics, *The Sanity of Art*. This little volume was an answer to a best-selling book of the early 1890s, Max Nordau's *Degeneration*, in which the author, a Hungarian physician, attacked nineteenth-century art in general as the decadent excrescences of diseased minds. Among those with whom Nordau dealt with unsparing scorn were Henrik Ibsen, Richard Wagner, Leo Tolstoi, John Ruskin, Victor Hugo, Algernon Swinburne, and the Pre-Raphaelites. "I could prove Nordau to be an elephant," asserted Shaw, "on more evidence than he has brought to prove that our greatest men are degenerative lunatics."

Shaw wrote his long essay in the form of an open letter to Benjamin Tucker, editor of an American paper called *Liberty;* and his epistle was first published as "A Degenerate's View of Nordau" in 1895. A revised version appeared in 1908 as *The Sanity of Art*, with a preface by Shaw in which he boasts that he and Tucker had vanquished Nordau forever.

II *Music Criticism*

In the summer of 1888, Shaw as assistant to Belfort Bax of the *Star*, a paper recently acquired by T. P. O'Connor, began to write music reviews; and in February 1889 he replaced Bax as the music editor, a post for which he was peculiarly well fitted. He recalled that as a teenager he could "sing and whistle from end to end leading works of Handel, Haydn, Mozart, Beethoven, Rossini, Bellini, Donizetti, and Verdi."[17] Shaw's background in music from infancy onward, his learning of it from his mother and from Vandeleur Lee, his participation in concerts, his frequent attendance of performances, and his studies of Wagner in the British Museum had prepared him for this new career.

As a pseudonym for his articles, Shaw chose "Corno di Bassetto," the Italian name for a basset horn, an instrument not heard since Mozart's day.[18] When Shaw learned that the basset horn had "a peculiar watery melancholy" and "a total absence of any richness or passion in its tone," he regretted having chosen it for a character meant to be sparkling.[19] To make his articles sparkling and appealing to large numbers of readers, Corno used wisecracks, exaggerations, egotistical remarks, and other kinds of humor. As Shaw admitted, "I purposely vulgarized musical criticism, which was then refined and academic to the point of being unreadable and often nonsensical."[20] In the preface to *London Music* (1931), he described the contributions of Bassetto as "a mixture of triviality, vulgarity, farce, and tomfoolery with genuine criticism."

The most substantial single work of music criticism that Shaw produced was the book entitled *The Perfect Wagnerite*, which deals only with *The Ring of the Niblungs*, which consists of "The Rhine Gold (Prologue)," "The Valkyries," "Siegfried," and "The Night Falls on the Gods." Shaw sees a comparison between Wagner's great opus and Percy B. Shelley's "Prometheus Unbound" since both authors offer the panacea of Love "as the remedy for all evils and the solvent of all social difficulties."[21] Shaw believes, however, that Shelley's concept of love is more nearly like mercy and kindness, and that Wagner thinks of it more in terms of sexual passion, "the emotional phenomena of which he has expressed in music with a frankness and forcible naturalism which would have scandalized Shelley."[22] Shaw presents Wagner, who faced public scorn, as "the literary musician par excellence," one who "was not only a consummate musician, like Mozart, but a dramatic poet and a critical and philosophical essayist, exercising a considerable influence on his century."[23]

III   *Theatrical Criticism*

During this time Shaw became more and more interested in the theatre and continued to think of a career as a dramatist. In 1894, he began writing reviews of plays for the *Saturday Review*, a journal edited by the notorious Frank Harris, whose taste in literature Shaw admired. In "The Author's Apology" to *Our Theatres in the Nineties*, Shaw explains his point of view as a critic and warns his readers against misunderstanding his critiques. He admits to handling "many well-known public persons rather recklessly" in journalistic writings that are not to be mistaken "for final estimates of their worth and achievements as dramatic artists and authors." He then admits his own biased view: "I postulated as desirable a certain kind of play in which I was destined ten years later to make my mark as a playwright (as I very well foreknew in the depth of my own unconsciousness); and I brought everybody, authors, actors, managers, to the one test: were they coming my way or staying in the old grooves?" A battler who made no effort to be impartial, he did make "allowances for the difference in aim, especially in the case of personal friends."

While serving as music critic for *The World*, Shaw attempted to write a play. His friend William Archer urged him to become a playwright; but, since Shaw doubted he could invent the plot, it was arranged that Archer would supply the plot and that Shaw would invent the scenes, characters, and dialogue. In 1885, he began to write *Widowers' Houses;* but, when he soon ran out of material, he put the manuscript aside; Shaw was too much of an individualist for collaboration. Meanwhile, he continued to support himself by writing critical articles and to educate himself by reading in the British Museum and by participating actively in the Socialist movement. In 1889 he edited *Fabian Essays*, to which he contributed "the Economic Basis of Socialism" and "Transition to Social Democracy."

He also became deeply involved at this time in the controversy over Henrik Ibsen, whose plays Archer, as translator, was instrumental in bringing to the London theatre. The work of the great Norwegian dramatist aroused Shaw's enthusiasm, and Ibsen's dramas soon became a shaping influence on his thinking and writing. Though the Norwegian playwright was not a Socialist and took no part in partisan politics, Shaw brought Ibsen's social thought to the attention of his fellow Fabians. One evening in the spring of 1890 he gave a lecture on Ibsen, and from it came his first published book, *The Quintessence of Ibsenism* (1891), in which he tried to explain Ibsen's work and thought especially for the English public, which found Ibsen's plays strange and repulsive. Archer and Shaw were almost alone in espousing Ibsen when his plays were first produced in London.

Shaw was at his best when pleading for an artist in whom he believed. *The Quintessence of Ibsenism* presents Shaw's interpretations of twelve dramas, beginning with *Brand* and ending with *Hedda Gabler*. Shaw agreed with Ibsen's view of the New Woman and the failure of modern marriage. He put great stress on Ibsen's concept of moral freedom for both men and women: "What Ibsen insists on is that there is no golden rule, that conduct must justify itself by its effect upon happiness and not by its conformity to any rule or ideal."[24]

Ibsen's great rival for acceptance in the London theatre was, of course, William Shakespeare. Nineteenth-century dramatists were, in William Irvine's words, "hypnotized by the gigantic reputation of Shakespeare." Since these current dramatists were discouraged from writing about contemporary life, they reproduced the Elizabethan rather than the modern world. "Great actors," Irvine declares, "either hacked up Shakespeare to fit their own talents or hired nonentities to fashion them a tailor-made part out of whole cloth." As Irvine also observes, a change came in the 1890s "when Shaw asserted the rights of the dramatist by carrying on a personal war against Sir Henry Irving."[25] Although Irving was largely responsible for the popularity of Shakespeare in this era, Shaw's fire was not directed exclusively at Irving the actor; he aimed it primarily at Shakespeare the playwright. He liked to use the word "Bardolatry" to imply that the worship of Shakespeare was a superstition, a vice, and a blight to the modern stage.

No more striking essay appears in Shaw's dramatic criticism than the one entitled "Better than Shakespeare," which is a review of the stage version in four acts of John Bunyan's *The Pilgrim's Progress* as a mystery play with music. Bunyan, he asserts, was far too great a dramatist for the English theatre. Shakespeare, on the other hand, wrote for it because "he understood nothing and believed nothing"—and created not a single hero in his thirty-six big plays.

"Only one man in them all who believes in life, enjoys life, thinks life worth living, and has a sincere unrhetorical tear dropped over his deathbed, and that man—Falstaff!" Shaw's scathing denunciation follows about all the characters in Shakespeare's plays as strange figures "who mistake themselves (and are mistaken by their author) for philosophers." Others are "princes without any sense of public duty, futile pessimists who imagine they are confronting a barren and unmeaning world when they are only contemplating their own worthlessness, self-seekers of all kinds, keenly observed and masterfully drawn from the romantic-commercial point of view." He asserts that what the audience missed in Shakespeare it could find in Bunyan, "to whom the true heroic came quite obviously and naturally."

Yet Shaw actually was not anti-Shakespeare, for he had been from his boyhood onward a student of the great dramatist and poet. Over and over again he expressed his veneration for the music in Shakespeare's language. He insisted that the way to present Shakespeare was to play him by ear, to reproduce his plays with full attention to the verbal music, because he believed that no other dramatist—not even Shaw—could match the beauty of Shakespeare's lines. Too often, by concentrating on the trappings of the theatre, the glory of the Bard's genius was lost. Without qualification, Shaw asserted that "Shakespeare as far as sonority, imagery, wit, humor, energy of imagination, power over language, and a whimsically keen eye for idiosyncracies can make a dramatist, was the king of dramatists."[26]

As in his art and music critiques, Shaw wrote drama reviews with levity, humor, and disarming candor by assailing what he believed to be the amateurish and the mediocre. For example, he lambasted a performance of Arthur Pinero's play *The Notorious Mrs. Ebbsmith* as "bad," "tedious," "insufferable." He recommended that Pinero "air his ideas a little in Hyde Park or the Iron Hall, St. Luke's, before he writes his next play." Shaw then reached the zenith of his candor when he added, "But my criticism has not, I hope, any other fault than the inevitable one of extreme unfairness." These remarks are a good example of the tongue-in-cheek G.B.S. persona who was writing to attract attention and to make a point by exaggeration. Nonetheless Shaw was utterly serious in his attitude toward the theatre; he looked upon it as "a factory of thought, a prompter of conscience, an elucidator of social conduct, an armory against despair and dullness, and a temple of the Ascent of Man." Indeed, he regarded the stage as superior to the church in its potentialities for good in the world.

IV   *The Beginning Dramatist*

While continuing his work as journalistic critic, he attempted to launch his career as a playwright. He resumed his work on the manuscript of *Widowers' Houses*, which he had begun in 1885, tried vainly to finish in 1890, and finally completed in 1892. The play was based partly on his studies of the economic theories of Henry George and Karl Marx. "*In Widowers' Houses*," says Shaw, "I have shewn middle class respectability and younger son gentility fattening on the poverty of the slum as flies fatten on filth. That is not a pleasant theme."[27] Subtitled *An Original Didactic Realistic Play, Widowers' Houses* is satirical in tone and spirit. Although Shaw took his title from Mark XIII, 38 - 40, in which Jesus admonishes his followers against the Scribes "which devour widows' houses," Shaw reversed the situation: the rich widowers with their houses exploit the poor.

As the play opens, Dr. Harry Trench, a recent medical-school graduate, is touring Europe with a friend, William de Burgh Cockane. They meet Sartorious, a widower and the wealthy landlord of the London slums, who is traveling with his beautiful but spoiled daughter Blanche. Dr. Trench falls in love with her and proposes marriage, but her father, a self-made man who feels inferior socially, hesitates, at first, about giving his permission for her marriage to one who is her social superior; but, when Trench produces letters of congratulations about his marital plans from his relatives, all is well. In the meantime, Sartorius dismisses his rent collector, Lickcheese, for spending twenty-four shillings on unnecessary repairs. By chance, Lickcheese meets Trench, reveals his former employer's "slum landlordism," and the young doctor reacts by telling his fiancée that he cannot accept any money from her father. After five pages of discussion Blanche, who is unwilling to live on Trench's income only, indignantly breaks the engagement. It is revealed, however, that unknown to Dr. Trench part of his income is derived from mortgages on Sartorius's houses. The physician is dazed, embarrassed, and "morally beggared" by this revelation.

In the third and final act, which occurs four months later, Lickcheese, who has become well-to-do by buying slum property at low cost and reselling it, talks to Sartorius about joining him in a get-rich scheme. Lickcheese has learned that the city intends to acquire land for a new street to be extended in the area of Sartorius's tenements. When Dr. Trench is requested to give his necessary consent on his mortgages, at first the physician refuses to cooperate, but after a lengthy discussion he agrees. Left alone, he looks longingly at a picture of Blanche; he takes it from its easel and starts to kiss it just as Blanche herself enters the room. In a charming scene in which she speaks with mock shrewishness, it "suddenly flashes on him that all this ferocity is erotic: that she is making love to him"—and thus they are reconciled.

Widowers' Houses cannot justly be considered a Socialist tract, for Shaw handles the dialogue and the characters cleverly and, to an extent, artistically; but he does fail to present any person, with the possible exception of Cockane, about whom the playgoer or reader really cares. Blanche is so unpleasantly hot-tempered and egotistical that it is hard to understand why Trench would be attracted to her. Trench himself is a spineless young man and a poor representative of the liberal cause, and Sartorius and Lickcheese are unscrupulous businessmen. There is no overt socialistic message. Like Shaw's novels, Widowers' Houses was a failure so far as public acceptance was concerned. Its chief significance lies in the fact that it is the first of Shaw's more than fifty contributions to the theatre.

In Widowers' Houses the impact of Charles Dickens's novels is noteworthy. In the character of Sartorius there is a tenuous similarity to Christopher Casby in Little Dorrit; and between Mr. Pancks, Casby's rent collector, and Lickcheese there is even a closer resemblance.[28] Archibald Henderson once wrote, "There is a palpable Dickensian atmosphere about Shaw; there is almost always a Dickens type somewhere in the offing. . . ."[29] And Shaw himself affirmed that "My works are all over Dickens and nothing but the stupendous illiteracy of modern criticism could have missed this glaring feature of my methods—especially my continual exploitation of Dickens's demonstration that it is possible to combine a mirror-like exactness of character drawing with the wildest extravagances of humorous expression and grotesque situation."[30] But Dickens's characters, scenes, satire, and social criticism, rather than his plots, appealed to Shaw in writing his novels, in Widowers' Houses, and also in his later dramas.[31]

V The Philanderer

Undaunted by the failure of his first play but pleased by the furor it had created, Shaw wrote in 1893 *The Philanderer: A Topical Comedy* that was based on the controversy then raging in London over Ibsen. *The Philanderer*, in Shaw's words, is about "the grotesque sexual compacts made between men and women under marriage laws which represent to some of us a political necessity (especially for other people), to some a divine ordinance, to some a romantic ideal, to some a domestic profession for women, and to some that worst of blundering abominations—an institution which society has outgrown, but not modified, and which 'advanced' individuals are therefore forced to evade."[32] These ideas came directly or indirectly from such Ibsen plays as *Love's Comedy, A Doll's House, Ghosts, Hedda Gabler, Rosmersholm,* and *The Master Builder.*

Generally speaking, Ibsen's plays gradually gained acceptance in England despite the opposition of the timid and the prudish. In fact, there developed in London an Ibsen cult which included many dilettantes of the type Shaw had satirized in *Love Among the Artists;* and such cultists, many of whom did not read or understand Ibsen, also drew Shaw's satiric barbs in *The Philanderer.* But the play deals seriously with the basic ideas of the Norwegian dramatist, and Shaw particularly supports the rise of the New Woman and the supremacy of the individual over institutional morality.

In the opening scene, Leonard Charteris, the philanderer (a character derived in large part from Shaw himself), is making love to Grace Cransfield, a widow, as they discuss their previous affairs quite candidly. Charteris proposes to Grace, saying he wishes to marry her so that Julia Craven will cease pursuing him. When he tells her that her "mission [is] to rescue" him from Julia, Grace refuses to be so used, saying she will not steal him from another woman. At this point, Julia quite unexpectedly enters and boldly starts a row with Charteris, who restrains her from physically attacking Grace. When Mrs. Cransfield quietly withdraws from the scene, she asks Leonard to get Julia away as soon as he can. This scene, by the way, is based on an actual happening between two of Shaw's lovers, Mrs. Jennie Patterson, who initiated Shaw into the rites of love on his twenty-ninth birthday, and her successor in his heart, Florence Farr, an actress.

Leonard and Julia have a heated argument in which he asserts that, as an Ibsenian woman, she must surrender him: "Advanced views, Julia, involve advanced duties: you cannot be an advanced woman when you want to bring a man to your feet, and a conventional woman when you want to hold him there against his will. Advanced people form charming friendships: conventional people marry." She pleads, cajoles, and threatens; but Leonard is adamant about his freedom. Julia, who does not give up easily, then goes to Grace, falls at her feet, and begs her to give up Leonard. Grace assures her she has no intention of marrying Leonard. When Charteris proposes to Grace, she refuses to accept him on the grounds that she loves him so much that he would have a "terrible advantage" over her. (This scene is reminiscent of the incident in *An Unsocial Socialist* in which Agatha Wylie tells Trefusis she does not love him and he insists, "Then you must marry me. If you were in love with me I should run away.")

Such is the main line of action in the play; but at least one other character should be mentioned, Dr. Percy Paramore, who is the first of several physicians whom Shaw satirized in his plays, an attitude based on Shaw's grave doubts about the medical profession. The doctor, "barely forty" and "highly self-satisfied intellectually," becomes a ridiculous figure when it is revealed that a kidney disease which he had "discovered" and named Paramore's Disease" did not actually exist. Aside from being an object of satire, Dr. Paramore has an important function in affording the means for Charteris to escape from the clutches of Julia Crave. For the physician, at Leonard's suggestion, successfully woos Julia. At the end, there seems to be no prospect that Leonard will marry Grace, who utters the final words of the play, "Never make a hero of a philanderer."

The Philanderer marks an advance in artistry over *Widowers' Houses*. The dialogue is brighter and wittier; the characters, on the whole, are more clearly and more originally drawn than such figures as Lickcheese and Sartorius. Though there are points at which the action slows, particularly in the arguments of the two fathers and Charteris, *The Philanderer* has movement and verisimilitude. It remains, however, something of a period piece and a minor part of Shaw's contribution. *The Philanderer*, as theatre, suffered a worse fate than its predecessor. Written in 1893, it waited until 1907 for its first public production.[33]

VI Mrs. Warren's Profession

Shaw wrote to William Archer August 3, 1893, that he was finishing the first act of his new play—*Mrs. Warren's Profession*—in which he had blended the plot of Arthur Pinero's *The Second Mrs. Tanqueray* and Shelley's *The Cenci.*[34] This statement was, of course, an exaggeration; for only a slight resemblance exists between what Shaw was writing and the two plays he cited. Though the second Mrs. Tanqueray was, like Mrs. Warren, "a fallen woman," that is where the similarity ends. The theme of incest prominent in Shelley's tragedy is mentioned only as a possibility in Shaw's comedy.

Though Shaw describes Mrs. Warren as "an organism of prostitution—a woman who owns and manages brothels in every big city in Europe and is proud of it," the play presents no scenes in or near the brothels. Shaw is concerned in this drama with the reasons for his protagonist's unsavory operations and especially with their effect on her attractive and brilliant daughter, Vivie, who is portrayed as an example of the New Woman. Again, as in *Widowers' Houses*, Shaw confronts the theme of "tainted money." With the profits from her brothels Mrs. Warren is able to support a high standard of living which includes the education of Vivie, whose aptitude in mathematics makes it possible for her to compete successfully in contests with men and to attend Cambridge University. Vivie, as the play begins, is utterly ignorant of the source of her munificent income; and her discovery of the fact and its effect on her and her relationship to her mother is the crux of the drama.

In Act I (there are no separate scenes) the action occurs in a cottage garden near Haslemere, Surrey, where Vivie Warren has arrived for a reunion with her mother after a long absence. The girl's "advanced" attitude is revealed in her conversation with Praed, the first man to arrive for the weekend party. She informs him she has come down to read law in preparation for her life work. "I hate holidays," she tells. When he asks, "Are you to have no romance, no beauty in your life?" she replies, "I don't care for either, I assure you. . . . I like working and getting paid for it. When I'm tired of working, I like a comfortable chair, a cigar, a little whisky, and a novel with a good detective story in it." Praed, an unattached artist and friend of Mrs. Warren, is quite impressed with Vivie.

As the other characters assemble, they include: Mrs. Warren herself, who is described as "rather spoiled and domineering, and decidedly vulgar, but, on the whole, a genial and fairly presentable old blackguard of a woman"; Sir George Crofts, a "gentlemanly combination of the most brutal type of city man, sporting man, and man about town"; Frank Gardner, a "pleasant, pretty, smartly dressed, cleverly good-for-nothing, not long turned twenty"; the Reverend Samuel Gardner, Frank's father, a beneficial clergyman of the Established Church, who is "that obsolescent social phenomenon, the fool of the family dumped on the Church by his father the patron."

In the first act, Frank, a friend of Vivie, is invited to join the party. Sir George Croft, though "about fifty" and Mrs. Warren's business partner, falls in love with Vivie. Mrs. Warren recognizes the minister as the man who had once offered her fifty pounds for a packet of letters that he had written to her when she was a barmaid.

In Act II, Frank Gardner flirts with Mrs. Warren while revealing he is interested romantically in Vivie. Observing Croft's attentions to Vivie, Mrs. Warren warns him against proceeding. In the course of the evening Vivie quizzes her mother, who candidly reveals the secret of her profession. There is a good deal of self-recrimination and anguish on Mrs. Warren's part, but her daughter accepts the explanation coolly and gracefully, saying, "Let us be friends now." At the end, they embrace.

In Act III, however, Vivie learns to her consternation that her mother has deceived her into thinking that the prostitution syndicate was no longer operating. Sir George Crofts offers to settle a large legacy on Vivie if she will marry him. Angered by her refusal and by her apparent preference for young Frank, Crofts tells them that they are half-brother and half-sister and that the Reverend Samuel Gardner is their father. Dismayed and disguisted, Vivie departs for London after saying good-bye to Frank.

The events of Act IV take place in Honoria Fraser's chambers in Chancery Lane. Honoria, Vivie's friend and now her business partner, does not appear in the play. Young Gardner calls at the office to try to persuade Vivie to resume relations with him, but she declines. Praed also stops by to urge Vivie to put some romance and beauty into her life by traveling with him, but she rebuffs him, too. When Mrs. Warren appears ("She is pitiably anxious and ill at ease: evidently panic-stricken") Frank Gardner and Praed leave the mother and daughter to themselves. As Vivie reveals that she has returned her monthly allowance check to the bank because she wishes to support herself henceforward, Mrs. Warren becomes angry, a feeling which increases when Vivie tells her that Crofts had disclosed the continuing of the syndicate. After Vivie says she has decided they must not meet again, Mrs. Warren accuses her of "stealing" the college education from her. Vivie declares she is bidding her mother good-bye not because she managed the brothels but because "You are a conventional woman at heart." Mrs. Warren refuses to shake hands as she departs, "slamming the door behind her." Vivie turns to her work "and soon becomes absorbed in its figures."

Shaw neither ridicules nor glamorizes prostitutes; he presents no overt sex scenes, no double-entendres, no prurient suggestion; he insisted on his serious purpose in writing about the economic basis of prostitution. Women would not need or desire to sell themselves if they had an opportunity to earn a fair wage in legitimate businesses. "What is demonstrated," writes Martin Meisel, "is not only the inextricable involvement of all in prostitution, but prostitution's inextricable involvement in the whole economic and social fabric."[35] Society, which is responsible for the white-slave traffic because women are made to be the dependents of men, is the only villain in *Mrs. Warren's Profession.*

No other of Shaw's plays caused so much controversy as did *Mrs. Warren's Profession.* The epithets hurled against it and its author must have reminded him of those that greeted Ibsen's *Ghosts,* for Shaw had collected a long list of words and phrases of abuse directed at Ibsen and had reprinted them in *The Quintessence of Ibsenism.* In addition to the treatment of commercialized sex and the suggestion of incest in *Mrs. Warren,* opponents raised objection to the portrayal of the Reverend Mr. Gardner as an attack on religion. On this point Shaw retorted, "According to this view Subaltern Iago is an attack on the army, Sir John Falstaff an attack on knighthood, and King Claudius an attack on royalty."[36]

All the explaining and defending, all the memories of eight straight failures in his creative works tried Shaw's patience but did not discourage him to the point of reaching despair. He did not at any time lose faith in himself and his mission. Like Walt Whitman, he could wait for his public, trusting in the "amplitude of time."

CHAPTER 3

First Success: The Coming of Recognition

I On War and the Soldier

"M AN is a creature of habit," wrote Shaw. "You cannot write three plays and then stop."[1] He resolved, however, to stop writing unpleasant plays which commercial producers would only reject time after time. Accordingly, his next venture was a play about a subject that appeals strongly to the Romantic imagination—war and the soldier. This play was to be different from its three predecessors, first, because it was to be virtually devoid of Henrik Ibsen's ideas and, second, because it was not to be written with a socialistic bias. To avoid offending London playgoers, he decided to write of a war in which the British army was not even remotely involved.

The portrayal of his military men was based in part on the writings of two generals who had observed soldiers in battle: Lord Wolseley, a Dublin-born field marshal who was instrumental in building the modern British army; and General Horace Porter, who was one of U.S. Grant's men. Both these generals wrote that the common fighting man does not actually enjoy being under fire but prefers a haven of safety to a hail of bullets.[2] Accordingly, Shaw portrayed his military characters as men "with no stomach for unnecessary danger." Much as he wished to avoid offense, he gave it by picturing a soldier "as a man with a stomach for necessary food" who preferred chocolates to cartridges.[3] A majority in his audiences saw the comedy, but their laughter was more gratifying to the cast than to Shaw, for he feared the playgoers were missing the serious intent of his drama. This fact, which gave him deep concern, diminished his pleasure in his first success and plagued him, as we shall see, many times throughout his life.

The scene of *Arms and the Man* is a family home in a small town near the Dragoman Pass. The war between the Serbs and the Bulgarians is getting hotter and nearer to the town. Raina Petkoff, a young lady in her nightgown but covered with a mantle of expensive furs, is gazing at the Balkans "intensely conscious of the romantic beauty of the night, and of the fact that her own youth and beauty are part of it." Her mother, Catherine Petkoff, "a woman over forty, imperiously energetic, with magnificient black hair and eyes," interrupts Raina's reverie to announce excitedly that there has been a great victory and that Sergius, Raina's sweetheart, was the hero of it. Catherine says: "Oh, if you have a drop of blood in your veins, you will worship him when he comes back." Raina answers: "What will he care for my poor little worship after the acclamations of the whole army of heroes? But no matter: I am so happy! so proud! It proves that all our ideas were real after all." Raina and her mother are, in Shaw's view, typical of all women who glamorize war and patriotic heroism.

There is gunfire in the streets that night as the Serbs are fleeing from the battlefield. Raina, alone in her boudoir, realizes that a man has entered. As she starts to cry out, he threatens her. "Don't call out or you'll be shot. Be good and no harm will come to you." The intruder is a Serbian artillery officer who admits he is trying to avoid being killed. When Raina goes for her cloak, he snatches it from her, saying, "I'll keep the cloak; and you'll take care that nobody comes in and sees you without it. This is a better weapon than the revolver: eh?"

Someone had seen the enemy soldier scaling the drainpipe to Raina's balcony, but when a searching party appears, she suddenly decides to conceal the man from his pursuers. After the searching party leaves, he promises lifelong gratitude, says he wishes he had joined the Bulgarian army instead of the Serbian one, and reveals that he is a Swiss mercenary.

The dialogue between the young intruder and Raina is one of the cleverest in the play. In his account of the fighting, the soldier reveals that Sergius, whom he identifies from Raina's photograph of him, was actually a ridiculous figure in the battle. This fact is disillusioning and upsetting to Raina, but she keeps her composure. Seeing that the soldier is half starved, she feeds him the only food she has at hand—chocolate creams, which he assures her he prefers to bullets. Seeing that he is extremely weary, she cannot bring herself to drive him out. Exhausted, he falls asleep on her bed. Mrs. Petkoff raises no objection.

In Act II, which transpires four months later, the war has ended.
When Major Petkoff and Sergius return, they narrate the story, told
by a Swiss officer after the exchange of prisoners, of how his life was
saved by two Bulgarian women. Sergius, after professing his un-
dying love for Raina, admits to Louka, the serving girl, that it is
"very fatiguing" to keep up the "higher love" for any length of
time. He tries to kiss her; she leads him on; and he avoids a compro-
mising action just as Raina appears. Soon Bluntschli—"chocolate
cream" soldier—appears to return the coat Raina had lent him
when he made his escape. Petkoff and Sergius recognize and
welcome him; the women pretend they never saw him, but it is
Catherine and Raina who persuade him to stay for dinner.

Meanwhile, in Act III, he and Raina have a talk which brings
them closer together. After Bluntschli tells Raina that he doubts her
when she insists that she has told only two lies in her life, she asks,
with a babyish familiarity, "How did you find me out?" Bluntschli
answers, "Instinct, dear young lady. Instinct, and experience of the
world."

RAINA (wonderingly). Do you know, you are the first man I ever met who
did not take me seriously?

BLUNTSCHLI. You mean, don't you, that I am the first man that has ever
taken you quite seriously?

RAINA. Yes: I suppose I do mean that. (Cosily, quite at her ease with
him.)

Meanwhile, Sergius becomes more and more involved with Louka:
and Raina tells him that she is aware of his romance with Louka and
reminds him Nicola, another servant, is her fiancé. But later, since
Nicola is willing to give her up because his doing so will be advantageous to him financially if she marries into the nobility, Sergius
and Louka become engaged. Bluntschli seeks and wins the hand of
Raina after it is revealed that her "chocolate soldier" has inherited
two hundred horses, seventy carriages, six palatial establishments,
three hundred servants, among other things. As the Swiss departs
vowing to return in a fortnight, Sergius exclaims, "What a man! Is
he a man!"

Arms and the Man, which he wrote between November 26, 1893,
and March 30, 1894, was Shaw's first even mild success as a creative
writer. The play opened April 21, 1894, at the Avenue Theatre,
London, and ran almost three months. On the first night, Shaw
heard the sweet sound of loud applause and the cry, "Author!" As

he responded to the curtain call, he heard a strong "Boo" from the gallery. Turning to the heckler, Shaw said: "My dear fellow, I quite agree with you; but what are we two against so many?" It is characteristic of Shaw that he later helped the heckler (identified as Golding Bright) by writing him many letters of advice about how to become a critic.[4] Gratifying as the applause was, the play brought as yet no munificent monetary return. A larger recompense came from the Richard Mansfield production in New York at the Herald Square Theatre later in the summer. This play was the first Shaw drama to appear on an American stage.[5]

As drama, this satire on romance, particularly the romanticizing of war and its glory, marks another step upward artistically in Shaw's career. On the whole, the characters are drawn with greater deftness than in the earlier plays; and they are revealed through the clever dialogue rather than through their action. For example, in Act II, in a passage already mentioned, Raina and Sergius protest their "higher love," which is quite obviously more "ideal" than real.

> SERGIUS. My lady and my saint! *He clasps her reverently.*
> RAINA, *returning his embrace.* My lord and my—
> SERGIUS. Sh-sh! Let me be the worshipper, dear. You little know how unworthy the best man is of a girl's pure passion!

Louka appears, the lovers release each other, and Raina says she will get her hat and then they can go out until lunch time.

> SERGIUS. Be quick. If you are away five minutes, it will seem five hours.

Immediately thereafter, Sergius directs his attention and his lust toward Louka.[6] The witty and formalized dialogue here and elsewhere in the play brings to mind scenes in Oscar Wilde's *Lady Windermere's Fan* and *The Importance of Being Earnest.*[7] The characters—especially Bluntschli, Sergius, Petkoff, and Louka—almost seem like figures out of Chekhov's *The Three Sisters* or *The Cherry Orchard.* The plot, however, especially the "business" about the cloak and the photograph, is directly in the tradition of the "well-made" plays of Scribe and Sardou, despite Shaw's practice of scorning these once-popular French playwrights.[8]

As an antiwar play, *Arms and the Man* is of low voltage; it bears no resemblance to Maxwell Anderson and Laurence Stallings' *What*

Price Glory? or to R. C. Sherriff's *Journey's End;* nor does it make any pretense of being such. Shaw avoids portraying the horror of the battlefield, and the only mention of death is Bluntschli's account in Act III of his friends's death by fire in a woodyard. Shaw's strategy is not Realism or Naturalism; his weapon, as we have noted, is satire that is directed at the romanticizing of war and at the glamorizing of the soldier. Characteristically, Shaw seeks to appeal to the intelligence rather than to the emotions of his audiences.

Arms and the Man resembles a comic opera without musical notes. Oscar Straus, the famous Viennese composer of operettas, made an unauthorized musical version, *Der Tapfere Soldat*, whose English title became *The Chocolate Soldier*, which brought in more money than *Arms and the Man*. Several times Shaw was offered a share of the royalties, but he absolutely refused to have anything to do with it. He decided not to try to stop the performances, however, for they gave employment to artists and others as well as enjoyment to the public. "Then," Shaw added magnanimously, "there was Straus to be considered. He was not to blame, as he evidently knew nothing about the copyright question. So I let them alone; and they all flourished exceedingly." But when a motion-picture version was projected, Shaw brought legal action, stopping the filming, and won damages of eight hundred pounds, which he did not bother to collect.[9]

II   Candida

Quite in contrast to *Arms and the Man* is the next play, a domestic comedy entitled *Candida: A Mystery*,[10] in which the influence of Ibsen is strongly evident. In fact, Shaw referred to it as *A Doll's House* in reverse since the "doll" is the husband rather than the wife. There is, however, a greater farcicality and less discussion than in Ibsen's social dramas. Though it ends in a discussion, *Candida* is not a true Discussion Play, a genre which Shaw was to develop to a great degree later.[11] In fact, Shaw adopts for his purpose one of the age-old conventions of domestic comedy—the triangle. Tom Taylor's *Still Waters Run Deep* (1855), his *Victims* (1857), Sardou's *Nos Intimes* (1861), and W. S. Gilbert's *Patience* (1881), all present triangles in which young men who often possess poetic tendencies court the wives of older husbands. Indeed, adultery and the possibility of adultery were "a leading dramatic subject in the nineteenth century."[12]

Shaw's chief characters, besides Candida herself, are her husband, the Reverend James Morell, and Eugene Marchbanks, a poet,
aged eighteen. Morell is a Christian Socialist minister of the
Established Church, and he is greatly in demand as a speaker before
women's clubs and other organizations. Being absorbed in his
career, he is neglectful of his wife, whom he takes for granted.
Marchbanks, who is greatly attracted to Candida, feels that she is
unappreciated; and Candida responds to his friendliness as their
relationship deepens. Candida is the kind of woman who needs to
"mother" someone. For the moment, she and Marchbanks seem to
need each other. In the course of time, Morell surmises that the
poet is becoming involved emotionally with Candida, and she with
him. Actually Marchbanks announces to Morell, "I love your wife,"
a statement which arouses Morell's uncontrollable laughter, but it is
followed by his anger. At one point Morell is on the verge of
physically attacking the young poet, but the fight is averted when
Marchbanks expresses his horror of physical contact with Morell.
Morell calls him a "little snivelling cowardly whelp."

Later, Candida astonishes Morell by saying that she must choose
between the two men. This decision leads to the famous "auction"
scene in which the two men present their cases to her, their bids for
her love. When she says that she will choose the weaker of the two,
Morell is almost certain that Candida means she will turn to
Marchbanks. After Morell argues that he needs her more that his
rival, Candida ruthlessly reminds him of his past in which he was
the center of attention in his family, surrounded as he was by
women. She decides that Morell is the one who needs her the
most—after he confesses his sins and weaknesses. Marchbanks
accepts her decision calmly since he has come to the decision rather
suddenly that it seems, after all, that, as an artist, he does not need
domestic happiness. This realization is "the secret in the poet's
heart" as he leaves the Morells saying, "Out, then, into the night
with me!" The artist's necessary independence is a theme to which
Shaw devoted a great deal of thought.

The play has three minor characters who play important parts in
developing the personality of Morell, but each is interesting in his
own right. Burgess, Candida's father, is a middle-aged Babbitt who
contrasts with Morell's liberal attitude. He speaks with a Cockney
accent, confronts Morell, and is regarded by him as a scoundrel who
underpays his employees. Although Burgess calls Morell a fool, the
two men shake hands, after quarreling violently, for they respect
each other.[13] Another minor but not unimportant character is

Morell's secretary, Miss Proserpine (Prossy) Garnett, "a brisk little woman of about thirty of the lower middle class," who adores Morell—hopelessly. The sixth and last character is the university-trained curate, the Reverend Alexander Mill, "a conceitedly well-intentioned, enthusiastic, immature novice," who gives Morell "a doglike devotion." Like Prossy, he helps to sustain Morell's ego. Aside from their relationship to Morell, these minor characters contribute, as well as others, to the comic effects of the play.

In a conversation with Proserpine Garnett, Marchbanks verbalizes one of the universal themes of poets and playwrights when he says he is constantly seeking the love which is pent up in others but which he cannot find because of his shyness: "And I see the affection I am longing for given to dogs and cats and pet birds, because they come and ask for it. . . . All the love in the world is longing to speak; only it dare not, because it is shy! shy! shy! That is the world's tragedy." As he continues in this vein, Prossy demurs and speaks for the Philistine world: "Look here: if you don't stop talking like this, I'll leave the room, Mr. Marchbanks: I really will. It's not proper."[14]

Candida herself is part of Prossy's world. In one of his G.B.S. exaggerations, her author, as we have already noted, referred to her as the Virgin Mother. At another time he compared her to Wagner's Siegfried, whom Shaw described as a "type of healthy man raised to perfect confidence in his own impulses by an intense and joyous vitality."[15] Gradually, Shaw changed his opinion of Mrs. Morell, for he was quoted as saying in 1920 about "the Candida secret": "What business has a man with the great destiny of a poet with the small beer of domestic comfort and cuddling and petting at the apron-string of some dear nice woman?"[16]

Clearly she is not as impressive as Vivie Warren or as Lady Cicely, the chief character in *Captain Brassbound's Conversion*. Candida is an unintellectual person who cannot respond to Marchbanks's poetry; as the poet reads to her in the beginning of Act III, he, seeing she is dozing, lets his manuscript fall to the floor. With "maternal humor" she accepts his adulation, of which she is obviously unworthy. When Morell returns from a meeting and declares that he had never spoken better in his life, Candida replies: "That was first rate! How much was the collection?" It is not surprising that, at the end of the play, she has settled back into her cozy domestic situation—and has failed to exhibit the attributes of the New Woman. Candida, after all, is a static character; she does not change appreciably in the whole course of the play. She is, however catalytic; for she brings about the changes in the two men in her life by helping them to see themselves as they are. As Arthur Nethercot has shown, Candida is the Philistine; Morell, the idealist; and Marchbanks, the realist as Shaw defines these terms in *The Quintessence of Ibsenism*.[17]

Critics have puzzled as to who was the prototype of Marchbanks. When Beverly Baxter wrote a notice of *Candida* in which he announced that the poet was the playwright himself, Shaw said the news had given him "a shock that would have killed any other man of my age." He said that, when he began writing the part, he had in mind Thomas De Quincey's account of his adolescence in his *Confessions of an English Opium Eater*. Nevertheless, Archibald Henderson, Shaw's official biographer, identifies Marchbanks as Shaw. Another poet mentioned as a possible prototype is Shelley, whom, as we have seen, Shaw deeply admired.[18] It seems probable that Shaw drew upon all three—himself, DeQuincey, and Shelley—in creating the character of Marchbanks.[19]

III *A Play About Napoleon*

As if to exhibit his versatility, Shaw's next play, *The Man of Destiny*, was about Napoleon. "In an idle moment in 1895," as he put it, "I began the little scene called The Man of Destiny, which is hardly more than a bravura piece to display the virtuosity of the two principal performers."[20] He wrote this one-acter especially for Richard Mansfield and Ellen Terry.[21] Reminiscent of the historical romances of Scribe and particularly Sardou's Napoleon in his "well-made" play *Madame Sans-Gêne, The Man of Destiny* is subtitled *A Fictitious Paragraph of History*.[22] In a letter to the actress, Janet A. Church, he referred to it as a harlequinade in the style of *Arms and the Man*.[23]

As Shaw conceives him, Napoleon is twenty-seven and not yet famous; but, as the Little Corporal, he is at an inn shortly after his victory at Lodi and is anxiously awaiting his dispatches. When a young sublieutenant arrives to report that a youth had conned him into surrendering the missives, the furious Napoleon orders the arrest of the sublieutenant, who just then hears a voice which he recognizes as that of his betrayer, a woman disguised as a soldier. The rest of the story concerns Napoleon's forceful action in retrieving the dispatches, which include a letter revealing Josephine's infidelity, which the Strange Lady, as she is identified, had been sent to intercept.

This little *tour de force* is not important except that it marks Shaw's first use of a historical figure in his creative work. Incidentally, it also illustrates the author's ability to mix comedy and discussion. Toward the end there is a long duologue in which the two of them decide the English are a "stupid" people whose weak point is that they are "full of scruples: chained hand and foot by their morality and respectability."[24]

At the same time he was writing *The Man of Destiny* Shaw was working on another comedy entitled *You Never Can Tell,* which was completed in 1896. It is an avowed potboiler, for Shaw referred to it as "an attempt to comply with many requests for a play in which the much-paragraphed brilliancy of *Arms and the Man* should be tempered by some consideration for the requirements of managers in search of fashionable comedies for West End Theatres."[25] To divert an audience Shaw at times introduced unusual—not to say, outlandish—properties on the stage. In this instance, it happens to be a dentist's chair in an operating room which the opening curtain discloses.

The scene is a seaside resort. Valentine, the young dentist, falls in love with Gloria Clandon, a young woman conditioned by a suffragette mother to exalt reason and to descry passion. Their affair does not progress smoothly; for, though Gloria is "all passion," she suffers from an "obstinate pride" and an "intense fastidiousness" which result in "a freezing coldness of manner."[26] Yet she is attractive, a channel of the Life Force, which in the end makes her irresistible to that "duellist of love," Valentine.

The most memorable character in the play is William, the waiter, who is dependable, efficient, and wise. It is he who voices the theme of the comedy: the unexpected happens, "You never can tell, sir: you never can tell." When Valentine's landlord Crampton turns out to be Gloria's long-lost father and Bohun, the Queen's Counsel who is called in to settle the family's legal entanglements, is revealed as the waiter's son, the coincidences seem too much contrived. All in all, *You Never Can Tell* is unworthy of ranking with Shaw's major plays. It was three years after its composition that its first presentation took place.[27]

IV   *Publication of the Plays*

One advantageous result of Shaw's difficulty in finding theatre managers who would take a chance on his plays was his decision to have them published. In a letter of September 9, 1895, to T. Fisher Unwin, the publisher, he inquired if there was "any public as yet which reads plays" and added "if I thought that people were picking up the French trick of reading dramatic works, I should be strongly tempted to publish my plays instead of bothering to get them performed."[28] The publication of contemporary dramas was not common in England in the 1880s and 1890s, but William Archer had pioneered in translating and publishing Ibsen's plays beginning in 1888 with *Prose Dramas (Pillars of Society, Ghosts, and An Enemy of the People)*, and *A Doll's House* had followed in 1889.[29] Shaw's *Widowers' Houses* was printed in 1893, a year after its first performance by "Henry & Company" (actually J. T. Grein, the play's first producer). None of his other early dramas was published until 1898 when two volumes of *Plays Pleasant and Unpleasant* appeared under Grant Richards's imprint.[30]

Shaw arranged for simultaneous publication of the two volumes in America by Herbert Stone of Chicago.[31] Stone, a young Harvard graduate, worked hand in hand with Grant Richards in putting Shaw's plays into book form. Stone, who was known for his emphasis on beauty in the design and in the printing of his books, had a rich father to whom he could go for subsidies when the books did not pay for themselves. Besides the plays Stone also published the novels of Shaw, particularly *Cashel Byron's Profession* (with *The Admirable Bashville*, the play Shaw made from it) and *Love Among the Artists*.[32]

In preparing his plays for publication, Shaw, partly as a result of his association with William Morris, whose Kelmscott Press produced books famous for their beauty as well as their utility, insisted on having his own way in many matters of printing, format, and typography; and he even ruled over details relative to punctuation and spelling.[33] As far as possible he avoided the use of apostrophes in contractions, preferring *werent* to *weren't*, *dont* for *don't*, *wont* for *won't*, *theres* for *there's*, but not *its* for *it's* meaning *it is;* indeed, he used the apostrophe only when it averted confusion. He chose to spell *whilst* rather than *while* and *shew* instead of *show*. In words like *humor* and *candor*, he followed the American custom rather than the English *our* ending. His great predecessor's name he invariably spelled *Shakespear*.[34] He did not italicize the titles of books and plays.

An outstanding and characteristic feature of Shaw's printed dramas is the addition of the prefaces. Although he regarded the dramas as the most effective platform for the promulgation of his ideas, the prefaces were an extension of that platform. In them he expanded on the themes, on himself, on the staging of the play, and on matters often remote from the characters, scenes, or ideas of the play. For example, he used them for the explanation of any subject he thought needed explanation, as in "Cleopatra's Cure of Baldness." In *Androcles and the Lion,* for example, the preface is more than twice as long as the play; for the lengths of the prefaces varied from a few to a hundred pages. "I write prefaces as Dryden did, and treatises as Wagner," Shaw seriously declared, "because I *can;* and I would give half a dozen Shakespear's plays for one of the prefaces he ought to have written."[35] Though he acknowledged Shakespeare's preeminence, he asserted that the Bard "left us no intellectually coherent drama" because he did not prepare his plays for publication in competition with novels.[36]

Like novelists, Shaw introduced in his prefaces each character in his plays with great particularity as to background, dress, and traits; and he did not include in his printed scripts any Cast of Characters or Dramatis Personae. His endeavor was to evoke in the reader a pictorial sense of the characters, scenes, and actions in what has been called "the theater of the mind." By practice, the reader, with the help of Shaw's words, learns to "see" the play as if on the stage or on the motion-picture screen. Not everyone can accomplish this skill, but the reward is gratifying for those who do. With the mounting costs of stage production and with the limited number of theatres even in centers such as London and New York City, the opportunity to attend plays is more and more restricted; and the publication of dramas greatly expands the possibility of experiencing drama. For each person who can see a Shaw play on the stage, thousands can read it in a book. In the more than three quarters of a century since Shaw began issuing the volumes of his plays, other playwrights have followed the custom so that today almost every work of aspiring as well as established dramatists is available to readers.

V   *A Melodrama of the American Revolution*

Shaw's third book of dramas he entitled *Three Plays for Puritans.* The first of these is *The Devil's Disciple,* whose scenes are laid in a New Hampshire town at the time of the American Revolution, 1777. Historically, Burgoyne and his troops were never in New

Hampshire. In the early scripts of the play Shaw has the general say that he has marched "south from Boston" and plans to "effect a junction at Albany" with General Howe "and wipe out the rebel forces." Perhaps the strangest slip of all is Shaw's referring to Burgoyne's soldiers as "the Continentals."[37] But incorrectly presenting the facts of history, in which Shakespeare afforded ample precedent, does not seriously mar the value of this comedy as a work of art.

The play, subtitled simply *A Melodrama,* does indeed contain all the stock ingredients of the traditional melodrama—the reading of a will, heroic sacrifice, court-martial, gallows, eleventh-hour reprieve, and the orphan who is befriended—"and all complete," as Shaw added, with "just that little bit of my own that makes all the difference."[38] What saves it from being merely a melodrama is its presentation of some of the advanced thought of the time.[39] Moreover, Shaw's use of the old form for his new purpose demonstrates his virtuosity as a playwright.

Richard Dudgeon, the protagonist, is a young man who rebels against the narrow creed of his mother, a pious, blue-nosed, cruel Puritan; and he announces that he is a disciple of Satan. When his father unexpectedly dies on his way home after seeing a brother hanged by the British, Richard appears for the reading of the will. He learns that all the property is left to him with a stipulation that "he shall not let my brother Peter's natural child starve or be driven by want to an evil life." Because Mrs. Dudgeon has mistreated Essie, the unfortunate child, Dick becomes at once the girl's protector and friend. He shockingly informs his family and their minister, the Reverend Anthony Anderson and his beautiful wife, Judith, that he is a follower of the Devil, his "natural master and captain and friend." He adds: "I saw that he was in the right, and that the world cringed to his conqueror only through fear. I prayed secretly to him; and he comforted me, and saved me from having my spirit broken in this house of children's tears." He turns to Anderson, saying, "So I hear you are married, Pastor, and that your wife has a most ungodly allowance of good looks."

ANDERSON (*quietly indicating Judith*) Sir: you are in the presence of my wife. (*Judith rises and stands with stony propriety*).
RICHARD (. . . *with instinctive good manners*) your servant, madam: no offence. (*He looks at her earnestly*). You deserve your reputation; but I am sorry to see by your expression that you are a good woman.

Richard announces that the British army is only a few miles away, and all except Essie and Dick depart. As his mother leaves, she utters a "dying curse" upon her son, who calls after her, "It will bring me luck. Ha ha ha!"

The events of Act II take place in the home of the Andersons. The minister tells his wife that he has called at Dudgeon's home to warn Richard of his imminent danger because the British are approaching with the idea of hanging him. Finding Dudgeon away, Anderson leaves word for Richard to come to the Anderson home; and Judith says she hopes he does not come because she "hates him." Anderson assures her she is not so wicked as she thinks. "The worst sin toward our fellow creatures is not to hate them, but to be indifferent to them; that's the essence of inhumanity."

Richard appears, but before Anderson can warn him of his danger, Christy, Dick's oafish young brother, bolts in to say his mother is seriously ill. Because she has sent for Anderson, not for Richard, Anderson asks Dick to stay with Judith until he makes his pastoral call. Reluctantly, the dutiful wife accepts the situation; and a squad of British soldiers appears outside not long after Anderson's departure. When a sergeant and two privates enter and arrest "Anthony Anderson" as a rebel, Dick pretends he is Anderson, speaks endearingly to Judith, kisses her good-bye, and she swoons away. When the pastor returns, he finds her still unconscious. Learning of Dudgeon's arrest Anderson takes to horse, leaving Judith to think that he is fleeing for his life.

In the meantime, the military court-martial takes place. General Burgoyne, a historical figure, "Gentleman Johnny" (whom Shaw miscalls "Gentlemanly Johnny"), is in charge. He is an intellectual and a playwright who appealed strongly to Shaw. In contrast to him is Sergeant Swindon, a typical militarist, and a stickler for formality and discipline. Burgoyne is almost apologetic in dealing with the prisoner, for the rules of war dictate that the captive must die, especially when Dudgeon (as Anderson) makes no defense but seems, in Burgoyne's words, "determined to be hanged." When Richard expresses a preference for death by firing squad, Burgoyne warns him that the marksmanship of His Majesty's army is such that half of them would miss him and that the rest would make a mess of the business. "Whereas we can hang you in a perfectly workmanlike and agreeable way. (*Kindly*) Let me persuade you to be hanged." Dudgeon withdraws his objection to the rope.

BURGOYNE (*smoothly*) Will 12 o'clock suit you, Mr. Anderson?
RICHARD. I shall be at your disposal then, General."

But, since Anthony Anderson arrives under an official safe-conduct to stop the proceedings just as the noose has been adjusted, Dudgeon is released. It is revealed that Burgoyne's cause is lost; his defeat at Saratoga is certain through no fault of his own, for the British War Office had failed to send orders to bring him the needed reinforcements. Thus Shaw seeks at the same time to correct history, to bring justice to a brave commander, and to satirize the military. In the end, Anderson and Dudgeon have reversed their roles: the minister has joined the militia as a captain and has invited Richard to occupy his pulpit, a typical Shavian paradox.

The love interest in the play is presented likewise in a manner typical of Shaw. Judith Anderson, in spite of herself, is drawn to Richard particularly after his offer to sacrifice his life (like Sidney Carton) on the gallows. She tells him, "Well, save yourself for my sake. And I will go with you to the end of the world." He replies that he was not dying for her or her husband, but only to fulfill a law of his nature. "I should have done the same," he declares, "for any other man in the town, or any other man's wife." Since the play presents a case of love denied, Shaw justifiably called it "a play for Puritans" and could refer to "the devil's disciple" as "a Puritan of the Puritans."[40] In his note "On Diabolonian Ethics," Shaw acknowledged his indebtedness to Charles Dickens, whose Clennam household in *Little Dorrit* was the model for Mrs. Dudgeon's, she herself being "a replica of Mrs. Clennam with certain circumstantial variations and perhaps a touch of the same author's Mrs. Gargery in *Great Expectations*."[41] For example, Mrs. Dudgeon's cold-heartedness toward Essie parallels Mrs. Clennam's cruelty to Little Dorrit.

No summary or interpretation of *The Devil's Disciple* can do full justice to it as a sparkling comedy capable of holding the interest of the playgoer or the reader from beginning to end. The chief characters are masterfully drawn; the dialogue is natural, witty, and sprightly; and the ideas are driven home with the sure hand of an artist. Consequently, *The Devil's Disciple* brought Shaw a larger monetary return than any other of his works up to that time. Its first production was in Albany, New York, with Richard Mansfield, for whom the role of Richard Dudgeon was intended. Three evenings later he transferred the play to New York City, where it enjoyed a run of sixty-four performances. American playgoers supported the play to a gross of £ 25,000, of which Shaw received ten percent. He exulted, "I should have had to write my heart out for six years in the *Saturday [Review]* to make as much."[42] The American success of *The Devil's Disciple* made it possible for its author to do two things: to resign from critical journalism and to think of himself as being financially able to consider marriage.

CHAPTER 4

Marriage and the Road to Greatness

DURING the time that Shaw was achieving success as a playwright, he continued as a member of the Fabian Society; for he was working, lecturing, and discussing the issues of the day with his friends Beatrice and Sidney Webb, Graham Wallas, Sidney Olivier, and others. A newcomer to the Fabians was Miss Charlotte Payne-Townshend, a young Irish woman of great wealth with advanced views about social issues. Having read *The Quintessence of Ibsenism*, she found the views it expressed congenial to her own way of thinking.[1] The Webbs not only introduced Shaw to Miss Payne-Townshend but also arranged for them to be together at a house party during six weeks of a summer vacation of the Fabians at Saxmundham in 1896. The two unattached guests bicycled together; they found many strong interests in common; and, by the following December, he was addressing her half-banteringly, "oh best beloved."[2] A month later she sent him flowers and a book[3] and still later a shawl. In a letter to her, January 9, 1897, Shaw wrote: "Thanks for the shawl. Far from recuperating, I contemplate Nature a shivering wreck."[4] As the closeness of their relationship increased, Charlotte became his "nurse" at the time of ailments and accidents to which he seemed to be prone, and, she also served him voluntarily as typist-secretary.

When they were apart, he wrote brief but cordial letters to Charlotte; but, at the same time, he continued his copious epistolary romance with the queenly actress Ellen Terry, a correspondence which began in 1892. In his garrulous preface to their published letters, Shaw twice mentions the fact that the thought of becoming Ellen Terry's husband had entered his mind but that theirs had been nothing more than "a paper courtship."[5] Shaw explains in the same preface that the ardor of his sentiments in the

letters to Miss Terry are to be ascribed to the openness with which
people of the theatre express their feelings toward each other and
that what seems like wholesale promiscuous kissing is a professional
custom.[6] (That it has not changed, anyone who watches "show
business" people on television knows well enough.) One of his
letters to Ellen Terry (September 8, 1897) ended with these words,
"I love you soulfully & bodyfully, properly and improperly, every
way that a woman can be loved."[7]

In fact, the two of them hardly met except across the footlights.
Even when they did meet, Shaw noted that "she was always a little
shy in speaking to me; for talking, hampered by material circumstances, is awkward and unsatisfactory after the perfect
freedom of writing between people who *can* write."[8] Shaw explained that he and Ellen Terry lived "within twenty minutes of
each other's doorstep, and yet lived in different worlds: she in a
theatre that was a century behind the times, and I in a political
society (the Fabian) a century ahead of them."[9]

In contrast to this relationship, Shaw and Charlotte Payne-
Townshend shared the same world. During a protracted absence, he
wrote that he missed her "in lots of ways." Ten days later he addressed her "Ever dearest" and recounted a bicycle accident in
which he "got just enough hurt to make you tender to me."[10] The
Shaw letters clearly indicate that Charlotte was the hunted, not the
huntress. She did not force her attentions on him during the
courtship, which lasted two years, until she became concerned
about his health after she had observed the dirt and squalor in
which he was living at 29 Fitzroy Square, West.[11] One day, after
seeing that he was haggard and ill and on crutches, she invited him
for a talk in her quarters at 10 Adelphi Terrace; for the time had
arrived for drastic action because of his need for rest and country
air. When she offered to rent a house in which she and a staff of
nurses could give him proper care, he countered by proposing
marriage.[12]

Charlotte accepted; and the wedding took place on June 1, 1898,
at the register office in the district of the Strand. As Shaw describes
the occasion, it is one of the oddest nuptial ceremonies on record.
He was very ill, "altogether a wreck on crutches and in an old jacket
which the crutches had worn to rags." He had invited two
friends—Graham Wallas, a Fabian and a member of the London
School Board, and H. S. Dequincey—to serve as witnesses. Both
came "dressed in their best clothes." Taking Shaw as "the in-

evitable beggar who completes all wedding processions," the registrar proceeded to marry Charlotte to the tall and handsome Wallas, who, in Shaw's words, "thinking the formula rather strong for a mere witness, hesitated at the last minute and left the prize to me."[13]

The bridegroom was forty-two; the bride, forty-one. From all accounts it was, by and large, a happy marriage. It fulfilled an idea Shaw developed in *The Philanderer;* namely, that the best marital relation must be based, not on romantic love, but on a sound economic foundation with mutual convenience and mutual respect. Their marriage had a solid basis of intelligence, consideration, and, on the whole, congeniality.[14] Just as the marriage gave Shaw an improved environment in which to live and work, it gave Charlotte for the first time a positive purpose in life.

I *Two Major Plays and a Prophecy*

Coincidentally, Shaw entered with his marriage upon the most important epoch of his career. It was the era he had had in mind when, in talking with American critic John Mason Brown, he had referred to himself as "the historic Shaw, the man of my middle years, the Shaw the world will remember."[15] Ahead of him lay the high road to greatness through the writing of his major plays that presented, with artistry, the ideas of his philosophy and religion to the world. Whatever else he was, Shaw was a man with a mission and a message. According to G. K. Chesterton, who knew Shaw and understood him well, all the plays were "plays for Puritans."[16] Chesterton emphatically declares: "There is at least one outstanding fact about the man we are studying; Bernard Shaw is never frivolous. He never gives his opinions a holiday; he is never irresponsible even for an instant."[17] The G.B.S. persona, as we have noted, was only an attention-getting device, a publicity agent.

Since Shaw conceived of himself primarily as a teacher, his writings were to be didactic. He declared that for art's sake alone he would not face the toil of writing a single sentence.[18] All great art, he insisted, is propaganda, by which he meant it was for the propagation of ideas. Accordingly, his dramas are designated by such terms as "the comedy of ideas," the "discussion play," and "corrective comedy," terms that apply likewise to the work of Ibsen and Chekhov. The discussion play (sometimes called the dialectic or disquisitory play) and the comedy-of-ideas plays are based on the premise that *ideas* can be as dramatic as love-making or murder on the stage; for action, to be dramatic, need not be overt.

M. Augustin Hamon in his book *The Twentieth Century Molière: Bernard Shaw*, makes a useful distinction between "material action" and "intellectual action." In the material-action play, a progression of outward events occurs—rising action, climax, and denouement—as in the well-made plays of France. In Molière and Shaw's intellectual dramas, according to Hamon, the overt action is subordinated to events resembling "real life, where nothing begins and nothing comes to an end."[19] As for "corrective comedy," it is another way of describing dramatic satire, a form of writing which employs laughter for the purpose of amelioration. Shaw knew that in order to instruct he must also entertain his audience or his readers, lest they sleep. With imagination and cleverness, he used the devices which the theatre, past and present, afforded him; and all these points are well illustrated, as we shall see, in his next play.

II   "Better Than Shakespeare?"

Bernard Shaw is undoubtedly the only author in history to get married while writing a play whose theme is the denial of romantic love. It was entitled *Caesar and Cleopatra*, the second of the *Three Plays for Puritans*, and was by far the most ambitious and most elaborate drama he had attempted up to that time.[20] But the wedding and other events slowed for a while his progress on the manuscript, which he had started two months before. The thoughtful bride rented a pleasant house in Haslemere, Surrey, for his recuperation from his foot injury and from his overwork.

To Grant Richards he wrote: "My wife is having *such* a delightful honeymoon! First my foot had to be nursed and the day before yesterday, just as I was getting pretty well, I fell downstairs and broke my left arm close to the wrist." He recovered in due course.[21] The leisurely life in the country, with its clean air and occasional sunshine, reinvigorated him; his tensions subsided, and he slept better than he had for years. In October, he reported that he was having difficulty in getting drama out of the story of *Caesar and Cleopatra*—"nothing but comedy & character."[22] But by the end of the year he informed Ellen Terry that he had finished "the first & only adequate dramatization of the greatest man that ever lived."

Shaw frankly declares that he offers his Caesar to the public as "an improvement on Shakespear's."[23] It was an improvement, however, not because Shaw believed he could write a better play than the Bard, but because the nineteenth century had shed new light on Julius Caesar. Shaw credits the German historian Theodor Mommsen with giving the world a new and sounder concept of the great Roman general than the Elizabethans had had at their disposal.[24] Mommsen stresses the concept of Caesar as a statesman rather than a military leader.

Unlike Shakespeare's pompous "great Caesar," who seems almost as if stepping down from a pedestal, the protagonist in Shaw's play is an original man who behaves in a natural manner. "Having virtue, he had no need of goodness."[25] In other words, his ideas of morality and success transcend the notions popularly held. The ambition ascribed to him by Plutarch and Shakespeare was "an instinct for exploration" such as we find in Christopher Columbus and Benjamin Franklin.[26] Moreover, he possesses a delightful sense of humor, there being, according to Shaw, "abundant evidence of his light-heartedness and adventurousness."

Shaw's Caesar is a statesman who acts like Lincoln and, above all, a philosopher who thinks like the playwright himself. This fact led William Irvine to refer to Caesar as "an idealized picture of Shaw in a toga."[27] The great conqueror can, like the Emancipator, forgive an enemy and work for the peace and reconciliation: he is a teacher who has the good of the world at heart. In his efficiency, he has been compared to Henry Ford, John D. Rockefeller, and Cecil Rhodes. "And yet," to cite Irvine again, "though a Shavian paragon, he has with great artistic skill been made sympathetic and convincing. . . . Caesar is frugal, rheumatic, out of humor when he is hungry, and sensitive about his age and baldness. He views himself and the world with indulgent amusement."[28] In a paradox typical of his creator, he is a world conqueror who advocates non-violence. G. K. Chesterton regards Caesar as Shaw's greatest reach of artistic creation.[29]

In *The Sanity of Art*, Shaw makes a significant statement about his concept of characters in the drama.

I deal with all periods, but I never study any period but the present, which I have not yet mastered and never shall; and as a dramatist I have no clue to any historical or other personage save that part of him which is also myself, and which may be nine tenths of him or ninety-nine hundredths, as the case may be (if indeed I do not transcend the creature), but which, anyhow, is all that can ever come within my knowledge of his soul. The man who writes about himself and his own time is the only man who writes about all people and about all time.[30]

As a result of this view, Caesar is at least nine-tenths Shaw. What of Cleopatra? Is she more than a foil to emphasize the greatness of Caesar? She is, as Shaw presents her, a kittenish girl of sixteen with more charm and egotism than docility and intelligence. Like Elizabeth I, she lives in fear for her throne, for her rival is her younger brother Ptolemy. Though historically, according to Plutarch, she bore a son (Caesarian) to the conqueror, she is no Circe, no sexpot; for she bears hardly any resemblance at all to the amorous queen of Shakespeare's play. Shaw's focus in *Caesar and Cleopatra* is on a middle-aged Caesar—he is fifty-five—who undertakes to teach one who is "as yet but a child that is whipped by her nurse" how to become the ruler of a nation.[31] This fact brings to mind another way in which the play as a historical drama shows an affinity to the history plays of Shakespeare.[32] The Henry and Richard plays particularly represent Shakespeare's attempts to portray both the negative and positive sides of the good monarch.

Of the minor characters in *Caesar and Cleopatra* a few deserve special mention. Britannus, Caesar's secretary, is described as "a Briton, about forty, tall, solemn, and already slightly bald."[33] As a rather stodgy and imperceptive man, he typifies the English of Shaw's day, not Caesar's. An instrument of satire, he is the butt of Caesar's jokes; and he often evinces horror at his master's unconventional actions. Appollodorus, a Sicilian who is "a dashing young man of about twenty-four, handsome and debonair," is an aesthete, a believer in "Art for Art's sake," who pays earnest suit to Cleopatra.[34] Ftatateeta, the queen's chief nurse, is "a huge grim woman, her face covered with a network of tiny wrinkles, and her eyes old, large, and wise; sinewy handed, very tall, very strong; with the mouth of a bloodhound and the jaws of a bulldog." Her imperious, haughty bearing is impressive; and she usually rules Cleopatra with an iron hand.[35]

Ptolemy XIV, Cleopatra's brother and husband, is six years her junior; and Theodotus is Ptolemy's tutor. Belzanor, a warrior of fifty, is captain of the queen's guard. Pothinus, also aged fifty, is Ptolemy's guard, a eunuch, and a schemer. Rufio is a Roman officer, "a burly, black-bearded man of middle age, very blunt, prompt and rough." A favorite of Caesar's, but no sycophant, he is appointed governor at the end of the play. Lucius Septimus, another of Caesar's officers, boasts that he killed Pompey, an act that horrifies Caesar.

In the opening scene of *Caesar and Cleopatra,* the huge shape of a sphinx "pedestalled on the sands" dominates the stage. Between its paws a young girl—Cleopatra—lies asleep. When Caesar approaches and addresses the brooding sculpture, he concludes by saying significantly: "My way hither was the way of destiny; for I am he of whose genius you are the symbol: part brute, part woman, and part god—nothing of man in me at all. Have I read your riddle, Sphinx?" In this speech, we find more than a hint of Shaw's conception of Caesar as a Superman.

From the paws of the Sphinx Cleopatra, not knowing who has been speaking, calls, "Old gentleman: don't run away. . . . Climb up here quickly; or the Romans will come and eat you up." Later she is astonished to discover that the "old gentleman" is indeed the dreaded Caesar. He becomes her teacher, though he is so busy with affairs that he cannot give her much attention. Yet she becomes more and more dependent on him as the play progresses. At one point (Act III), Caesar, leaving the queen behind, goes to the Island of Pharos, after ordering its capture; and Cleopatra is determined to follow him. By boat, Appollodorus delivers to Caesar a carpet as a present from Cleopatra. When the carpet is hoisted up and unrolled, Cleopatra steps out.

Though she becomes more and more impressed with Caesar's greatness and grows in dignity and status, she is not altogether an apt pupil. Motivated by fear, she tries to find security through power rather than through wisdom; for Caesar's wise ways as a statesman-soldier do not transfer to Cleopatra. For instance, when Pothinus plots against his life, Caesar forgives him and disarms him with friendliness; but Cleopatra, acting behind Caesar's back, orders Ftatateeta to kill Pothinus. Caesar's reaction to this murder is the climax of the play, and his speech about it is one of the most memorable passages in all of Shaw's dramas. Outraged at the assassination of "our prisoner, our guest," Caesar turns and looks at Cleopatra, who confesses: "He was slain by order of the Queen of Egypt. I am not Julius Caesar the dreamer, who allows every slave to insult him." After Rufio, Lucius, Appollodorus, and Britannus each in turn voice support for Cleopatra's order, Caesar speaks:

. . . (*with quiet bitterness*) And so the verdict is against me, it seems.

CLEOPATRA. (*vehemently*) Listen to me Caesar. If one man in all Alexan-

dria can be found to say that I did wrong, I swear to have myself crucified
on the door of the palace by my own slaves.

CAESAR. If one man in all the world can be found, now or forever, to
know that you did wrong, that man will have either to conquer the world as
I have, or be crucified by it. (*The uproar in the street again reaches them*).
Do you hear? These knockers at your gate are also believers in vengeance
and in stabbing. You have slain their leader: it is right that they shall slay
you. If you doubt it, ask your four counsellors here. And then in the name
of that right (*he emphasizes the word with great scorn*) shall I not slay them
for murdering their Queen, and be slain in my turn by their countrymen as
the invader of their fatherland? Can Rome do less than slay these slayers,
too, to show the world how Rome avenges her sons and her honor. And so,
to the end of history, murder shall breed murder, always in the name of
right and honor and peace, until the gods are tired of blood and create a
race that can understand.[36]

"A race that can understand" is essentially what Shaw meant by
the Superman, a concept that was to assume an important place in
all his later thinking and writing. Indeed, although opposition to
violence, vengeance, and war became Shaw's ruling passion he does
not condemn all killing. As if in fulfillment of Caesar's prophecy,
Cleopatra at the end of Act IV finds Ftatateeta lying dead with her
throat cut on the altar of Ra. Rufio has slain her, as it turns out, with
Caesar's approval; for he had evidently thought his pupil incapable
of learning a lesson in any other way. As Caesar departs for Rome
coolness exists between him and Cleopatra; but she becomes reconciled when he promises to send her a son of Rome, one who is unlike Caesar, "brisk and fresh, strong and young, hoping in the
morning, fighting in the day, and revelling in the evening."
Palpitatingly, Cleopatra asks "His name, his name?" Caesar asks,
"Shall it be Mark Anthony? (*She throws herself into his arms.*)"
Something strangely symbolical appears in Cleopatra's (the world's)
preference for physical pleasure instead of the spiritual teachings of
Caesar (Shaw).

Assuredly this play represents a lofty reach of artistic achievement, and exemplifies Shaw's powers at their best.[37] To begin with,
the characters are masterfully drawn, each serving as a contrast to
the central figure, Caesar. Cleopatra's immaturity emphasizes
Caesar's wisdom; and Appollodorus's narrow estheticism, his "Art
for Art's sake" slogan, contrasts with Caesar's broader vision of the
possibilities of art as the servant and transformer of life. Britannus's
limitations as a provincial-minded "little Islander" with a fanatical

concern for "British respectability" bring out in full relief his master's cosmopolitan mind and personality. Rufio is a conventional soldier who contrasts to Caesar's imaginative, inspirational military methods. The scenes of *Caesar and Cleopatra* are beautifully evocative, and the incidents are cleverly wrought. The dialogue includes some of Shaw's wittiest and most impressive lines. The ideas, especially those of nonviolence and forgiveness, are highly significant. In no other play does Shaw more skillfully combine instruction and entertainment.

An effective motion-picture version of *Ceasar and Cleopatra* opened what appeared to be almost "limitless possibilities," as Shaw himself put it in 1945 when the play was being filmed under the direction of Gabriel Pascal. Seeing the huge Sphinx pictured, Shaw exclaimed: "When I look back on my work as a young man with my colleagues in the theatre, it seems to me we were like children playing with wretched makeshift toys. Here you have the whole world to play with!"[38] But the playwright's enthusiasm for the filming of *Caesar and Cleopatra* ended in partial disappointment when the screen production was commercially unsuccessful. It was not, however, an artistic failure; for Claude Rains was excellent as Caesar, and Vivien Leigh was more than competent as Cleopatra. Happily, the movie reproduced the dialogue almost as Shaw wrote it. An important point is that millions who otherwise would have had no opportunity to see it experienced *Caesar and Cleopatra*.

III   *A Play for Ellen Terry*

Shaw tells us that *Captain Brassbound's Conversion*, the last of the *Three Plays for Puritans*, resulted from Ellen Terry's remark upon receiving news of her son's first child, "Now I am a grandmother, nobody will ever write a play for me." Shaw wrote the play, as she said, "out of a natural desire to contradict."[39] He created Lady Cicely, the leading role, out of his knowledge of Miss Terry through her letters to him; and he had no firsthand knowledge of Morocco, the locale of *Brassbound*, when he wrote this play. The main source, however, is Cunninghame Graham's (in Shaw's words) "excellent book of philosophic travel and vivid adventure entitled Mogreb-el-Acksa (Morocco the Most Holy)." Shaw declares that he was "intelligent enough to steal its scenery, its surroundings, its atmosphere, its knowledge of the east, its fascinating Cadis and Krooboys and Sheiks and mud castles."[40]

Shaw once referred to *Captain Brassbound* as "that excellent Christian tract" and thus illumined the main theme, which is the foolishness of vengeance and violence.[41] The influence of Shelley on this play is unmistakable, not only in the reference to the Atlas Mountains but also in the basic ideas of the play. The theme of vengeance is found both in Shelley's "Witch of Atlas" and in Shaw's *Captain Brassbound's Conversion*. As Roland Duerksen puts it, "Had Shaw chosen to supply his play with a motto, he could scarcely have found one more suitable than Shelley's lines:

> The magic circle of her voice and eyes
> All savage natures did imparadise.

Shelley's witch, like Lady Cicely, introduces a new spirit of confidence, trust, and selflessness into a world which knows only the old codes of fear, aggression, and revenge."[42] A subsidiary theme in *Brassbound* is the backwardness of a judicial system which is based on vindictiveness and retribution, and still another theme of the play is what might be called, in Ashley Montague's phrase, "the natural superiority of woman."

When Lady Cicely Waynefleet travels to Morocco in the company of her brother-in-law Sir Howard Hallam, a prominent judge, they are the guests of Leslie Rankin, a Presbyterian missionary, since there is no hotel in the seaport of Mogador. When Lady Cicely expresses her desire to travel in the nearby Atlas Mountains, she is warned about the danger of travel in the interior; but she insists and, on the recommendation of an unprincipled person, Felix Drinkwater, Captain Brassbound (known as the Black Paquinto, a brigand) of the schooner *Thanksgiving* and his crew are engaged as escorts. The English travelers do not know what they are to experience, though Brassbound warns Hallam not to go on the expedition: "You are safe here. I warn you, in those hills there is a justice that is not the justice of your courts in England. If you have wronged a man, you may meet that man there. If you have wronged a woman, you may meet her son there. The justice of those hills is the justice of vengeance." The Black Paquinto warns, "Take care. The avenger may be one of the escort." But Sir Howard, like Lady Cicely, is unafraid.

As it turns out, Brassbound, a nephew of the judge, has for many years sought vengeance against Hallam for allegedly defrauding Brassbound and his mother out of their rightful inheritance and for thus indirectly causing his mother's death. Consequently, Brass-bound has his uncle arrested in a Moorish castle and turns him over to Sheik Sidi el Assif as a slave. At this point, Lady Cicely begins Captain Brassbound's conversion when her tact, charm, and logic convince him that he should give up his vendetta against his uncle. When Brassbound goes to the sheik, whom Lady Cicely had met and captivated, and offers to buy Hallam back at whatever price he chooses to name, Sidi says: "It is well. You shall keep this man and give me the woman in payment." With this arrangement Lady Cicely says she would be delighted.

Before Sidi el Assif can depart with his prize, an American navy cruiser, the *Santiago*, arrives in the harbor. Captain Hamlin Kearney in the name of the United States demands that the prisoners be returned to him. Meanwhile, the Cadi of Kintafi comes and upbraids the sheik for capturing the travelers. He releases Lady Cicely and Hallam, but he makes prisoners of Brassbound and his crew. The whole episode smacks of a *deus ex machina* and is one of the weaknesses of the play.

The next scene is back in Leslie Rankin's house where a room has been arranged for the judicial inquiry with Captain Kearney as the presiding officer. Lady Cicely is determined to do all she can to help Brassbound, as he has requested her to do. After all, he has forgiven Sir Howard, as she emphasizes in a discussion with the missionary. When the prisoners are brought in for the inquiry, Brassbound appears dressed fashionably, spotlessly, elegantly; and Lady Cicely, who is responsible for his transformation, walks with him, arm in arm. She promptly takes charge of the proceedings, tells a story of the happenings, sufficiently to Kearney's satisfaction that he releases the prisoners. When Hallam reminds Lady Cicely that she has not told "the whole truth," she replies: "What non-sense! As if anybody ever knew the whole truth about anything." So Captain Kearney is spared the story of the reconciliation of Brassbound and Sir Hallam. Since Brassbound sees this reconcilia-tion as the end of his life's purpose, he forthwith turns to Lady Cicely, says he needs a commander, and proposes that she marry him. As she is almost ready to accept him, they hear gunfire from the *Thanksgiving*, and Brassbound knows his fate is sealed and that he must bid her farewell. As he returns to his gunboat, she exclaims: "How glorious! How glorious! And what an escape!"

This play, which Shaw subtitled *An Adventure*, is the most exotic of his dramas until the end of the century. Also, despite its noble themes it is the least important of the *Three Plays for Puritans*. The most definite achievement of *Captain Brassbound's Conversion* is the characterization of Lady Cicely, one of Shaw's memorable evocations, who possesses that quality of efficiency which Shaw admired wherever he found it. There is a great deal of Shaw's Caesar in her as well as something of Shaw himself, for Shaw, like his heroine, hated violence and had "no element of vindictiveness in him."[43] Without its lone woman, this comedy would be a failure; only an actress with force and vivacity could carry the play to success on the stage.

Accordingly, Shaw was deeply disappointed when Ellen Terry disdained the part that he had created for her. He assured her that Lady Cicely was radically different from Cleopatra, who depended on her passions to control men, and from Candida, "with her boy and her parson, and her suspicion of trading a little on the softness of her contours." Lady Cicely's superiority is not sexual, but moral; with this power, by implication, she could control empires and forward civilization itself in ways military might could never do. He ended the letter with: "Oh, Ellen, Ellen, Ellen, Ellen. This is the end of everything."[44] But it was not the end; she played Lady Cicely seven years after the part was offered to her. Ellen Terry was fifty-eight at the time.[45]

Max Beerbohm's adverse comment on *Captain Brassbound's Conversion* elicited one of Shaw's most self-revealing admonitions. He said: "Stick to my plays long enough, and you will get used to their changes of key & mode. I learnt my flexibility & catholicity from Beethoven; but it is to be learnt from Shakespear to a certain extent. My education has really been more a musical than a literary one as far as dramatic art is concerned. Nobody nursed on letters alone will ever get the true Mozartian joyousness into comedy."[46]

IV   *A Fabian Manifesto and A Prophecy*

But the joyousness of comedy, Mozartian or otherwise, at times gave way to Shaw's civic duty. From 1897 to 1903, he served on the St. Pancras Council or Vestry, as it was called in those times. Regarded as a liberal and a radical, as well as a Fabian Socialist, his stance is indicated by his statement: "A vigorous County Council, spending freely on public health, convenience, and safety, saves the rate-payer more than it costs him. It is better to pay a shilling more to the rate collector than a couple of pounds more to the doctor."

One of the reforms he advocated as a vestryman was that women should be represented on a committee in charge of providing public facilities in the city. For his efforts, he gained only accusations of being "indecent", and the public toilets remained "For Men Only."[47] This fact disgusted Shaw, who was an advocate of Women's Rights from first to last.

Out of his experience as a Borough Councillor came a Fabian tract *The Common Sense of Municipal Trading* and a background for some of the political considerations in his plays as well as in his nonfiction books. He ran as a Labour candidate for the London County Council in 1904, and that unsuccessful campaign ended his political career. This defeat, however, did not end his interest in political affairs, which took an international turn partly because of the Boer War (1899 - 1902). Shaw was born early enough to remember the American Civil War; he had read about the Franco-Prussian War of 1870 and about the Spanish-American War; he lived through World Wars I and II; and the fighting in the Korean conflict began before his death in 1950. It was, however, the Boer War in South Africa which first led not only Shaw but his fellow-Fabians to take a firm stand on the issues of armed conflict and imperialism. Heretofore, their concern had been largely with domestic problems.

To bring together the English Socialist concepts of international issues, Shaw served as editor of *Fabianism and the Empire*, a tract which, as it turned out, was also a manifesto and a prophecy. Though it is not within the scope and province of this book to deal with Shaw's voluminous Fabian tracts, this work is pertinent because it sets forth the playwright's views about peace, a subject that was to concern him the rest of his life. *Fabianism and the Empire* was ostensibly a summary and synthesis of the party's views on world problems; but, though he submitted the manuscript to other members for their scrutiny and suggestions, actually it was mostly Shaw's own thoughts. E. R. Pease, the chief historian of the Fabian Society, considers it to be the best of Shaw's political pamphlets.[48]

As to the South African war, Shaw surprisingly favored the British rather than the Boers; for he reasoned that England had a superior civilization, by which he meant a better soil in which socialism could grow. According to *Fabianism and the Empire*, the expansion of powerful nations is a natural development in the dividing of the waste places of the earth; and this development is a fact which is to be accepted. Since no nation has the right to isolate itself and to do what it pleases with its own territory, it must recognize the rights of its neighbors to trade and travel within its borders.[49] The Boer War was a tragic error which the government did not intend. The tract, consistently with Shaw's opinion, assailed militarism and the British army. Soldiers were underpaid and were also often brutalized by military discipline, which was sometimes used to cover up the selfishness and inefficiency of the officers.[50] Moreover, the Fabian tract adversely criticized the English military establishment for its ineptitude, which resulted in many unnecessary casualties.

Deploring the Boer War and all wars, Shaw believed that armed combat was a social phenomenon that had to be faced when it happened. No absolute pacifist, G.B.S. did not oppose war on moral grounds, but on its economic wastefulness. He considered war to be a "costly and intolerable nuisance" which the nations should banish from the earth.[51] Therefore, he held that, until peace was established, disarmament was an act of foolishness; and he advocated that Britain build up its military power.

Might, however, did not make right; but a superior civilization and a greater efficiency were, in Shaw's view, what entitled a country, large or small, to its rights in the world. In the administration of foreign affairs, the aristocracy of ability had to be recognized. The consular service had, however, to be revised in order to make it the servant of peace, not war. In particular, England had to achieve good relations with India and its Congress party and grant all her colonies political liberty. His warning about the possible dissolution of the Empire proved to be amazingly prophetic.

CHAPTER 5

"Comedies of Science and Religion"

I Man and Superman

IN a time when automobiles were so rare as to be objects of curiosity, Shaw put one on the stage in Act II of *Man and Superman* (1901) in his usual effort to give amusement as well as to evoke thought. To him, the motorcar was symbolic of the new age of mechanical wonders at the dawn of the twentieth century. In this play, subtitled *A Comedy and a Philosophy*, the comedy is found mainly in the love affair of John Tanner, a member of the English idle-rich class, and his ward, Ann Whitefield. She is a woman of social standing and personal force, but she is by no means Tanner's equal intellectually. Tanner, whose character is reminiscent of Trefusis in *An Unsocial Socialist*, is the author of "The Revolutionist's Handbook" and "Maxims for Revolutionists," both of which are printed with the play.

Shaw reverses the usual social order by making the woman the huntress and the man the hunted.[1] After Ann takes aim on Tanner, he has no escape. A mild complication develops in the love of Octavius Robinson, a poet, for Ann; but she soon makes clear her preference. Tanner, who is by far the stronger of the two suitors, is the better candidate for the fatherhood of Ann's children. Her love actually is more eugenic than sexual though she has abundant physical attraction. John, for whom Don Juan is the prototype, manages to elude Ann's lures during Act I and Act II, as well as in most of Act IV, but at the very end of the play he fully succumbs. Indeed, as Charles A. Carpenter and Margery Morgan have shown, a great deal of sexual symbolism and natural history appears in those final pages of *Man and Superman*. In John and Ann's embrace—far different from the usual clinch at the end of romantic movies—Shaw presents his characters in the power of the Life Force, the true basis of sexual attraction.[2]

Shaw follows the practice of Shakespeare and others in creating a subplot in this play. It has to do with Violet Robinson, sister to Octavius, and a wealthy American, Hector Malone, Sr., whose son, Hector Jr., is in love with Violet. When it is reported that Violet is pregnant without benefit of clergy, various persons express degrees of shock: but Tanner defends Violet's right to have a child because of the promptings of Nature. When Roebuck Ramsden calls Violet's supposed seducer "a damned scoundrel" and agrees with Octavius that she must marry the father of her child, Tanner horrifies Ramsden with his view: "So we are to marry your sister to a damned scoundrel by way of reforming her character: On my soul, I think you are all mad."[3] Tanner also adds fuel to the flames by offering financial assistance to Violet in her plight. Later she reveals that she has been married to young Hector and that they have kept their wedding a secret for fear of offending his father who wished Hector to marry a title. Malone, Sr., becomes reconciled to the situation and all goes well.

The difference in aim and outlook between the Malones, father and son, is one among several instances of Shaw's use of contrast, a literary device he had probably learned from Dickens. Similarly, there is a striking contrast between Ramsden and Tanner. Ramsden is an elderly business man who becomes, along with John, co-guardian of Ann Whitefield after the death of her father. An archconservative, who insists on his "advanced views," he is shocked and repelled by Tanner's revolutionary opinions. Octavius, a poet, likewise serves as a foil to Tanner; for he is unromantic in his thought and behavior. He is a "genius" character who accepts and fears the Life Force and who is indeed remarkably like Shaw himself. Robinson, on the other hand, is conventional, ineffectual, sentimental—the type of man whom, as Ann sees, the Life Force has eluded. One of the liveliest situations in the play is Tanner's assuring Tavy that Ann is merely playing "hard to get" but that she really intends to trap Robinson; for she is really pursuing Tanner himself all along.

Mendoza—the exotic hold-up man and poetaster who was deliberately stolen by Shaw, as he admitted, from Conan Doyle—is a marked contrast to all other characters in *Man and Superman*, except that, like Octavius, he had a disappointing love affair. Wholly apart from any romantic entanglements is Henry Straker, Tanner's chauffeur, an important character whose diversity from all the other characters is also striking. After a discussion of education, labor, and socialism with Straker, Tanner refers to him when he says to the effete Octavius: "That's a momentous social phenomenon. Here have we literary and cultured persons been for years setting up a cry for the New Woman . . . and never noticing the advent of the New Man. Straker's the New Man."[4] Straker is a direct fictional descendant of Edward Conolly, the protagonist of *The Irrational Knot*, whose employer referred to him as "a genius as an electrician."[5] Though the prototype of Straker was Leporello, valet to Mozart's Don Giovanni, Shaw transforms him into "an intentional dramatic sketch for Wells's anticipation of the efficient engineering class which will, he hopes, finally sweep the jabberers out of the way of civilization."[6]

Shaw shows great admiration for practical men of efficiency and perhaps intends a satirical jibe at his own profession. Still, he would not put the engineers who created the Atomic Age and those who planned and accomplished the landings on the moon as the supreme heroes of our time. The artists and philosophers must also be respected and encouraged to serve the spiritual needs of men. As Eric Bentley has shrewdly observed, with Shaw on most questions it is not "Either/Or," but rather "Both/And."[7] He could see that engineers, efficient politicians, artists, and thinkers are all important in their varying capacities. Moreover, he could recognize that there was more than one side to any political, economic, sociological, artistic, or religious issue. To Shaw, truth was to be found, not on any altar of dogmatism, but on the anvil of discussion.

II   Don Juan in Hell

Discussion abounds in all Shaw's important dramas, but nowhere is it more interesting or more revealing than in the famous Act III of *Man and Superman*. This interlude or dream sequence can be and is often produced as a separate play, *Don Juan in Hell*. Act III opens on a group of brigands, tramps, Social-Democrats, an anarchist, and a bull-fighting inebriate who are led by Mendoza, a Jew, "a tall strong man, with a striking cockatoo nose, glossy black hair, pointed beard, upturned moustache, and a Mephistophelean . . . swagger."[8] They are located in a secluded spot in the Spanish Sierra Nevada Mountains where they are intent on holding up motor cars and in securing a more equitable distribution of wealth. When an automobile approaches and is stopped by nails strewn in the road, its occupants are Tanner and Straker; who have eluded

Ann and her party and who are fleeing madly across Europe to reach Marseilles, Gibraltar, Genoa, or "any port from which they can sail to a Mahometan county where men are protected from women."[9] Captured without a struggle by the brigands, they enter into a discussion mainly with Mendoza, who refers to himself as a Socialist. When the bandit chief, introduces himself with "I am a brigand: I live by robbing the rich," Tanner replies: "I am a gentleman: I live by robbing the poor."[10] After a while, Mendoza reads some original love poetry, which puts Tanner and Straker to sleep; and a dream accompanied by Mozartian music ensues. Nothing else in all Shaw's works surpasses the witty, humorous, incisive, and socially significant dialogue of the dream. Since no analysis can do it justice, it should be read or heard.[11]

The characters are: (1) The Old Woman, Donna Ana (Ann Whitefield); (2) Don Juan (Tanner); (3) The Devil (Mendoza); and (4) The Statue (Roebuck Ramsden), who in the Dream is Donna Ana's father and is known as the Commander. Ana is Everywoman, the eternal mother type;[12] but she is also a caricature of conventional piety. When she finds she is in hell, she regrets that she was not more wicked on earth and complains that all her good deeds were wasted. Shaw's Don Juan, who is quite unlike the usual concept of him as a ladies' man who spent most of his life in *amours* for which he achieved a shady reputation, is more like Mozart's, but he is indeed an original creation. In an early story entitled "Don Giovanni Explains" Shaw portrayed him as more of a Puritan than a libertine. Likewise, in the dream scene Juan is one who shuns women and seeks wisdom: he is, in truth, a philosopher rather than an erotic. The Commander, a Philistine who comes down to hell for relief from the boredom of heaven, is intellectually superior to the other characters just as he (as Ramsden) was in his earthly life. The Devil is presented in a sympathetic light (an idea derived partly from John Milton's concept of Satan) as an intellectual of depth, insight, and eloquence.

These four have a long discussion about many subjects—the nature of Heaven and Hell, of society and socialism; of war and the weapons of war; of love, politics, evolution, marriage, and the Life Force; of Man, Woman, and the Superman. Though written more than seventy years ago, the speech of the Devil about Man and his weapons reads as if published in the latest periodical of political comment: "Have you walked up and down upon the earth lately? I have; and I have examined Man's wonderful inventions. And I tell you that in the arts of life man invents nothing; but in the arts of death he outdoes Nature herself, and produces by chemistry and machinery all the slaughter of plague, pestilence, and famine. . . . There is nothing in Man's industrial machinery but his greed and sloth: his heart is in his weapons. This marvellous force of Life of which you boast is a force of Death: Man measures his strength by his destructiveness."[13] This speech, uttered by a skillful actor in a time when multiple billions are spent on hydrogen bombs and on defensive and offensive missiles with installations of stupendous costs, surely evokes a sense of the dramatic. It is the climax of the play.

For the idea of Creative Evolution, the pervasive theme in *Man and Superman*, Shaw is indebted to the French philosopher Henri Bergson, whose concept of the *élan vital* is similar to Shaw's Life Force. Shaw also owes a great debt to Wagner's *The Ring* with its emphasis on life as "a tireless power which is continually driving onward and upward."[14] In this upward spiral of the evolutionary process there is more of the Lamarckian than the Darwinian theory, as Shaw sees it. He learned much from Schopenhauer's *The World as Will and Idea* and from Nietzsche's Superman. Shaw's concept differed radically, however, from Zarathustra's and more closely resembled Carlyle's "able man" in *Heroes and Hero-Worship*, particularly the *Vates* who, "whether Prophet or Poet," has penetrated the divine mystery or open secret of the universe.[15] Samuel Butler, the author of *The Way of All Flesh* and *Luck or Cunning?*, also contributed a great deal to Shaw's concept of the Life Force. Like Butler, Shaw, who did not share the pessimism of Schopenhauer and Nietzsche, looked upon himself as a meliorist. He believed that through Creative Evolution man can slowly but gradually improve as literature, music, and the other arts refine and civilize the consciousness of the race. But everything depends on whether men can learn to cooperate with the Life Force in its effort to create that higher consciousness, the only hope of achieving a world without injustice and violence. Such is the message of *Man and Superman*.

Clearly, as in *Caesar and Cleopatra* and in *Captain Brassbound's Conversion*, Shaw no longer proposes socialism as the solution of the world's problems. He does not abandon socialism, but he ceases giving it the central place in his thought. Politics as a priority has given way to religion when he expresses his purpose thus: "As I have not been sparing of such lighter qualities as I could endow the book with for the sake of those who ask nothing from a play but an agreeable pastime, I think it well to affirm plainly that the third act, however fantastic its legendary framework may appear, is a careful attempt to write a new Book of Genesis for the Bible of the Evolutionists. . . ."[16] As Shaw conceives Him, God is not only a Being, but also a Becoming. "To me the sole hope for human salvation lies," he writes, "in teaching Man to regard himself as an experiment in the realization of God, to regard his hands as God's hands, his brain as God's brain, his purpose as God's purpose. He must regard God as a helpless Longing, which *longed* him into existence by its desperate need for an executive organ."[17]

By the time Shaw wrote *Man and Superman*, he was convinced that *homo sapiens* was a failure as a political animal. In the Epistle Dedicatory, which he wrote to Arthur Bingham Walkley, the critic who started it all when he urged Shaw the Puritan to do a Don Juan play, he said flatly: "I do not know whether you have any illusions left on the subject of education, progress, and so forth. I have none. The trouble was that voters who decided important issues were ill-informed and incapable, and the answer was to an electorate of capable critics."[18] "We must eliminate the Yahoo," says Tanner, "or his vote will wreck the commonwealth."[19] Eugenics is the method and the answer, as "The Revolutionists' Handbook" clearly shows.

Shaw, the preacher, directs his message to the world. As Professor Crompton states it in the closing of his essay on this play: "Shaw's dialogue is a profession of faith and a call to action intended to summon us from the art gallery, the concert hall, the foreign-movie house and the cocktail party to deal with the awkward and difficult problems of the real world."[20]

The power and appeal of *Man and Superman* lie partly in its lively and interesting gallery of portraits. John Tanner, Ann Whitefield, Violet Robinson, Octavius Robinson, Henry Straker are not easily forgotten. Although the four speakers in the dream sequence likewise are delineated with great skill through what they say, the dialogue in all four acts is witty, clever, and character-revealing. Another strength of the play—one that is also a weakness—is the astounding bulk of his philosophy which Shaw crowds into it. Important as his ideas are, Professor Henderson's remark that *Man and Superman* contains enough ideas for a dozen ordinary comedies is well taken. Despite the scintillating dialogue and impressive ideas, prolixity mars an otherwise masterly drama.[21]

Indeed, the play is so long that its full production requires almost eight hours. (*Hamlet* in its entirety occupies five hours, and O'Neill's *Strange Interlude,* given in the afternoon with an hour's intermission for dinner and resumed in the evening, is two hours shorter than Shaw's dramatic marathon.) Consequently, the dream scene in Act III usually has been omitted or presented, rightly enough, as a separate play; for it requires two hours in itself. The three noteworthy productions of *Don Juan in Hell* that have charmed audiences in many theaters on both sides of the Atlantic began when Robert Loraine and Lillah McCarthy first headed the cast in June 1907.[22] In 1952 Charles Laughton as the Devil, Agnes Moorehead as Ana, Charles Boyer as Don Juan, and Sir Cedric Hardwick as the Commander presented the dream sequence with great success in the United States and in the British Isles. A revival in 1973 featured Miss Moorehead again as Ana, Ricardo Montalban as Juan, Edward Mulhare as the Devil, and Paul Henreid as the Statue. *Man and Superman* has been Shaw's most lucrative play. On Broadway alone it had, up to 1975, 640 performances; and of these, 105 productions were of Act III as a separate play.[23] Over the years there have been many productions of one or the other of the two parts of *Man and Superman* throughout the civilized world.[24]

III *"Ireland Eternal and External"*

The resounding success of *Man and Superman* convinced Shaw that he had found his medium—"corrective comedy" and the discussion play in which he could present his views about any problem that faced humanity and get a hearing. Moreover, he felt sure that his audience thereafter was the world, or at least those parts of it that were capable of understanding the artistic theatre. Although he had reached the zenith of his prewar fame and although he had written twelve plays, several Fabian documents and books of criticism, not to mention five novels, four of them published, not one depicted his native land. The scenes of the plays were laid in England, America, Bulgaria, Morocco, Egypt, and Spain.

Yet that he loved Ireland and acknowledged her part in shaping his mind and outlook, no one familiar with Shaw's career could entertain the slightest doubt. Because his heredity and early environment made him Irish to the core of his being, Shaw meant it when at ninety he declared, "It is the beauty of Ireland that has made us what we are."[25] Writing in the *Atlantic Monthly* in 1949, at ninety-three, he said: "Eternal is the fact that the human creature born in Ireland and brought up in its air is Irish whatever variety of mongrel he or she may derive from, British or Iberian, Pict or Scot, Dane or Saxon, Down or Kerry, Hittite or Philistine: Ireland acclimatized them all. I have lived for twenty years in Ireland and for seventy-two in England; but the twenty came first; and in Britain I am still a foreigner and shall die one."[26]

Shaw watched with interest tempered with a degree of aloofness the rise of the Irish Literary Theatre, which began in 1899 and continued into the first years of the new century under the leadership of Lady Gregory, John B. and William Butler Yeats, Martyn Green, and others. This movement opened the way for the Celtic or Irish Renaissance, and one important outgrowth of the movement was the establishment of the famous Abbey Theatre in Dublin, which was to become known all over the world and which was to play a shaping role in the careers of many native dramatists, actors and actresses. The Abbey stressed Irish themes and sought to promote Irish talent.

With his sociological, international, and even cosmic interests and ideas, Shaw was not in sympathy with the emphasis on the Gaelic language and the Irish folklore that were promoted as parts of the Renaissance. Like his younger Irish compeer, Samuel Beckett, Shaw did not share the enthusiasms and problems of Yeats, Synge, and Lady Gregory. Nationalism, whether literary or political, he scorned as a "mode of self-consciousness, and a very aggressive one at that."[27] Actually, he was more friendly toward the founders and leaders of the Celtic Renaissance than he was toward the movement itself.

John Bull's Other Island, which he wrote in 1904 because he felt an obligation to do something for his native land and especially for the Literary Theatre, he described as "uncongenial to the whole spirit of the neo-Gaelic movement, which is bent on creating a new Ireland after its own ideal, whereas my play is a very uncompromising presentment of the real old Ireland."[28] Though Shaw said in the preface that it was William Butler Yeats who requested the play for the Irish Literary Theatre, Yeats did not remember suggesting it, but recalled that Shaw wrote it voluntarily.[29]

A political play, it explores several themes, among them capitalism with its imperialism and exploitation, the long conflict between England and Erin, and the contrast between the English and the Irish. In drawing this contrast, it seems to me, Shaw is guilty of the fallacy of false generalization; but he attempts to avoid it by presenting varied types of character from the two countries, especially Ireland.

Once again he uses the literary device of contrast. Tom Broadbent, for example, is a Gladstonian liberal, a veritable John Bull, and something of a Babbitt. He is sure that Home Rule—under guidance from London—will save Ireland. Possessing a strong acquisitive bias, he puts his trust in the protective tariff and common sense; and it is mainly through Broadbent that Shaw satirizes the English. Broadbent's partner in their firm of civil engineers is Larry Doyle, who, Irish to his fingertips, is "a man of thirty-six, with cold grey eyes, strained nose, fine fastidious lips, critical brows, clever head, rather refined and good-looking on the whole, but with Broadbent's eupeptic jollity."[30] His romantic attitude is unlike Broadbent's realistic outlook, but it becomes tiresome as each man mentions over and over again the national characteristics of his country. Doyle laments the Irish tendency to dream: "Oh, the dreaming! the dreaming! the torturing heart-scalding, never satisfying dreaming, dreaming, dreaming, dreaming! . . . It's all dreaming, all imagination. He cant be religious."[31] He then says that he cannot be political either: "If you want to interest him [an Irishman] in Ireland youve got to call the unfortunate island Kathleen ni Hollihan [sic[and pretend she's a little old woman." This gentle jibe is at Yeats, who wrote a play entitled *Kathleen ni Houlihan* and who took generally a nonpolitical stance as a poet.

Like the antithesis of Broadbent and Doyle is the sharp contrast between the two Roman Catholic priests. Father Peter Keegan has a youthful, saintly countenance and a gentle manner. He is an odd mixture of St. Francis of Assisi, Henry Thoreau, and William Blake. Unfrocked because he gave absolution to a black man (an elderly Hindoo), Keegan has been called "the privileged 'madman,' the spokesman of the demi-urge, the oracle of supernal wisdom, and the God-intoxicated visionary."[32] He is a rebel, a critic, a good debater, as well as the maker of witty epigrams, many of which are scattered through the text. It is he who voices some of Shaw's favorite ideas. "My way of joking," he says, "is to tell the truth. It's the funniest joke in the world." In the final minutes of the play he asserts: "Every dream is a prophecy: every jest is an earnest in the womb of Time." More than once he expresses Blake's idea that this world of ours must be hell.[33] Keegan may be said to be "the conscience" of the play. He, Doyle, and Broadbent are the chief characters in the *dramatis personae*. As for Father Dempsey, the parish priest, he is a much less impressive figure intellectually than Keegan. He is rather acquisitive; and, though easy under the yoke of authority, he is jealous of his position. Father Dempsey is a stodgy individual; but, as Doyle says, "he has nothing to hope or fear from the State; and the result is he's the most powerful man in Rosscullen."[34]

Nora Reilly, the only young woman in the play, is, despite her natural Irish charm, a weak character compared to most of Shaw's other women. She is so naive as to think that Doyle is still in love with her though he has not communicated with her for eighteen years. The only other woman in the play is Aunt Judy, who is fifty, commonplace, lively, contented, and hospitable. Tim Haffigan is a young wastrel and alcoholic who in Act I with an artificial brogue gulls Broadbent into thinking he is a deserving Irishman and then vanishes from the play. Shaw calls him a "stage Irishman."[35] His uncle, Matthew Haffigan, a farmer, contributes to the pathos as well as to the humor of the story of Rosscullen and its plight. "The real tragedy of Haffigan is the tragedy of his wasted youth, his stunted mind, his drudging over his clods and pigs until he has become a clod and pig himself. . . ." So says Larry Doyle, adding "and let young Ireland take care that it doesn't share his fate."[36] Haffigan is a symbol of the Irish peasant class. Patsy Farrell, an inept young laboring man, is, like Matthew, brutalized by toil. Barney Doran, who is "stout-bodied, short-armed, roundheaded . . . [and] on the verge of middle age" lacks moral strength and benevolence. He is vulgar, untidy, "with an enormous capacity for derisive, obscene, blasphemous, or merely cruel and senseless fun, and a violent and impetuous intolerance of other temperaments and other opinions." Thus Shaw analyzes him.[37] Cornelius Doyle, Larry's father, is an old man, small wiry, with a hard-skinned, rather worried face. He feels shy around Broadbent but tries to appear genial. Hodson is Broadbent's old valet and the only other Englishman in the play.

Through these characters, *John Bull's Other Island* becomes a living entity, but the situation around which the play revolves is simplicity itself. In the beginning Tom Broadbent and Larry Doyle are about to depart for Rosscullen, Ireland, to arrange to take over for a syndicate some mortgaged farm lands on which the owners have defaulted. Larry is reluctant to return to his native soil after many years, mainly because he knows his former sweetheart, Nora Reilly, is waiting for him in the hope of renewing their love. Because he no longer reciprocates her feeling and is relieved when his partner shows an interest in her, the competititon for the hand of a beautiful Irish colleen—a rivalry which in the hands of another kind of playwright could have created a melodramatic love affair—misses fire. When Nora sees that Doyle is no longer interested in her, she accepts Broadbent's proposal. When she informs Larry of it a little later, he quite blandly responds: "But that was the very thing I was going to advise you to do." When she tells Doyle goodbye and leaves him, Larry watches her as she goes and exclaims: "Oh, that's so Irish! Irish both of us to the backbone: Irish! Irish! Iri—"[38] Within twenty-four hours Broadbent wins not only the girl, but also the nomination to represent Rosscullen in Parliament. It was first offered to Larry Doyle, who declined to be the candidate.

The drama seems to be plotless if compared to the well-made plays of Sardou and Scribe, but, as in Chekhov's *The Cherry Orchard* or *The Sea Gull*, Shaw's *John Bull's Other Island* has an observable, ordered progression and structure, a parallelism of episodes, a subtle linking of ideas. Discussion often takes precedence over action; for, as Frederick P. W. McDowell has noted, "Shaw saw his play as a stream which gathers everything within it to flow with full force into the debates which conclude Acts III and IV. In the third act the discussion pertains to social and political Ireland, and in the last few pages of the play Doyle, Broadbent, and especially Father Keegan carry the debate into the universal aspects of Ireland's destiny."[39] Not only in this plotlessness which is more apparent than real, but also in the main lines of conflict, *John Bull's Other Island* is notably Chekhovian. For instance, there is the unrequited love of Nora Reilly and her acceptance of Broadbent for the security he could offer her. In every one of Chekhov's major plays the theme of unrequited love appears, and oftentimes his women are married to men they do not love.[40]

Another important conflict has to do with the exploitation and the commercialization of the land. Broadbent and Doyle, partners in a civil engineering firm, decide to build for their syndicate a resort hotel and golf course to replace the farms whose mortgages they have foreclosed in Rosscullen. Father Keegan, a forerunner of today's environmentalists, raises objections; but he is powerless in preventing the desecration. This situation recalls that of *The Cherry Orchard* in which Madame Ranevsky and her brother Gaev oppose the replacing of the beautiful cherry trees, an ancestral heritage, by a housing project. Like Keegan's their efforts are only verbal.

In passing, it should be noted, as hinted above, that *John Bull's*

88   GEORGE BERNARD SHAW

Other Island as a discussion play dealing with important issues,
social and spiritual, bears resemblance to all of Chekhov's major
dramas.[41]

As usual Shaw achieves his comic effects through clever, witty
dialogue and through (at times) outlandish action. For example,
Father Keegan's conversation with a grasshopper at the beginning
of Act II is an amusing bit of Celtic fantasy. More realistic is the farcical episode of Broadbent's effort to take Matthew Haffigan and
his newly purchased pig home in his automobile. The pig lands in
Broadbent's lap and causes him to lose control of his car and to
wreck part of the Rosscullen market. The narration of this incident—it is not staged—sends the natives into fits of raucous, un-
restrained laughter. But Broadbent is sure the incident will win him
votes in his candidacy for Parliament. Father Keegan, characteristically, feels repelled by it; with intense emphasis, he declares:
"It is hell: it is hell. Nowhere else could such a scene be a burst of
happiness for the people."[42] Another bit of farce is Nora Reilly's
ability to convince Broadbent that he is drunk, though actually he is
not, when he precipitately proposes to her at their first brief
meeting by the Round Tower.

But the Tower is not only a meeting place for lovers; it is also a
place for meditation to which Peter Keegan goes when he wishes to
think about Heaven. It might be considered also as a symbol of the
beauty of the old Ireland that Shaw sought to depict amid all the
comedy. He clearly conveys his consciousness of this beauty, for instance, in his description of the scene at the beginning of Act II:
"Westward a hillside of granite rock and heather slopes upward
across the prospect from south the north. A huge stone stands on it
in a naturally impossible place, as if it had been tossed up there by a
giant. Over the brow, in the desolate valley beyond, is a round
tower. A lonely white high road trending away westward past the
tower loses itself at the foot of the far mountains. It is evening; and
there are great breadths of silken green in the Irish sky."[43]

The beauty of the countryside is lost on all the characters save
Peter Keegan, who symbolizes the best side of the Irish mind and
spirit. It is he who frankly likens Broadbent to an ass who is "efficient in the service of Mammon, mighty in mischief, skilful [sic] in
ruin, heroic in destruction." "But he comes to browse here without
knowing that the soil his hoof touches is holy ground." Efficiency is
the enemy and despoiler of beauty. The mad saint, in response to
Broadbent's assertion that the world belongs to the efficient,

counters with this centrally important statement: "For four centuries the world has dreamed this foolish dream of efficiency; and
the end is not yet. But the end will come."[44]

The contrast between the English and the Irish mind Shaw draws
more fully in the "Preface for Politicians" (1906). Among other
things, Shaw writes about the "curse of nationalism," about natural
rights to Irish independence and Home Rule, about prohibitive tax-
ation on English trade, and about the importance of a standard
wage. He then attacks the military by saying: "A political scheme
that cannot be carried out except by soldiers will not be a permanent one. The soldier is an anachronism of which we must get
rid."[45] The Preface expresses a far-from-optimistic view of the Empire because of Britain's failure to mete out justice to Ireland and to
other members of the Commonwealth. He lengthily condemns
England for the notorious "Denshawai Horror" in which Egyptian
villagers were executed for defending against trespassing British
soldiers. In fact, Shaw proposes Home Rule for all countries in the
British Empire.

At the end of his addenda to the preface, he recalls that he urged
the Protestants of Northern Ireland to play their part in a single
Parliament that would rule an undivided country. Failing to convince them, he again exhorted Protestant and Catholic Ulster alike
to join in developing "into what the Americans call Congress, or
Federal Government on the whole island."[46] Had Shaw's counsel
been heeded, the tragic blood-letting in present-day Northern
Ireland could have been prevented.

John Bull's Other Island proved too large and too difficult for the
Irish Literary Theatre, for which it was written. But at intervals it
had five successful runs at the Court Theatre, London, from 1904 to
1906. Writing of these performances, Archibald Henderson notes
that "The real effect of the play was to attract the cultured and ex-
clusive class of English society, and, as Archer put it, to reveal
Shaw, once and for all, to the intelligent public."[47] The Honorable
Arthur James Balfour, the prime minister, went to see this play four
times, two of them in the company of political rivals, Sir Henry
Campbell-Bannerman and Hubert Henry Asquith, at his invitation.
King Edward VII ordered a command performance at which, it was
reported, he laughed so heartily that his chair broke down. (Years
later as part of the coronation festivities of King George V, Prime
Minister Asquith arranged for a presentation of the third act at No.
10 Downing Street; and the new King and Queen were highly

entertained by it.) London playgoers enjoyed *John Bull's Other Island* immensely, despite its satire of Broadbent as a typical Englishman and its trenchant comments on British policies. This play missed fire in America, however, as New York audiences and critics evidently found its issues uninteresting.[48] For the past half century it has suffered the fate of a neglected masterpiece.

While writing *John Bull's Other Island,* Shaw interrupted a holiday in Scotland to dash off a "trifling" little one-act playlet, *How He Lied to Her Husband,* which is a parody of *Candida* and a reply to "Candidamaniacs." Out of the stale, hackneyed plot of a domestic triangle and "knockabout" farce, Shaw boasted that he had made an original play.[49] Though trivial, it is fresh, clever, and witty; it is precisely the kind of thing that Oscar Wilde could have written; but it is a far cry from Shaw's more serious drama.

IV   *Money, Faith, and Power*

The third play of the series that Shaw designated as "comedies of science and religion" is *Major Barbara: A Discussion in Three Acts.* Commenting on it in a letter, Shaw referred to it as "all religion and morals and Fabian debates."[50] More specifically, the main issues of the debates are poverty, money (especially "tainted money"), capitalism, socialism, and the Salvation Army. The central theme might be stated in the words of Samuel Butler, the nineteenth-century novelist and one of Shaw's great admirations.[51] In *Erewhon* (1872), Butler declared poverty a crime and revised St. Paul's oft-quoted dictum, "The love of money is the root of all evil," to "The lack of money is the root of all evil," an idea with which Shaw fully agreed.

Money plays its part in the opening scene of *Major Barbara,* which takes place in the library of Lady Britomart Undershaft, who could have stepped right out of one of Wilde's domestic comedies. Fiftyish, well-bred, well-mannered, she is appallingly outspoken and sharp-tongued. Amiable yet high tempered, she is a typical managing matron of the capitalistic upper class. She and her son Stephen, a gravely correct, self-important, shy bachelor of twenty-five, engage in a delightfully humorous conversation about the family's economic and marital prospects. Lady Britomart has decided to call in her long-estranged husband, Andrew Undershaft, now a munitions tycoon, to enlist his financial aid for their two daughters whose fiancés are far from wealthy. Stephen's prospects are not bright, either, for he, being legitimate, cannot inherit any part of the Undershaft and Lazarus munitions factory which, by the strange terms of Undershaft's will, can go only to a foundling. This fact, among others, accounts for the estrangement of the father and the mother.

Undershaft dutifully arrives. "He is, on the surface, a stoutish, elderly, easy-going, patient, simple man . . . with formidable reserves of power, both bodily and mental, in his capacious chest and long head." In a letter Shaw describes him as "Broadbent and Keegan rolled into one, with Mephistopheles thrown in." Father Keegan's attributes are not clearly evident in Undershaft, but Broadbent's penchant for efficient action is observable in this impressive character who is, as Shaw continues, "diabolically subtle, gentle, self-possessed, powerful, stupendous, as well as amusing and interesting."[52] Like Dick Dudgeon, Undershaft is a disciple of the Devil. He springs from Blake's concept of Satan in *The Marriage of Heaven and Hell* and from Nietzsche's Dionysus in *The Will to Power.*

Lady Britomart finds that she must introduce her estranged husband to his own children, whom he has not seen since they were babies, as well as to his two prospective sons-in-law. Charles Lomax—a young man-about-town who is engaged to Sarah, the daughter who is overshadowed by her sister—has a frivolous sense of humor which leads him to ill-timed, uncontrollable laughter; but he plays a concertina in the Salvation Army band. Barbara's husband-to-be is Adolphus Cusins, a bespectacled Greek scholar, an intellectual who has a controllable sense of humor and much greater strength of character than Lomax. Cusins's prototype is Shaw's friend, the eminent scholar Gilbert Murray, famous for his translation of Euripedes.

Undershaft is most deeply impressed with Major Barbara herself as he elicits information about her work in the Salvation Army. At Barbara's invitation, he agrees to visit her shelter and to march in a parade if she will inspect his factory; and she accepts his condition. Undershaft sees the seamy side of life at the shelter when Bill Walker, a ruffian, comes to the center to find his girl, whom he thinks the Salvationists have lured away. He is rude to some of the inmates and, in his frustration, strikes a Salvation Army lass. Two deadbeats confess their trick of admitting to nonexistent sins as a means of obtaining free meals at the center. All this low behavior is ascribed to poverty.

In contrast, Undershaft's factory is a kind of Utopia in which the workers are like one large happy family. He argues that it is better to have weapons, and the wars in which they are sold and used, than to have the crime and curse of poverty, for money is the object of his religion. He offers to "buy" the Salvation Army, but Barbara disapproves. When her colleague Mrs. Baines accepts a large contribution from a whiskey manufacturer along with Undershaft's offer to match it, Barbara resigns in protest. Her father argues that organizations like the Salvation Army are dependent on tainted money, for all money at its source is suspect. Though she expected to convert him to the Salvationist cause, she paradoxically becomes converted to his kind of religion. She will no longer devote her life to the slum-dwellers, but will do service among the people who work for Undershaft and Lazarus.

In the meantime, her father has become fond of Adolphus Cusins, who makes himself amenable to Undershaft's way of life. When Cusins reveals that his parents were never married according to English law, he is clearly a foundling and hence qualified to succeed Undershaft at the cannon foundry. This discovery makes Barbara surer than ever that he is the one for her to marry; and, when the play ends, she is house-hunting.

All seems to end happily as pure comedy must, but *Major Barbara* leaves certain questions unanswered. To begin with, what is Shaw's real attitude toward Undershaft? The answer is clarified in the preface, particularly in the part entitled "The Gospel of St. Andrew Undershaft" in which Shaw repeats what he said in the preface to *Immaturity:* "The universal regard for money is the one hopeful fact in our civilization, the one sound spot in our civilization." He goes on to say: "Money is the most important thing in the world. It represents health, strength, honor, generosity, and beauty as conspicuously and undeniably as the want of it represents illness, weakness, disgrace, meanness and ugliness. . . . And the evil to be attacked is not sin, suffering, greed, priestcraft, demagogy, monopoly, ignorance, drink, war, pestilence, nor any other of the scapegoats which reformers sacrifice, but simply poverty."[53]

As an economic play, *Major Barbara* recalls *Widowers' Houses* and *Mrs. Warren's Profession,* two other portrayals of objectionable professions in a capitalistic society.[54] In a sense, poverty is the overriding theme in all three of these plays. In the earlier two plays, Shaw puts the blame on society for the evils exposed; in *Major Bar-*

bara, Shaw does not assign blame but implies that the poor are at fault for tolerating poverty. In the two earlier plays, Shaw implies that Fabian Socialism is the way out of political difficulties; in *Major Barbara,* he acknowledges and explores the advantages of capitalism before presenting the greater advantages of Marxism. This fact is not surprising when it is noted that *Man and Superman* proposes eugenics, not socialism, and puts faith in the coming of Superman as the only hope of the world.

Though Undershaft is not Superman, he possesses some of his attributes. Shaw presents Undershaft in a favorable light for his efficiency—a quality Shaw admired more and more—and for his mysticism, "his constant sense that he is only the instrument of a Will or Life Force that uses him for purposes wider than his own." Shaw's admiration for a munitions maker who sells his instruments of death and destruction to any nation that wishes to buy them indicates that the playwright was moving away from his Fabian socialism and toward Karl Marx's concept of force as a means of social betterment. By far the greatest reason for Shaw's admiration for Undershaft is his making war on poverty, "the vilest sin of man and society," by providing ample money for his workers and his family. To Barbara he could say, "I saved your soul from the seven deadly sins!"

BARBARA. The seven deadly sins!
UNDERSHAFT. Yes, the deadly seven. Food, clothing, firing, rent, taxes, respectability, and children. Nothing can lift those seven millstones from man's neck, but money; and the spirit cannot soar until the millstones are lifted. I lifted them from your spirit. I enabled Barbara to become Major Barbara, and I saved her from the crime of poverty.[55]

The daughter is deeply impressed—"hypnotized" is the word Shaw uses at one juncture—with her father's arguments; but her conversion is the greatest weakness of the play because Shaw fails to prepare the reader or the playgoer for it. Nothing in Barbara's character until she visits Undershaft's factory accounts for her final decision to join her fortunes with him and his employees in the model town. To break with the Salvation Army because of the tainted-money issue is one thing, but to continue her abandonment of the poor is another. She had done good work with Bill Walker, Rummy Mitchens, Peter Shirley, Snobby Price, and the other derelicts who needed her—and continued to need her. It would have been more in character for her to have changed her mind on the financial issue and to return to the Salvation Army, where her superior, Mrs. Baines, was the kind of person who would have welcomed her back.

Indubitably, the Salvation Army does great good in the world. Shaw's unfavorable portrayal of its West Ham operation ignores the organization's work in rehabilitation, but it supports his contention that such work tends to make poverty tolerable. When her father sarcastically tells her, "Leave it to the poor to pretend that poverty is a blessing," Barbara might have answered that few if any of them do; that most people accept poverty because they must; and that only exceptional persons, like St. Francis and Thoreau, embrace it as a blessing. Surely Shaw knew that the eradication of poverty is a longtime, ultimate goal. Meanwhile, the indigent and the wayward poor continue to be a problem and opportunity for charitable institutions so long as governments do not provide adequately for them. To abandon such unfortunate persons to their fate is clearly unchristian and inhuman. Shaw fails to face this issue in *Major Barbara*.

The Barbara who worked with Mrs. Baines and Jenny Hill to help the poor might also be expected to argue that money, desirable and necessary as it may be, is not an absolute good any more than the lack of it is an absolute evil. She might have perceived that the comfortable Utopia that her father erected at Perivale St. Andrews, a Utopia built of millions made on the sale of armaments to kill and destroy, could hardly be a place for her. But she is willing to sluff off her Christianity like a serpent its skin, to embrace the religion of the Life Force, to turn her back on the poor, and to try, as she said, to bring salvation to the "fullfed [*sic*], quarrelsome, snobbish, uppish creatures, all standing on their little rights and dignities, and thinking that my father ought to be greatly obliged to them for making so much money for him—and so he ought."[56] Her decision seems precipitant and unconvincing. In Acts I and II, Barbara is a young woman who thinks and acts in her own right, but in the last scene she becomes a puppet for the expression of Shaw's philosophy.

Nevertheless, *Major Barbara* is a strong, brilliant, entertaining comedy which presents a rewarding discussion of issues. It says many things which, as Broadbent said of Father Keegan's remark about heaven and hell, salvation and damnation, "cannot be said too often." It remains fresh and modern, and Sir Winston Churchill testified about its amazing effectiveness. On seeing it a second time after an interval of two decades, "the most terrific twenty years the world has known," he noted that "in *Major Barbara* there was not a character requiring to be redrawn, not a sentence nor a suggestion that was out of date." He called it "the very acme of modernity."[57]

V   The Doctor's Dilemma

Shaw thought of publishing *Man and Superman, John Bull's Other Island,* and *Major Barbara* under the title "Comedies of Science and Religion." He decided against this collection, however, because of the great length of *Man and Superman.* So this play appeared in print separately, and the other two were published together. His next play, though devoid of religion, could be considered at least a "comedy of science." *The Doctor's Dilemma* owes its beginning directly to Mrs. Shaw. One day in 1906 the Shaws were talking with Sir Almroth Wright, an eminent physician, at St. Mary's Hospital, London, when an assistant asked Sir Almroth if he could add another tuberculosis patient to the limited number he could treat with his new opsonic method. "Is he worth it?" the physician asked. Later Charlotte reminded Shaw that there was a play in that situation. "I believe you are right," he replied. "Hand me my tablet and I will go to work on it at once."[58]

William Archer also was partly responsible for suggesting the kind of play *The Doctor's Dilemma* turned out to be. When he twitted Shaw for not writing about death and reminded him that he could not be considered a great dramatist unless he wrote a tragedy, Shaw accepted the challenge.[59] He subtitled *The Doctor's Dilemma* "A Tragedy" chiefly because, as he put it, the theme of " 'a man of genius who is not also a man of honor' is the most tragic of all themes to people who can understand its importance."[60] But surely this is not a tragedy in the sense of Aristotle's, Shakespeare's, Arthur Miller's, or anyone else's use of the term. It is true that Dudebat dies on the stage; but with his asking with his dying breath if the newspaper man is still around to report his death, the event can hardly be tragic if, in fact, it is pathetic. The proper category is tragicomedy, a form invented by Plautus in antiquity and developed in modern times first by Ibsen and Chekhov, and later, among others, by Sean O'Casey, Samuel Beckett, and Eugene Ionesco.

In addition to its tragicomic elements, *The Doctor's Dilemma* is a

satire and a discussion of the medical profession, the Bohemian artist, and the foolishly adoring wife; and these three themes are
skillfully interwoven. The first scene discloses two minor characters,
a medical assistant and an elderly female servant, who are discussing the chief character and the events which we need to know—a
familiar expository, introductory device in Ibsen and countless other
dramatists, including Shakespeare. Act I, which takes place in Dr.
Ridgeon's consulting room, is largely devoted to the introduction of
the six doctors and of the artist's wife, but it also clarifies the main
situation, the nature of the "dilemma." Dr. Ridgeon, who is based
on Shaw's friend Sir Almroth Wright, has just become Sir Colenso
Ridgeon in honor of his discovery of a new cure for the dread disease tuberculosis, which was formerly considered to be fatal. Since
accounts of his knighting appeared in London newspapers, it was
natural that his colleagues should appear to offer him congratulations.

Shaw individualizes the five physicians mainly through their
various ways of treating disease—cures that range from inoculation
to the compulsory removal of everyone's "nuciform sac" (a
theatrical pseudonym for the vermiform appendix). One of the five
is Dr. Blenkinsop, an impoverished physician but also the most
sincere character in the play. He has lost touch with the scientific
side of medicine and obviously regards himself as a failure, but he
has had a great deal of clinical and bedside experience. He reveals
that he is afflicted with tuberculosis.

While the five doctors have been congratulating Ridgeon and discussing with him their various theories, nostrums, and experiences,
a beautiful woman has been waiting in the anteroom; and she has
come there to appeal to Sir Colenso on behalf of her husband, Louis
Dudebat, an artist who is seriously ill with tuberculosis. Jennifer
Dudebat, "an arrestingly good-looking young woman," "has
something of the grace and romance of a wild creature," but she has
"a good deal of the elegance and dignity of a fine lady."[61] Ridgeon,
smitten by her charms in spite of himself, nevertheless informs her
he cannot possibly accept another patient. He explains that, since
the number he can save at a time is ten, he must choose each of
these on the basis of his worthiness. When Mrs. Dudebat assures
him that her husband is worthy and unpacks a portfolio of his paintings to prove it, Dr. Ridgeon relents enough to invite her to bring
her husband to a dinner that his colleagues are giving in honor of
his knighthood. If the doctors present agree that Dudebat is deserving, Ridgeon will give him the cure.

Following the dinner, the doctors compare experiences and find that Dudebat has borrowed varying amounts of money and a gold cigarette case. (Later when Dr. Walpole asks Louis to return the case, he presents a pawn ticket for Walpole to redeem.) Before the physicians leave the dining room, Minnie Tinwell, a maid at the hotel, reveals that she is Louis Dudebat's lawfully wedded wife, whom he had deserted after a few weeks' honeymoon that had been partly financed by her savings. This revelation is more than enough to convince Ridgeon and the others that Dudebat is not worth saving, especially not when to do so would doom good old Dr. Blenkinsop.

Ridgeon hardly feels that he can play false to his promise to Mrs. Dudebat, but he decides to turn his cure over to Dr. Bonington to treat Dudebat, a decision that means almost certain death for the artist. Ridgeon, despite his desire to marry the widow—or because of it—follows through with this plan. Consequently, after a time Dudebat dies in the presence of all the doctors, his wife, and a doddering newspaper man, whose presence pleases the egotistical painter. This death, the first to take place on the stage in any of Shaw's plays, is highly sentimentalized. Not long before he draws his last breath, Dudebat says, "I've fought the good fight. And now it's all over, theres [sic] an indescribable peace. (*He feebly folds his hands and utters his creed.*) I believe in Michael Angelo, Valasquez, and Rembrandt; in the might of design, the mystery of color, the redemption of all things by Beauty everlasting, and the message of Art that has made these hands blessed. Amen. Amen." While dying with his head resting on his wife's bosom, he asks if the newspaper man is still around! As the group of physicians depart, Mrs. Dudebat shakes hands with all except Ridgeon.

Act V takes place in one of the smaller Bond Street Galleries, and Jennifer Dudebat is there for two purposes: to exhibit her late husband's paintings and to promote her new book about Louis, *The Story of a King of Men* By His Wife. Sir Colenso Ridgeon, who enters before the exhibition is scheduled to open, intends to select for purchase a number of Dudebat's pictures and, more importantly, to restore himself in the good graces of the lovely Jennifer with the idea of proposing to her. Their interview, in which he admits that he was responsible for the artist's death in order to marry his wife, is fantastic and astounding. At the same time, he confesses that he had saved Dr. Blenkinsop's life with the same cure which Dr. Bonington had bungled in Dudebat's case. Jennifer is outwardly more friendly and forgiving than Ridgeon deserves, but the final irony is hers. When he announces he has marked in the catalogue five pictures he intends to buy, Jennifer announces that her husband already has bought them for her as a birthday gift. When her remarriage takes Ridgeon completely by surprise, she reminds him that those who have happily married once always marry again; and he exclaims immediately before the curtain falls: "Then I have committed a purely disinterested murder!"—a signal, surely, that we should not take the play too seriously.

One weakness of the play is that the "dilemma" is artificial and contrived. Though Shaw said he knew of one or two physicians who faced Ridgeon's problem, the whole business of the doctors' inviting Dudebat to the dinner at which they decide his fate does not ring true. The whole "ten-men-in-a-lifeboat" dilemma is a fabrication.[62] It should be noted also that Jennifer does not accept Sir Colenso's cure as absolute. When she refers in the last act to Ridgeon as the little man who tried to kill a great one, he retorts: "Pardon me: I succeeded."[63] Like many of Ridgeon's speeches, this assertion seems unnatural and outlandish.

Still another serious defect in the play is that not one of the male characters, with the possible exception of Dr. Blenkinsop, the physician to the poor, elicits sympathy. Shaw not only characterizes all the doctors; he also caricatures them. Mrs. Dudebat and Emmy, the only two women in the cast, are somewhat more sympathetically drawn despite the fact that Shaw disliked the possessive and sentimental wife.

The Doctor's Dilemma is in an age-old tradition of plays and other types of literature that make light of medical practitioners. Comic doctors appeared in early Greek comedy; they appeared also in mummers' plays in the Middle Ages and in later folk drama such as the Punch and Judy shows. Doctors were ridiculed for their pretentiousness also in Renaissance comedy. The greatest direct influence on Shaw was Molière, who in the seventeenth century wrote several plays, including *L'Amour medicin* and *Le Malade imaginaire*, which ridiculed doctors. Molière, like Shaw, was the enemy of quackery in whatever form he found it.[64]

Except for its social criticism and ideas, found chiefly in the preface, *The Doctor's Dilemma* does not differ in its effect from one of Molière's comedies about doctors. It is in the preface that the preacher, teacher, and "artist-philosopher" in Shaw attacks the medical theories, discoveries, and practices of his day.[65] He begins by declaring that it is not the fault of doctors if medical service is a murderous absurdity. He goes on to say: "That any sane nation, having observed that you could provide for the supply of bread by giving bakers a pecuniary interest in baking for you, should go on to give a surgeon a pecuniary interest in cutting off your leg, is enough to make one despair of political humanity."[66] Doctors should be paid by the state to keep the people well, but Shaw does not emphasize socialized medicine in the preface.

He does go deeply, however, into the evils of professionalism in medicine. There is, Shaw contends, a kind of trade-unionism among physicians which prevents them from exposing one another's failures and which thereby permits evil practices to be perpetrated on innocent patients. Ultimately the solution of all medical problems is to be found, Shaw believes, in socialism which alone of all forms of government can provide everyone with enough money to obtain the nutrition, the sanitation, and the beauty necessary for the healthy life.

By far the greater part of the preface is devoted to an attack on vivisection. Back in 1887 Shaw had first written in opposition to the use of live animals in the search for medical truth which will save human suffering. Since vivisection is experimental, it is not at all certain that the result of cutting up an animal will prevent any suffering whatever. "The question," he wrote, "is really one of the acknowledgement of a moral relation between man and beast. Deny such relations, and men may clearly be as cruel to animals as they please. Admit it, and you still have a right to make a horse work for its living, but not to torture it."[67] Shaw argues that the attempt to justify vivisection is based not on legitimate curiosity but on outright cruelty. If the practice of it on animals is accepted, the next horrible step is to apply it to human beings. (In this view Shaw was a prophet, as the experiments on men and women in Nazi Germany evinced.)

The Doctor's Dilemma, though interesting, is dated, outmoded, and unworthy of a high place in the canon of Shaw's dramas. There is evidence that the author himself did not look upon it as one of his major achievements. In 1915, when he wrote a prefatory note to *Major Barbara* to be distributed to the press, he mentioned *Man and Superman, John Bull's Other Island,* and *Major Barbara* as "three plays of exceptional weight and magnitude on which the reputation of the author as a serious dramatist was first established, and still mainly rests."[68]

CHAPTER 6

A Miscellany of Prewar Plays

I N order to understand Shaw's thinking in the years before World War I, we need to take a brief look at history. The
period from 1905 until the outbreak of the war was known as the
Liberal Regime, an era of domestic controversy but of international
peace. Several important reforms in Britain took place during the
administrations of Sir Henry Campbell-Bannerman and Herbert
Asquith. These included a change in the Education Act of 1902 in
favor of the Non-Conformists, national control of the liquor trade,
the legislation of peaceful picketing, a Workingman's Compensation Act, an Old-Age Pension Law, a National Insurance Act, including Unemployment Insurance, and a Minimum Wage Law.
Since the Fabians had advocated most of these measures in the late
nineteenth century, Shaw and his friends took satisfaction in seeing
the fruits of some of their endeavors; but they were unwilling to
concede that the millennium had arrived.

Parliament was unable to resolve the important issue of Home
Rule for Ireland before the outbreak of the European conflict. The
House of Commons twice passed the bill in 1913 and the House of
Lords twice rejected it. Meanwhile, Ulster's opposition to Home
Rule became increasingly virulent; 150,000 Ulstermen met and
passed a resolution to oppose the arrangement by arms if necessary.
By the end of 1913, Ulster had raised 100,000 volunteers. In the
following year, Asquith proposed a compromise in which Ulster was
to continue under British government; so, in September, the Home
Rule bill became law with the provision that it was not to be put
into force until after the war.[1]

Opposing the Ulster partition, Shaw once more pleaded with his
countrymen to work together for the weal of Ireland. In a speech
(1912) at a Home Rule rally in Memorial Hall, London, he spoke of
his "wild and inextinguishable pride" in being an Irishman.
Although he welcomed the infusion of religion into politics and

"the turbulence of controversy" which would result, he opposed all feuds and the violence they bring with them. Shaw proposed a resolution which reads as follows: "That this meeting expresses its strong desire to see the end of the racial and religious feuds in Ireland, and Irishmen of all creeds and classes working together for the common good of their native country."[2] It applies to the Irish problem today.

I *Again the Problem of Marriage*

The Irish question was seldom out of Shaw's mind, but other issues engaged his creative energies in the years before World War I. One of these was the problem of marriage, about which he had written in his novels, particularly in *The Irrational Knot* and in *Love Among the Artists,* and in the preface to his first volume of dramas, *Plays Pleasant and Unpleasant.* It also was a dominant theme, as we have already noted, in *Man and Superman.* After all, sex and marriage are the only instrumentalities so far devised by which the Life Force can keep the human race going. Following *The Doctor's Dilemma,* in which he examined and exposed an institution, the profession of medicine, Shaw turned his attention once again to marital relations in *Getting Married.*

In this play Shaw demonstrates anew, as in *Don Juan in Hell,* that discussion can be a form of dramatic art. Though there is plenty of overt action, he subtitles the new play *A Conversation* or *A Disquisitory Play.* Since this drama is not divided into acts or scenes, it is probably the longest one-act play in theatrical history.[3] Shaw observes the classic unities of time and place, but not the unity of action, since several different actions take place as the groups of characters interact with one another while discussing their attitudes and problems. Still, the action is centered on one subject—marriage—and the theme is expressed in one idea: namely, that marriage (as Winston Churchill said of democracy) is the worst arrangement we could have. Critical as he is of the English laws governing marriage and divorce, Shaw does not advocate abandoning monogamy for its alternative, free love.

The discussion in *Getting Married* takes place entirely in the twelfth-century Norman kitchen in the palace of Bishop Bridgenorth of Chelsea. It seems fitting as setting for a series of conversations about domestic life; and, besides, it is one of the finest rooms in the house. Mrs. Bridgenorth and William Collins, a greengrocer who serves as alderman and as factotum for the Bridgenorths, are planning a wedding and dinner for the last of the five Bridgenorth daughters. Collins, who closely resembles William the waiter in *You Never Can Tell*, seems to have everything under control.

The wedding, for which guests have already begun to arrive, is to join Edith Bridgenorth and Cecil Sykes. But unexpected obstacles arise. The morning post brings two pamphlets, Belfort Bax's essay *Men, Wrongs*, addressed to the bridegroom, and another entitled *Do You Know What You Are Going to Do? By a Woman Who Has Done it*, addressed to Edith. After they both have locked themselves in their rooms to read the pamphlets and then have reappeared after the time appointed for the wedding, they decide they cannot take the vows. She is appalled to have learned that she cannot divorce Cecil even if he commits a murder, forges, steals, or becomes an atheist. He is equally horrified that he must pay any damage suits of Edith, who has an alarming way of making slanderous statements. The other characters attempt hastily to draw up contracts which would protect one party from the other.

A great amount of argument occurs in which each of the elders, with the exception of the bishop, looks upon any contractual arrangement from a selfish point of view. Romantic ideas about marriage come in for a heavy barrage of satire, but it is agreed in the end that the institution itself deserves support as well as criticism and change.[4] It is Collins who contributes the strongest words of advice: "Marriage is tolerable enough in its way if youre easygoing and dont expect too much from it. But it doesnt bear thinking about. The great thing is to get the young people tied up before they know what theyre letting themselves in for. . . . If you once start arguing, Miss Edith and Mr. Sykes, youll never get married. Go and get married first: youll have plenty of arguing afterwards, miss, believe me." In a short time, Edith and Cecil compose documents satisfactory to each other, and sneak off to the empty church where a curate marries them. So ends the central story.

But other characters reveal and discuss their marital situations and attitudes throughout the play. In the preface to *Getting Married*, Shaw explores the relationship of sex and marriage, along with many other allied subjects. For many of his ideas about the problems of domestic life Shaw acknowledges his debt to Samuel Butler, author of *The Way of All Flesh* and of *Erewhon*. Butler held that family ties often stunt the growth of personality; but Shaw, who agrees, goes beyond the strictures of Butler and asserts: "Marriage remains practically inevitable; and the sooner we acknowledge this, the sooner we shall set to work to make it decent and reasonable."[5]

Always the staunch advocate of woman's rights, Shaw insisted that "family life will never be decent, much less ennobling, until this central horror of the dependence of women on men is done away with."[6] No present-day women's liberation leader could outdo Shaw in pleading for economic equality. "Place the work of a wife and mother on the same footing of labor worthy of its hire and provide for unemployment [compensation] in it exactly as for unemployment in shipbuilding or any other recognized breadwinning trade."[7] When Shaw has Edith Bridgenorth say that, after marriage, she expects to be paid as much money as a hired housekeeper, he inveighs against the English law which assumes that woman has her "sphere"—housekeeping—and that man has his—all the rest of human activity—and that the only point at which the two spheres touch is in the replenishing of the population. Accordingly, there can be no companionship between men and women. Here we can see the influence on Shaw of such pioneers in feminism as Mary Wollstonecraft, John Stuart Mill, and August Bebel.[8]

Just as Shaw attacked the idolaters of Shakespeare and war, he assailed what he calls "the idolaters of marriage."[9] Since there is nothing magical or sacred about the conjugal tie, it should always be subject to change. In a typical Shavian paradox, G.B.S. flatly declares: "Divorce, in fact, is not the destruction of marriage, but the first condition of its maintenance." Each divorce could result in two new marriages as the couples find new mates. "Divorce only reassorts the couples; a very desirable thing when they are ill-assorted."[10] These considerations lead Shaw to favor cheap and easy divorce simply on the grounds that one or both parties desire it, thereby averting court battles, collusion, and unsavory publicity.[11]

To Ivor Brown, Shaw's views on divorce constitute a Bill of Rights indeed—for the adults. "But," he asks, "what of the juniors?"[12] Shaw's answer is that the interests of the children constitute a powerful argument for divorce. "An unhappy household," he insists, "is a bad nursery." Brown cogently argues that such an environment is, in some cases, not so bad as removing them to a detested boarding school or to a foster home approved ("and sometimes carelessly and disastrously approved") by a local authority who is perhaps incompetent to cope with the intricacies and subtleties of the problem. Shaw's proposal of cheap and easy divorce would so vastly increase the burden of "the bureaucrat as distributor and guardian of the parentless children"[13] that the task would become an insurmountable one that would be fraught with anguish if not disaster. The sociological effect of increasing numbers of broken homes on increasing numbers of children is one which Shaw does not take sufficiently into account. It is so stupendous a problem today in England and in the United States—not to mention other parts of the world—that it does not admit of a simplistic solution. This fact, however, does not detract from the play as an interesting and significant contribution to drama as well as to the history of ideas.

II   A Second Play About America

The Shewing-up of Blanco Posnet (Shaw preferred the archaic "shewing" for "showing"), though not one of Shaw's major plays, is interesting for at least four reasons: (1) it is the second of Shaw's two plays whose setting is in America; (2) it was first presented by the Abbey Theatre, Dublin, and the first of his plays to have its debut in his native city; (3) it presents an interesting expression of Shaw's view of God as fallible and of man's place in God's (the Life Force's) plans; and (4) its suppression in England by the Lord Chamberlain led to Shaw's writing one of his important prefaces about censorship.

"This little play," its author says in the preface, "is really a religious tract in dramatic form,"[14] and its subtitle is *A Sermon in Crude Melodrama*. Because *Blanco Posnet* owes a great deal also to Tolstoy's *The Power of Darkness*, particularly to the character of the old soldier, who brings about the redemption of the protagonist, Nikita, Shaw wrote Tolstoy that he remembered nothing in the whole range of drama that fascinated him more.[15] Another important influence on *Blanco Posnet* is the fiction of Bret Harte, whose stories of California often portrayed gamblers and prostitutes who were revealed at the end of the narratives to have hearts of gold.[16]

The scene of Shaw's play is a large room, "not unlike an English barn, furnished as a court house, where a party of women, their dress and speech those of pioneers of civilization in a territory of the United States, are shucking nuts." The likelihood of such an activity in a court house of the West is indeed remote, as is the use of the sheriff as prosecutor and judge in the trial, which runs counter to

American court practices. The man on trial is Blanco Posnet charged with horse-stealing, a major crime in the early days of the West before justice was regularized. Although Blanco was brought to trial after having been seen with a horse stolen from the sheriff, he had actually taken it from Elder Daniels, Blanco's brother, who had borrowed the sheriff's horse.

Blanco's brother, it turns out, comes as near to being a villain as anyone in Shaw's work. He is hypocritical and so unfeeling, like several of the rough characters, that he seems to take satisfaction in the prospect of Blanco's hanging. Feemy Evans, the town's prostitute, angered by Blanco's words of contempt, is ready to swear that she saw him on the horse. At this point, a commotion occurs at the door of the courtroom. The horse has been found, and a woman enters to say that Blanco had lent her the horse to take her desperately ill child to a doctor. The child dies, but Feemy has a change of heart and declines to testify against Posnet. Having escaped the gallows, he preaches a sermon about the two games that are played in the world, the rotten game and God's perhaps silly but greater game. Not through the moralizing of his brother, whom he despises, but through the experience of trying to save the child, Blanco becomes a better man. He believes it is God's way of dealing with him. There is nothing blasphemous in all this, but it is the language Blanco uses that offended the Lord Chamberlain. Speaking of God's way with men, Blanco says: "He's a sly one. He's a mean one. He lies low for you. He plays cat and mouse with you. He lets you run loose until you think youre shut of Him; and then, when you least expect it, He's got you."

But that is not all. Toward the end of the play, Blanco preaches a sermon about God and evil, the croup that has taken the life of the child. "What about the croup?" Blanco asks. "It was early days when He made the croup, I guess. It was the best He could think of then; but when it turned out wrong in His hands He made you and me to fight the croup for Him." Shaw said that to him the whole purpose of the play lay in the problem, "What about the croup?" On the question of the origin of evil and the mystery of pain he added that "My doctrine is that God proceeds by the method of 'trial and error,' just like a workman perfecting an aeroplane."[17] As these words indicate, Shaw's ideas about God diverge sharply from the Judeo-Christian concept, for veneration has no place in his religion. To him, God is not perfect, not omniscient, and not omnipotent. He needs and merits the help of human beings, whom He unceasingly creates for the purpose of striving for higher and higher goals toward Godhead.[18] It is chiefly for these religious ideas that *Blanco Posnet* remains noteworthy.

In *Press Cuttings,* another short play which Shaw wrote in the prewar interim, he reverted to the already-mentioned cause that was near to this heart—the rights of women. Besides these rights, which include women's suffrage and women's rights to serve in the armed services, Shaw interjects a prophecy of man's landing on the moon. In this play, Balsquith (a name derived from Asquith and Balfour) is the prime minister, and General Mitchener (Kitchener), as a typical militarist, is in the war office when a suffragette enters bearing a letter from the P.M. "She" is revealed to be Balsquith himself disguised as a woman, the only way he could get through the lines of women demonstrators. When General Sandstone of Mitchener's staff advocates the exclusion of women from an area within a two-mile radius of Westminster, Mitchener, who thinks only force can solve anything, approves of the plan and says "Shoot 'em down." When the Prime Minister contends that public sentiment would not accept the shooting, his view is rejected; and Sandstone resigns.

Meanwhile, martial law is declared. Balsquith meets a deputation of Anti-Suffrage Leaguers, and Mitchener talks with the char-woman who cleans his office. She argues that the child-bed is more dangerous than the battlefield. Two Anti-Suffragettes enter and inform him it is the right to military service, and not the vote, that they favor. They assert that Bismarck and Napoleon, as well as other strong men in history, have been women in disguise, and that Queen Elizabeth was a man dressed as a woman. The play becomes more and more farcical as Sandstone proposes to Mrs. Banger, a masculine woman of forty, and Mitchener offers his hand in marriage to Mrs. Farrell, the charwoman, and she accepts him. The beautiful and romantic Lady Corinthia must content herself with being Balsquith's Egeria, his teacher and helper.

Press Cuttings, though its lines contribute to our understanding of his social thought, does not add anything to its author's stature as a dramatist. Other dramatic writings that flowed from Shaw's teeming brain at this time were *The Fascinating Foundling,* which he dubbed "A Disgrace to the Author," and *The Glimpse of Reality: A Tragedietta.* Like *Press Cuttings,* which has more substance than the other two, Shaw classed them as "tomfooleries," for which he made no apology, saying, "Irresponsible laughter is salutary in small quantities."[19]

III   Misalliance

Shaw's next serious and important drama is *Misalliance: A Debate in One Sitting*. It is a delayed sequel to *Getting Married* and is like its predecessor in two ways: (1) it is not divided into scenes or acts; and (2) the curtain is lowered twice solely for the convenience of the audience. This play, with a small bow to Turgenev's *Fathers and Sons*, could well have been entitled *Fathers, Mothers, and Children*, for the main issue is modern parenthood. Shaw presumably chose *Misalliance* as the title because of the unhappy marital and family relationships which it portrays.

Johnny Tarleton, thirtyish, a young businessman, is spending his usual long weekend at the Surrey home of his wealthy father, John Tarleton, the manufacturer of Tarleton's Underwear. Johnny is reading a novel when Bentley Summerhays—"one of those smallish, thin-skinned youths, who from 17 to 70 retained unaltered the mental airs of the later and the physical appearance of the earlier age"—enters. Probably because Bentley is socially a grade above Johnny, the two of them hurl epithets and insults at each other until they almost come to blows. Young Johnny, who is physically the stronger, menaces Bentley, who bursts into sobs, tears, and piercing yells.

Hearing this commotion, Hypatia Tarleton, the girl whom Bentley is hoping to marry, enters with her mother. They comfort Bentley and reprove Johnny for his brutal behavior. As Lord Summerhays enters, he discusses his son's weaknesses and his possible merits with Johnny; and, when Bentley reappears, he is ridiculed by his father as a shameful "baby." The three men go for a walk, leaving Hypatia and her mother to discuss at length a variety of subjects, including Hypatia's feelings about men in general and about Bentley in particular. She states that, although she is not in love with Bentley, she will probably marry him because she supposes she must marry somebody.

When the elder John Tarleton and young Bentley Summerhays enter, they are arguing about youth and age; and Tarleton urges Bentley to improve his mind: "Read your Darwin, my boy, Read your Weismann." An advocate of ideas and culture, he sprinkles his conversation with friendly commands: "Read Browning. . . . Read Ibsen. . . . Read Mill. . . . Read Jefferson. . . . Read Chesterton." He worries because members of his family, especially Johnny, do not cultivate their minds. As an industrial mogul, he is an interesting contrast to the powerful Andrew Undershaft.

The action of the play centers chiefly in the story of Hypatia, whom Shaw describes as "a typical English girl of the sort never called typical" and adds: "she has an opaque white skin, black hair, large dark eyes with black brows and lashes, curved lips, swift glances and movements that flash out of a waiting stillness, boundless energy and audacity held in leash." She is bored with her life in which it seems nothing happens except talk, talk, talk. At one point she says: "If parents would only realize how they bore their children! Three or four times in the last half hour I've been on the point of screaming." When Lord Summerhays reveals that he has fallen in love with her, she tells him that she will be grateful to him all her life because his declaration was the first time anything really interesting had happened to her. When he calls her "a glorious young beast," she responds: "I like that. Glorious young beast expresses exactly what I like to be."

Her father says that Hypatia is always looking for adventure to drop out of the sky, and that is precisely what happens. An airplane that crashes off stage into the Tarletons' glass house and flower garden damages the vinery but luckily injures no one. Two persons—Joseph Percival, a handsome young aviator, and Lina Szczepanowska, a good-looking Polish acrobat—emerge from the plane. Percival, it turns out, is a friend of Bentley's, and Lina is from a family in which it is a tradition that some member must risk his or her life daily. She is bright and attractive, and John Tarleton promptly declares to her that he would like to make a fool of himself over her. Lina puts his name and age (fifty-eight) in the little book of her romantic offers.

At this point a strange young man carrying a revolver enters and hides in a new Turkish bath on the stage as Hypatia and Percival appear. Unaware that they are watched, she attempts to make love to Percival, but he eludes her and runs away with her in pursuit. As John Tarleton comes in, the intruder emerges from the Turkish bath and threatens him as the deceiver and deserter of the gunman's dead mother. Tarleton diverts the young man from his fatal intention by means of sparkling conversation. Lina enters and deftly assists Tarleton in disarming the gunman, who turns out to be a disgruntled clerk.

Tarleton introduces him to Mrs. Tarleton as Mr. Gunner and the name sticks. Though he pictures himself as a submissive and miserable nine-to-six cashier, Gunner becomes aggressively outspoken. He reveals that he saw Hypatia and Percival in what he calls "a scandal and an infamy." To him they typify "the morals of the capitalist class" and the "rotten bourgeoisie." When Mrs. Tarleton objects to such "bad" language, her husband assures her that it is only socialism.

As Hypatia and Percival reappear, he is chasing her. When Bentley learns what Gunner has been saying of him and Hypatia, he forces the intruder to sign a document retracting his "slanderous statements." Shortly thereafter Mrs. Tarleton takes an interest in Gunner when she learns the name of his mother, whom she had once befriended. Tarleton persuades him to take a drink of sloe gin after which Gunner talks volubly of socialism and about his restored sense of manhood. Finally, he tells the men: "Understand, I don't give a damn for the lot of you," and departs.

The Tarletons and the Summerhays decide that it is time to talk about Hypatia's future. Bentley loses control of his feelings when he sees that his friend Joey has taken Hypatia from him. Percival explains he cannot afford to marry; Hypatia tells her father, "Buy the brute for me"; and he complies as he offers to support them at least temporarily by providing fifteen hundred pounds a year. At this point, Lina Szczepanowska seeks to prepare the airplane for a take-off, feeling that she can no longer stay in a house of people who think of nothing but love-making. In a long speech she recalls that the Tarletons, father and son, and the Summerhayses, father and son, have all made advances to her. She is determined to fly the plane and to take Bentley, in whom she has tried to instill courage, with her; and he hesitantly agrees to go. Tarleton starts to talk to Lina and then to Lord Summerhays but breaks off the conversations, saying that there is nothing more to be said, whereupon Hypatia fervently exclaims, "Thank goodness!" as the curtain falls.

The preface to *Misalliance*, which is longer than the play itself, is entitled "Parents and Children." Like the play, it deals with "the generation gap" in which Shaw's sympathies are altogether on the side of the young. The idea of a child as the property of the parents is abhorrent to him, for it has tended to justify child abuse and child slavery.[20] Shaw defines a child as a "fresh attempt to produce the just man made perfect: that is to make humanity divine."[21] So the worst of all sins against children is any attempt to shape and control their minds. "Every child has the right to its own bent" even if it means disliking mother, father, sister, brother, uncle, or aunt.[22]

Recalling his own unhappy school days, Shaw looks upon school as in some respects more cruel than a prison. Textbooks were a horror to Shaw, a hideous imposture. "It is a ghastly business, quite beyond words, this schooling."[23] He would not abolish schools, but he would revolutionize them. He would forbid all forms of corporal punishment, a common disciplinary measure in 1909; and he would permit the greatest possible freedom to school children in their natural pursuit of knowledge and wisdom. Asked to give a prize to the Ayot St. Lawrence School, G.B.S. offered to endow a handsome one for the worst-behaved boy or girl with the provision that records be kept of his or her subsequent career and compared with that of the best-behaved. The offer was refused.[24]

Concurring with Samuel Butler again, Shaw regarded the ideal family as "a humbug and a nuisance." Because the ties of family life are often a restrictive force in the lives of children, many of them, brought up at home, are not fitted for society.[25] He summarizes his viewpoint at the end of the preface in these words: "Liberty is the breath of life to nations; and liberty is the one thing that parents, schoolmasters, and rulers spend their lives in extirpating for the sake of an immediately quiet and finally disastrous life."[26] *Misalliance*, presenting memorable characters and dealing with important issues that are still alive, assuredly deserves a considerable place in the Shaw Canon.

IV   *A Playlet About Shakespeare*

Shaw followed *Misalliance* with a playlet about Shakespeare, *The Dark Lady of the Sonnets*. In the preface, which is more than twice as long as the play, Shaw refers to it as a "little *piece d'occasion* written for a performance in aid of the funds of the project for establishing a National Theatre as a memorial to Shakespeare" and explains why he identifies the Dark Lady as Mary Fitton. When Frank Harris, who had written a play about Shakespeare and Mary Fitton, accused Shaw of plagiarism, Shaw retorted that Thomas Tyler, a reading companion of his in the British Museum and the first promulgator of the Fitton Theory, had told Shaw of it before Harris had learned of it. Shaw admitted there is reason for doubt that Mary Fitton was the Dark Lady, but he "stuck" with her nevertheless.[27]

In the playlet, he presents Will Shakespeare as human enough to make love to a closely cloaked woman who actually, unknown to him, is Queen Elizabeth. When the Dark Lady sees her lover philandering with the cloaked woman, she strikes them both. On learning the Queen's identity, she is aghast. Shakespeare scolds her for having smitten him. The Bard softens the Queen's anger with sweet words and asks of her a boon: a National Theatre. She declares that to present such a gift is impossible, but she agrees to pray for its establishment in some future time.

The Dark Lady is valuable mainly in evincing Shaw's continuing interest in Shakespeare; for, as already noted, Shaw was a member of the New Shakespeare Society in the 1880s; and later he was an active member of the General Committee of the Shakespeare Memorial National Theatre organization. It is a myth that Shaw considered himself superior to Shakespeare. Presumably the clearest of all his statements on the subject is his answer to a biographer who, misled by a G.B.S. pronouncement, implied that he had declared his plays better than Shakespeare's. Said Shaw: "It was the overwhelming contrast with Ibsen that explains my *Saturday Review* campaign against the spurious part of Shakespear's reputation. But the notion that I ever claimed crudely that my plays, or anybody's plays, were better written than Shakespear's, is absurd."[28]

V The Generation Gap

Fanny's First Play: An Easy Play for a Little Theatre is a farce which Shaw frankly called "a potboiler."[29] Nevertheless, it merits attention, first, because it presents in Margaret Knox a modern young woman almost worthy of ranking with Vivie Warren and Barbara Undershaft. Second, its theme of the "generation gap" is so modern that the play could have been written a month or so ago. Here, again, as in *Getting Married,* Shaw is plainly on the side of the young. A third reason for considering this play is its distinction of having had the longest run—622 performances—of any of Shaw's dramatic works.

It is a neat little package of a play. First of all, the three acts are framed by an introduction and by an epilogue. The introduction sets the scene and the action to come in Florence Towers, near Cambridge, where Count O'Dowda has curtained off the end of a saloon to form a stage for a private performance. The count has promised his daughter Fanny to stage her play, to do so anonymously, and to invite real-life critics, as a birthday gift.

In Act I, which takes place at the Denmark Hill home of Mr. and Mrs. Gilby, they receive a letter from a friend informing them that

their son Bobby, missing for a fortnight, is in some kind of trouble;
but the particular kind is not mentioned. Their footman Juggins
brings in a card bearing the name "Miss D. Delaney. Darling
Dora," and she enters and reveals, to Bobby's parents' consternation, that she had met Bobby in police court and had left him in jail
following a brawl. Dora tells the Gilbeys: "You see you've brought
Bobby up too strict; and when he gets loose theres no holding him."
The Gilbeys are worried about how they can face Mr. and Mrs.
Knox to whose daughter, Margaret, Bobby is engaged.

In Act II in the drawing room of their home the Knoxes are ap-
prehensive lest the Gilbeys have found out about Margaret, who has
been missing a fortnight. Like Bobby, she has behaved scandalously. At a boat race she and M. Duvallet, a young married Frenchman
whom she casually met, fought with the police. Margaret broke two
teeth of an officer and was proud of it, though it cost her two weeks
in Holloway Gaol. Margaret declares that her "descent into hell"
has set her "free from this little hole of a house and all its
pretenses." When Knox begs her to keep secret what she has done,
Margaret insists that she will "tell everybody."

As the last and third act opens in the Gilbeys' dining room, Bobby consults Juggins about how to break his engagement delicately
without appearing to jilt Margaret. At this juncture, the young
woman in question enters and begins to prepare Bobby for the news
that she wishes to break the engagement. When they exchange accounts of their escapades, including their prison experiences,
Margaret confesses to a feeling of relief; but Bobby feels scandalized. "But you know," he says, "it's not the same for a girl. A
man may do things a woman maynt." After Juggins has announced
the arrival of Miss Delaney, Dora and Margaret recognize each
other as prison mates. Though Bobby has kept company with
"Darling Dora," he snubs her; and, when Margaret calls him "a
young beast," the two of them wrestle angrily. Helpless to separate
them, Dora calls for Juggins who throws open the door and announces M. Duvallet, a Frenchman whom Margaret had met, liked,
and danced with in prison. When Mr. and Mrs. Gilbey are seen
coming up the street, the young people flee to the pantry. When
Juggins gives notice to Mr. Gilbey that he will quit his employment,
Gilbey thinks this decision is a consequence of Bobby's disgraceful
behavior; but the reason turns out to be that Juggins's older
brother, who has asked him to quit domestic service, is a duke.

Meanwhile, the Knoxes appear again; and the parents all discuss the state of the world and the question of Margaret's and Bobby's future. The young people reappear and find their own answers: Bobby announces he will marry Darling Dora; and Juggins, whose real name is Rudolph, proposes to Margaret, who says that she has loved him since the first day she beheld him. Duvallet is sure that all this could have happened only in "la belle Angleterre."

In the epilogue, Count O'Dowda expresses his deep disapproval of the play, which is altogether too modern for his taste. When the critics try to guess the playwright's identity, one mentions Shaw, another Granville Baker, and a third Pinero. Fanny is pleased and flattered. Finally, the fourth critic, Trotter, reveals two of Fanny's secrets: one is that she is the author of the play and the other is that, as a suffragette, she, like the young people in the play, spent time in jail. One of Shaw's chief purposes in the epilogue is to ridicule his critics; for Trotter, Gunn, and Vaughan are the thinly disguised names of London critics—Walkley, Cannon, and Baughan. Actually it is gentle satire, for Shaw, though often disagreeing with their verdicts, usually had respect for his journalistic reviewers.[30]

The preface to *Fanny's First Play* is only a page and a half long. In it, Shaw asserts that the lesson of the play is not unneeded. Since "our respectable middle class people are all as dead as mutton," it is better for the young "to have their souls awakened by disgrace, capture [*sic*] by the police, and a month's hard labor, than drift along from their cradles to their graves doing what other people do for no other reason than that other people do it, and knowing nothing of good and evil, of courage and cowardice, or indeed anything but how to keep hunger and concupiscence and fashionable dressing within the bounds of good taste except when their excesses can be concealed."[31] It appears that multitudes of young persons, consciously or unconsciously, have taken Shaw's advice in the 1970s. As usual, our author's thinking is in advance of his time.

VI *A Fable About Christianity*

One day when Shaw was at the theatre Lillah McCarthy, who was playing the role of Margaret Knox in *Fanny's First Play*, received a letter from Mrs. Sidney Webb in which she said: "I wish you could persuade G.B.S. to do a piece of serious work, and not pursue this somewhat barren tilting at the family." On showing the letter to him, the actress noted that for once he looked grave, and she added that "Shaw has a tremendous respect for Beatrice

Webb."[32] His next was "a serious piece of work"—*Androcles and the Lion: A Fable Play* (1912)—about Christianity; but, as usual with Shaw, the farcical was mixed with earnestness. That he had the deepest respect for Jesus is manifest in this play and in others of his writings; yet he writes of Christ and God without reverence. Indeed, it may confidently be said that reverence was no part of Shaw's mind or temper. When, partly in jest, he asked an amateur phrenologist to look for a bump of veneration on the Shavian head, the man exclaimed that it was a hole! At all events, in *Androcles* he presents the most serious subjects, such as martyrdom, with a vein of humor. As he commented to Archibald Henderson, "Here I take historical tragedy at its deepest: a point reached only by religious persecution. And the thing is done as if it were a *revue* or a Christmas pantomime, the chief figure being a pantomime lion."[33]

In the prologue, he retells the story of Androclus and the Lion by Aulus Gellius. Shaw not only changed the *u* in Androclus to an *e*, but he also changed the pagan slave into a Christian tailor, gave Androcles a quarrelsome Roman wife, and thereby introduced one of the oldest themes of comedy. After Androcles pulls the thorn from the lion's paw and starts waltzing with him, Megaera reminds her husband that he refused to dance with her. Androcles's wife, a defender of the religious status quo in Rome, deeply opposes his Christianity as a disgraceful divergence, a shameful apostasy, and as worse than being addicted to drink.

Likewise, in the main action of the play, the emperor regards the Christians as rebels against the established faith and as enemies of Rome. The chief candidates for martyrdom are Lavinia, a beautiful and intelligent young woman; Ferrovius, whose fierceness as a fighter is matched by his piety as a convert; and Androcles, the gentle, animal-loving tailor. A fourth less attractive and less important Christian is Spintho, a sensualist and a persistent sinner, who in trying to escape runs into the path of a lion, which devours him. Lavinia captivates a Roman captain, who offers her a way of escape which she steadfastly refuses to accept. She is willing to die, not for Christ, but for the God who is yet to be, one who, by the way, is quite close to Shaw's conception of the Diety.

Ferrovius's great problem is to fulfill the Christian dictum to love his enemies; for, when the Roman gladiators confront him in the arena, he slays all of them and wins the admiration of Caesar, who offers him a position in the Roman guards. Ultimately Ferrovius accepts and becomes a follower of Mars, but he refuses to do so in

the name of Christ. Like Lavinia, Ferrovius believes that the Christian God is not yet. "He will come when Mars and I are dust," says
the warrior; "but I must serve the gods that are, not the God that
will be." Ferrovius's joining the guard so pleases Caesar that he
decides to free all the Christians except Androcles, who is sent into
the arena to appease the crowd. But the lion recognizes his benefac-
tor and not only refuses to eat him, but even waltzes with him once
more. Shaw's Caesar is no tyrant, and the Roman persecution is
shown to be "an attempt to suppress a propaganda that seemed to
threaten the interests involved in the established law and order,
organized and maintained in the name of religion and justice by
politicians who are pure Have-and Holders."

Two plays by Shaw's contemporaries influenced the writing of
Androcles. The success of Barrie's *Peter Pan*, one of the most popular plays of Shaw's time, reached a climax when the famous bronze
statue of Peter Pan was erected in Kensington Gardens in 1912. It
may have been more than coincidence that Shaw wrote that same
year his first play for children, which, like Barrie's fantasy, appeals
to adults as well. Children have enjoyed *Androcles*, especially the
capers with the lion, but the play has never seriously rivaled *Peter
Pan* in popularity. In his later years Shaw looked back on *Androcles*
as an antidote to *Peter Pan*. He believed that a play for children
should never be oversimplified or condescending. Barrie's play,
Shaw felt, was a "sample of what adults think children like."[34]

Another play to which *Androcles* serves as an antithesis is *The
Sign of the Cross* (1895), a melodrama by Wilson Barrett, an
English actor-manager. Both the play and its author are now almost
forgotten. It is evident, however, that Shaw had not forgotten it
when he wrote *Androcles*, for Barrett's play presents a Roman patri-
cian who falls in love with a beautiful Christian girl who is about to
be thrown into the arena to meet death from the lions, a situation
which probably suggested the Roman captain's love affair with
Lavinia.

Androcles and the Lion lacks the elements of "corrective comedy" as found in *Major Barbara* or *Man and Superman*, for, as we
have seen, it is an amusing farce which Shaw vainly attempts to
turn into a serious fable. But, in a postscript to *Androcles and the
Lion*, Shaw castigated the English clergy for approving the war and
for continuing to conduct worship in the name of Jesus: "They have
turned their churches into recruiting stations and their vestries into
munitions shops. . . . They have stuck to their livings and served

Mars in the name of Christ, to the scandal of all religious man-kind." Shaw was particularly outraged on learning that a church was closed at Forest Hill because its service was in the German language. Quite in contrast to the clergy as they bow to the god of war are the Christian martyrs, whom Shaw portrays in *Androcles* as "people who are shown by their inner light the possibility of a better world based on the demand of the spirit for a nobler and more abundant life, not for themselves at the expense of others, but for everybody."[35] Here, as elsewhere, Shaw evinces his strong predilection for the Quaker faith.[36]

Much of the value of *Androcles* lies in the fact that it inspired one of its author's longest and most important prefaces. This preface, which fills a hundred pages in *The Complete Plays* (the drama has only forty-seven), is entitled "The Prospects of Christianity." Written in 1915 when World War I was in full blast, the preface is a plea for the teachings of Jesus Christ. These teachings have not fail-ed; the simple fact is they have not been tried. As Shaw expresses it: "I am ready to admit that after contemplating the world and human nature for nearly sixty years, I see no way out of the world's misery but the way which would have been found by Christ's will if he had undertaken the work of a modern practical statesman."[37] The preface parallels remarkably the ideas in Shelley's *Essay on Christianity*,[38] for both the preface and the essay contain the same list of Christ's doctrines. Among these are (1) the widening of the family circle to include all mankind under the Fatherhood of God; (2) the abandonment of revenge and punishment; (3) the counteracting of evil by good; and (4) the conception of society as an organism in which each person is not an independent individual but rather a member of the whole—"and each of you members of one another, as two fingers on a hand, the obvious conclusion being that unless you love your neighbor as your self and he reciprocates you will both be the worse for it."[39]

Though Shaw did not always acknowledge his indebtedness to other writers, he fully credited Shelley as having had a deep in-fluence on his work and thought. It was Shelley who made a vegetarian and a free-thinker of him. Yet Shaw disagreed with Shelley's emphasis on love as a panacea, calling it "amoristic superstition," and he wrote of Jesus not as the embodiment of love but as an economic and social philosopher. "Jesus remains un-shaken as the practical man," says Shaw, "and we stand exposed as the fools, the blunderers, the unpractical visionaries."[40] A little later he declared: "Decidedly, whether you think Jesus was God or not, you must admit that he was a first-rate political economist."[41]

Accordingly, Shaw makes a distinction between the essential social doctrines of Jesus and the historical development of Christianity. "The glaring contradiction between his teaching and the practices of all states and churches," Shaw asserts, "is no longer hidden."[42] The church has, in Shaw's view, wasted a great deal of intellectual energy on the miracles. He insists that, if it could be proved that not one of them had occurred, the proof would not invalidate one of his didactic utterances.[43] The reverse is likewise true. "Unfortunately, wherever Jesus went," Shaw continues, "he was assailed with a clamor for miracles, though his doctrine created bewilderment."

Not only in the miracles, but also in the ideas of Salvation, the Second Coming, Redemption, and the Atonement Shaw saw obstacles to the achievement of the true ends for which Jesus lived. The emphasis on the Cross has, in Shaw's belief, converted Christianity into "Crosstianity."[44] Thus the doctrine of the Atonement Shaw regards not as the chief value of Jesus's life, but as indeed the main impediment to the application of His ideas in the world. The whole preface, like the play, makes interesting and rewarding reading.

VII *A Play About Modern Love*

Shaw continued his work as playwright with a farcical one-act play or playlet far removed from war and rumors of war, for *Overruled* is a minor piece about a subject far ahead of its time, wife-trading. Originally entitled *Trespassers Will Be Prosecuted*, it contrasts two types of libertines and two types of attitude toward unconventional love-making. Two couples on a cruise fall in love with each other's spouses, an arrangement which proves to be pleasant all around.

As it not infrequently happens in Shaw, the preface which *Overruled* evokes is more valuable than the play itself. Writing on such topics as "The Alleviations of Monogamy," "The Convention of Jealousy," "The Pseudo Sex Play," and "Pruderies of the French Stage," Shaw presents a natural history of modern love with a sense of its moral and immoral aspects. "There is a continual and irreconcilable conflict," he declares, "between the natural and conventional sides of the case, between spontaneous human relations

118

GEORGE BERNARD SHAW

between independent men and women on the one hand and the property relation between husband and wife on the other, not to mention the confusion under the common name of love of a generous natural attraction and interest with the murderous jealousy that fastens on and clings to its mate (especially a hated mate) as a tiger fastens on to a carcass."[45] The daily newspapers continually narrate the homicidal consequences of this kind of pseudo-love.

<h2>VIII The Original of My Fair Lady</h2>

Shaw's next major play was one of his most successful and familiar dramas, *Pygmalion: A Romance in Five Acts*. It is based, first of all, on the ancient myth of a sculptor who produced a beautiful maiden, Galatea, fell in love with her, and prevailed on Aphrodite to give her life. Shaw was not the first to use the legend as the basis of a play. In 1871 W. S. Gilbert wrote *Pygmalion and Galatea,* but long before that Tobias Smollett wrote in his novel *Peregrine Pickle* about a young woman of low breeding whom a bachelor took in hand and trained to be a society princess. In Shaw's comedy the subject is phonetics, a topic near to Shaw's heart, and the theme is the power of speech training to break down the barriers of social status.

So widely known is the story of Professor Higgins, the speech teacher (Pygmalion), who discovers Eliza Doolittle, a Cockney flower girl (Galatea) and transforms her into a young woman who attends an ambassador's party and succeeds in passing as a lady, that it hardly requires a detailed synopsis. Aiding Higgins in the reeducation of Eliza is Colonel Pickering, an expert in Oriental languages. Both amusing and complicating is the intrusion of Eliza's father, a dustman, who has hitherto paid little attention to his daughter. Now he appears as the wronged father of a presumably "abducted" daughter and demands compensation. On finding that Higgins is no kidnapper and that the arrangement is on the level, Doolittle offers to sell Eliza for five pounds. The transformation of this renegade father into a well-dressed, middle-class bourgeois through the magic of money is the worst flaw of the play. On Higgins's recommendation, an American millionaire leaves Doolittle an income of three thousand pounds a year; and, as a result, the former vulgar dustman becomes respectable, and his personality makes a complete about-face. The whole idea is preposterous and unconvincing. On the contrary, Eliza, Higgins, and Colonel Pickering are skillfully drawn while Freddy Eynsford-Hill, Mrs. Eynsford-Hill, and Mrs. Higgins are presented with acceptable realism.

The play reaches its climax in the garden party at which Eliza displays the refinements of speech she has learned from Higgins. She scandalizes the uppercrust—and incidentally London playgoers also—by using the expression "bloody likely," but otherwise she acquits herself more than well enough. She makes the greatest impression, however, not on the older persons present, but on young Freddy Hill, who falls in love with her, though Eliza does not encourage him. Toward the end of the story, the chief concern hinges on the question, What will become of Eliza? When she speaks of returning to her old stall at the market, Higgins upbraids her: "If you cant stand the coldness of my sort of life, and the strain of it, go back to the gutter. Work till you are more a brute than a human being; and then cuddle and squabble and drink till you fall asleep. Oh, it's a fine life, the life of the gutter. It's real: it's warm: it's violent: you can feel it through the thickest skin: you can taste it or smell it without any training or any work. Not like Science and Literature and Classical Music and Philosophy and Art."[46] When she threatens to marry Freddy Hill, the professor tells her he will not let her throw away his masterpiece on Freddy.

At the very end of *Pygmalion,* when Higgins orders Eliza to buy him a ham, a Stilton Cheese, a pair of reindeer gloves, number eights, and a tie—"You can choose the color"—his requests indicate that he expects their relationship to continue and perhaps lead to marriage. When Eliza replies disdainfully, "Buy them yourself" and dashes out, Mrs. Higgins observes: "I'm afraid you have spoiled that girl, Henry. But never mind, dear: I'll buy you the tie and gloves." "Oh, dont bother," Higgins assures her complacently in the last speech of the play. "She'll buy em all right enough."

This ending seemed fitting to Shaw, but not to his friends, critics, and playgoers, who insisted on knowing what became of Eliza, whom did she marry, and what became of her relationship to Higgins and Pickering. Complaining of imaginations "enfeebled by their lazy dependence on the ready-mades and reach-me-downs of the ragshop in which Romance keeps its stock of 'happy endings,' Shaw reluctantly appended a novellike dozen pages to the text of *Pygmalion.* He explained that Eliza married Freddy Hill, that Colonel Pickering gave them five hundred pounds for their honeymoon, and that they later opened a flower shop which, with the addition of asparagus and other vegetables, prospered well enough. Eliza continued to have an amiable, but not intimate, relationship with the two bachelors on Wimpole Street.

It is ironical that this play, written partly to demonstrate that language (phonetics particularly) could contribute to understanding among men, should be closed because of the outbreak of World War I in July 1914.[47] After the war, *Pygmalion* resumed its place in the theatre and continued to augment Shaw's international fame. Looking back over its history before 1956, Lucile Kelling declared that it "emerges as a tremendous favorite almost the world over";[48] and it still holds a high place among Shaw's works. In fact, six years after his death, it became the basis of *My Fair Lady*, one of the most commercially successful musical comedies of all time. That Shaw would not have consented to the musical version there can be no doubt; for, thirty-five years before *My Fair Lady* captivated New York theatregoers, Shaw heard that Ferenc Lehar, author of *The Merry Widow*, planned to make an operetta of *Pygmalion;* and he directed Trebitsch, his German translator, to warn Lehar "that he cannot touch *Pygmalion* without infringing my copyright, and that I have no intention of allowing the history of *The Chocolate Soldier* to be repeated." Lehar gave up the idea, which Alan Jay Lerner and Frederick Loewe later succeeded in materializing.

Critical opinion of *My Fair Lady* ranges from Eric Bentley's comment that it is "Shaw reduced to the stereotypes of Establishment entertainment"[49] to the most extravagant praise. The truth lies somewhere in between. The musical is not so bad as Bentley's remark would make it, but neither is it an improvement over the original. Lerner and Loewe, who showed great respect for Shaw in their adaptation, used approximately sixty-five percent of the dialogue of *Pygmalion*. They produced scenes which Shaw only mentioned or described in his script, and they concluded the musical as Shaw first conceived of the ending: Eliza returns to Higgins rather than marrying Freddie Hill, as Shaw reluctantly conceded in his sequel.[50] The delightful songs that grace *My Fair Lady* are appropriate to the spirit of the play. The musical version does not supplant *Pygmalion;* each should be regarded as a separate artistic entity.

It was in relation to *Pygmalion* that the friendship and the love of Shaw and Mrs. Patrick Campbell, the actress for whom he wrote the part of Eliza, developed and flourished.[51] This is not the place to detail the story of that interesting affair, which was carried on mostly by correspondence; but one letter is worth citing since it exemplifies Shaw's compassion and expresses his disgust with the events of 1914. "This war," he wrote, "is getting too silly for words: they make no headway and produce no result except to kill, kill, kill. The Kaiser asks from time to time for another million men to be killed; and Kitchener asks for another million to kill them." Women, Shaw declared, should rebel against making any more men for fighting wars. "But alas," he added, "the women are just as idiotic as the men."[52]

When Mrs. Campbell informed Shaw of her son's death on the battlefield, he replied characteristically that he could not be sympathetic, but only furious, saying that he wanted to swear. "I do swear. Killed just because people are blasted fools." In response to the bereaved mother's reference to a chaplain's letter, Shaw fulminated: "It is not his business to say nice things, but to shout that 'the voice of thy son's blood crieth unto God from the ground.' "[53] It would be difficult to see how anyone could hate the waste and the horror of war more than did Shaw.

CHAPTER 7

The Climax of a Career

I   Heartbreak House

S HAW'S attitude toward World War I is plainly discernible in a drama entitled *Heartbreak House: A Fantasia in the Russian Manner on English Themes,* most of which he wrote in 1913 but which he continued to revise over a period of six years. Because it revealed the deterioration of English society, Shaw withheld it from the stage until after World War I on the grounds that to have produced it would have given aid and comfort to the enemy. He was not always so tactful or so careful, for his pamphlet *Common Sense About the War* was actually used by Germany to undermine British endeavors in the war. But *Heartbreak House* he considered too powerful a medicine for the time. "War," he declared, "cannot bear the terrible castigation of comedy, the ruthless light of laughter that glares on the stage." He added that the truth-telling was not compatible with the defense of the realm.[1]

He called *Heartbreak House* "cultured leisured Europe before the war," a phrase that expresses the main theme of the play. As he concentrated on the state of things in England just before 1913, he depicted the aristocracy as having greater interest in exciting amusements than in political responsibilities. Next to Heartbreak House stood Horseback Hall, a symbol of the well-to-do people's trivial preoccupations. The situation was like that in Russia in its so-called "twilight period" before the fall of the Czars, the era Anton Chekhov's dramas realistically portrayed.

Not long before writing *Heartbreak House* Shaw, while attending a performance of Chekhov's *The Cherry Orchard,* was so deeply impressed that he is reported to have said: "I feel as if I want to tear up all my plays and begin all over again."[2] His admiration was strengthened as he saw other dramas of the great Russian, who, like himself, was an advocate of nonviolence. Moreover, at this time

Shaw had also been reading Tolstoy's autobiographical and religious play, *The Light That Shines in Darkness*, which like *The Cherry Orchard* influenced Shaw's "fantasia in the Russian manner." But, though Tolstoyan in its moral earnestness, *Heartbreak House* is mainly Chekhovian in its tragicomic spirit and in its pervasive sadness. The time of the play—"a fine evening at the end of September"—recalls *The Cherry Orchard*, which takes place in the same month of melancholy overtones. In Chekhov's four chief dramas, the characters all gather under one roof, just as they do in *Heartbreak House*. In Chekhov's plays, the love relationships invariably go awry; similarly, in *Heartbreak House* all the flirtations come to nothing. Shaw's characters, like some of those in *Uncle Vanya*, *The Three Sisters*, and *The Cherry Orchard*, discuss the emptiness of their lives. In fact, the emphasis on discussion is the most obvious resemblance between the two dramatists. Still another similarity is Nurse Guinness, who resembles the privileged old nurse of Chekhov's *Uncle Vanya*.

Yet Shaw, like Shakespeare, was no slavish imitator of any other playwright; and *Heartbreak House*, accordingly, had its own distinctive flavor. In calling it "a fantasia," Shaw implies the play's freedom from dramatic restrictions. There is an atmosphere of weirdness that is conveyed at the outset by the setting. Captain Shotover's house, the only scene of the play, is in the form of "an old-fashioned high-pooped ship with a stern gallery." Its doors lead to a garden, and its windows command a view of the hilly country in the middle of the northern edge of Sussex.[3] It is a fitting environment for the strange persons who gather in the house.

First of all, there is Captain Shotover himself, a man of eighty-eight, wearing a reefer jacket with a whistle hanging from his neck. He is still hardy and hearty, with a way of uttering strange sayings through his ample white beard. He dominates the story although Ellie Dunn, a pretty young woman with intellectual tastes, is the character around whom most of the action revolves. As the play opens, she has come to visit Captain Shotover's daughter, Hesione Hushabye, who fails to greet Ellie at the appointed time. Shotover is indignant about his daughter's neglectfulness; but, when his younger daughter, Ariadne, appears after twenty-three years abroad, he receives her with a casualness that borders on the inhuman. When Hesione appears, she greets Ellie cordially; but, strange to say, she hardly notices her long-absent sister.[4] When

Ellie's father, Mazzini Dunn, enters, Captain Shotover invites him to help with a dynamite experiment in the garden.

In Act II, Ellie is shown to have hypnotic powers and a desire to marry Boss Mangan. After discussing their engagement, she and Mangan talk frankly about his supposed kindness to Ellie's father, whom Mangan has ruined financially. Mangan's confession that his "kindness" was insincere disillusions Ellie. When he reveals that he is in love with Hesione, Ellie discloses her love for Hector Hushabye, hypnotizes Mangan, and leaves him. Though Hesione disapproves of the match, Ellie persists in her determination to marry Mangan for his money. Recovering his senses, he has overheard the two women's conversation and is offended.

A pistol shot is heard outside as Hector, Randall, and Mazzini Dunn arrest a burglar who has stolen Lady Utterwood's jewels. The thief happens to be Billy Dunn, former husband of Nurse Guinness and Shotover's former dishonest boatswain. His plea for mercy falls on friendly ears as Mazzini proposes that the burglar set up as a locksmith, whereupon Billy asks his captors to take up a collection for him. As Hector hands him a pound note, the burglar starts to leave but encounters Shotover, who recognizes him and orders him taken to the forecastle. After the guests have left and Captain Shotover and Ellie are alone together, they discuss Ellie's prospective wedding to Mangan; but she proposes marriage to Shotover, who disenchants her with his drinking and talking of rum. When Randall and Lady Utterwood quarrel bitterly, Hector enters the verbal fray and is moved to ask, "Is there any slavery on earth viler than this slavery of man to women?"[5]

In the final act, the characters discuss their various kinds of heartbreak. Mangan, who threatens to strip and proposes that they all undress, is revealed as actually being poor. Hector laments the "powers of destruction" which Mangan and his mutual admiration gang wield. Hector's reference to the captain's house as "this ship we are all in" and "this soul's prison we call England" is reminiscent of the student's remark in *The Cherry Orchard* "All Russia is our garden." *Heartbreak House* ends with a bombing in which Mangan and the burglar—"two practical men of business"—perish and the nearby rectory is destroyed. Mrs. Hushabye and Ellie exult in the experience and express the hope that the planes will return the next night.

Symbolism permeates much of his play. The design of the captain's house may be taken to signify the Ship of State, and this concept gives warrant to Shotover's words near the end of the play. To Hector's question, "And what may my business as an Englishman be, pray?" the captain answers: "Navigation. Learn it and live; or leave it and be damned." There can be little doubt that he means political and social wisdom. The destruction of the rectory leads Shotover to remark: "The Church is on the rocks, breaking up. I told him [the rector] it would unless it headed for God's open sea."[6]

Apocalyptic, prophetic, and philosophic, *Heartbreak House* is one of Shaw's most interesting and most important plays. It is long, but never boring to anyone attuned to its nuances. It is dreamlike, but in no wise a dream play in the Strindbergian mode, in which time and space do not exist. Many of its speeches are harmonic and cadenced, and there is a pervasive musical quality in the dramatic design. Even the bombing at the end reminds Ellie and Mrs. Hushabye of Beethoven.[7] Shaw in his nineties spoke of *Heartbreak* as his "greatest play",[8] but whether the public will agree only time will tell. At all events, its "message" has a peculiar appropriateness for our time.[9]

In the preface Shaw does not deal with Shakespeare's influence on *Heartbreak House*, but Shaw late in life called this play his *Lear* "with his daughters all complete" so that, as Stanley Weintraub has shrewdly observed, "The play might be profitably viewed as a fantasia in the Shakespearean manner upon Shavian themes."[10] The evils of war constituted the main theme of the preface to *Heartbreak House*. "Hypochrondria," "The Wicked Half Century," "War Delirium," "Madness in Court," "The Rabid Watchdogs of Liberty," "The Sufferings of the Sane," "Evil in the Throne of Good," "The Mad Election"—these subheadings indicate the mood and tenor of the essay which precedes Shaw's masterly play. What war did to the British—and to some extent to the American—civilian is his main concern. He laments the loss of Shakespeares and Platos in the battles, adding that "to the truly civilized man, to the good European, the slaughter of the German youth was as disastrous as the slaughter of the English."[11] In the closing sections of the preface he deplores the effects of the war on the theatre and on the dramatic poet.

As early as 1912, Shaw had foreseen the possibility of armed conflict in Europe. He drew up a proposal which "urged vainly upon our English Foreign Office and on the German ambassador, of a combination of Britain, France, Germany, and America to impose peace on Europe."[12] The next year in an article entitled "Ar-

maments and Conscription: A Triple Alliance Against War," Shaw
proposed that England, France, and Germany enter into an
alliance, the terms being that, if France were to attack Germany,
England would combine with Germany to crush France; if Germany were to attack France, England would combine with France
to crush Germany.[13]

World War I and its aftermath exerted a long-lasting effect on
Shaw's thought and indeed on all his endeavors. Long ago he had
reached the conclusion that socialism, despite its merit and achievement, was not enough to set the world right. Ramsey MacDonald's
Labour government, partly an outgrowth of Fabianism, brought
further disillusionment. Shaw continued to believe that as a political
animal man is a failure. He became more and more convinced that
the answer to the world's plight lay in Creative Evolution, which he
dealt with in *Man and Superman*. Man's inhumanity to man in the
war led him more than ever to the belief that only a race of
Supermen would be endowed with humaneness and wisdom. He
came to feel that the life of the present human being is too brief for
him to achieve the necessary wisdom and maturity. Shaw could not
agree with those who put their faith in science; for science, he warned, endangers the species "by inventing weapons capable of
destroying civilization faster than we can produce men who can be
trusted to use them wisely." He added that we handle them like
children entrusted with nitro-glycerine or with chloride of
nitrogen.[14]

II *Antiwar Pamphlets*

His widely circulated *Common Sense About the War* (1914)
made Shaw many enemies and lost him many friends. The gist of
this sensational pamphlet was that the Kaiser and the German Empire were not solely to blame for the European war, but that Lord
Edward Grey and Great Britain were likewise accountable. Prussian
Junkerism must bear its share of guilt for starting the conflict, but
England was not without her Junkerism, too. These ideas so in-
furiated the majority of Englishmen against Shaw that even his distinguished friends reviled and opposed him. H. G. Wells compared
him to "an idiot child screaming in a hospital," and Henry Arthur
Jones published an open letter to Shaw, saying: "The hag Sedition
was your mother and Perversity begot you. Mischief was your
midwife and Misrule your nurse, and Unreason brought you up at

her feet—no other ancestry and rearing had you, you freakish homunculus, germinated outside of lawful procreation."[15] When Jones led a movement to expel Shaw from the Society of Authors, an organization which Shaw had been instrumental in founding, Shaw refused to accept the expulsion; he asserted that all animosity would be forgotten when reason was restored.

Still, his unpopularity stung him deeply, though he stuck by his guns. He deplored the invasion of Belgium, but blamed Britain for not intervening. Furthermore, he contended that, if Britain had made it clear to Kaiser Wilhelm that she would fight, he would not have moved against Belgium in the first place. To make an appeal for the Belgians, Shaw published an "Open Letter to President Wilson" urging him "to invite the neutral powers to confer with the United States of America for the purpose of requesting Britain, France, and Germany to withdraw from the soil of Belgium and fight out their quarrel on their own territories." It is noteworthy, and not possibly coincidental," as Archibald Henderson observes,

that Shaw in many of his public pronouncements anticipated Wilson on many points of policy. The assertion is made in full recognition of the fact that Wilson took no public notice of Shaw's open letter, and so far as is known, never referred to him or gave any hint—save broadly between the lines of his speeches, notes, and announced policies—of his influence. Historians, it is confidently believed, will some ·day recognize the pronounced influence upon Wilson of Shaw's views on many matters vital in Wilson's policies: The Fourteen Points, the League of Nations, Freedom of the Seas, direct dealing with the German people, and the Treaty of Versailles.[16]

To *Common Sense About the War* and to the "Open Letter to President Wilson" Shaw added a third polemical document, *Peace Conference Hints,* a work that attracted wide attention but that probably had no direct effect on the statesmen who drew up the Versailles Treaty. He argued that in wartime soldiers and civilians alike are fed propaganda in which the conflict is presented as a crude melodrama in which their nation is the hero and the enemy is the villain. When peace arrives, the time comes to exchange romance for reality.[17] War can no longer be looked upon as a "beneficent gymnastic, moral or spiritual" any more than can hurricanes or earthquakes.[18] He warned that the next war, if permitted to occur, would be a scientific attempt to destroy cities and kill civilians—an accurate prophecy of World War II, twenty and more years later, with its tragic culmination at Hiroshima and Nagasaki.

As early as 1907 Shaw had expressed the idea of keeping peace through an international organization backed by force; hence, he anticipated both the League of Nations and the United Nations; and, had these organizations followed Shaw's advocacy of a peace-keeping force, the history of the twentieth century might well have been different from what it is.[19] To Shaw, only an organization such as the League of Nations could put an end to war. It must be, he insisted, "A very vigorous organization of resistance to evil, like a municipal police force."[20] He agreed with Woodrow Wilson's description of the League as "not one group of nations set against another, but a single, overwhelming, powerful group of nations which shall be the trustee of the peace of the world."[21] Shaw believed that all nations in the group should be compatible and that no autocratic powers should be admitted.[22] The failure of Wilson to establish an effective and lasting League of Nations was a grave disappointment to Shaw,[23] who consequently felt that not only his *Hints* but all his writings in the advocacy of peace had fallen on stony ground.

III   *"A Metabiological Pentateuch"*

His Cassandralike mood led Shaw to turn his attention to non-political questions, and in dealing with them he came to the conclusion that man's failure as a political animal could be ascribed to the brevity of life. If man could live, say, three hundred years while retaining and increasing his wisdom, he might be able to solve problems like peace and justice, which now had formerly seemed insoluble. These issues Shaw deals with in his longest play, *Back to Methuselah*—which is, in truth, a cycle of five plays. The time extends all the way from the Creation to 30,000 years beyond the present. Here, as elsewhere, Shaw expresses anti-Darwinian ideas, but he supports Creative Evolution, the essence of his religion. That Shaw considered it a religious drama is indicated in the subtitle, *A Metabiological Pentateuch*. He stressed the importance of imagination and will, asserting that imagination is the beginning of creation. "You imagine what you desire; you will what you imagine; and at last you create your will. . . . To desire, to imagine, to will, to create." So, by willing it, men can live three hundred years or more, as they do in *Back to Methuselah*.[24]

Shaw conceived of this play, or cycle of plays, as being, like Wagner's *Ring*, "an allegorical music-drama in which ideas were made flesh."[25] He thought of it also as "a contribution to the modern Bible."[26] With its magnificent scope and universal theme *Back to Methuselah* ranges from the mythical beginning of the race to man's life as a disembodied spirit in the year A.D. 31,920. Part I, in which Shaw plays loosely with the story of Adam and Eve, is laid in the Garden of Eden. The first parents, coming on a dead fawn, are distressed and bewildered; for they have not encountered death before. They speak of endless existence and death. As Adam goes to cast the fawn's carcass into a river, the Serpent, gigantic and multicolored, raises its head and speaks to Eve. In a strangely seductive musical whisper, it talks of death, birth, and miracles. It introduces laughter, love, jealousy, fear, certainty, and marriage to Adam and Eve.

In Act II of "In the Beginning," Cain appears and finds his father digging and Eve spinning. Though both have lost their youth and grace, they are nevertheless in the prime of life. The conflict between father and son is at once evident; for Cain is proud to be the first murderer, the first hunter, the first warrior, the first conqueror, while Adam is content to be the first farmer. Eve closes this act with the observation that man need not live by bread alone and that, when he learns what his true objective is, there will be no more digging and spinning, no more fighting or killing. Cain, as the symbol of military might and war, is central to "In the Beginning," which is the most effective and most artistic section of the whole play.

Part II presents "The Gospel of the Brothers Barnabas," two biologists who have concluded that life is too short for men to achieve their social ends and that "the term of human life must be extended to at least three centuries." Shaw here introduces two politicians (loosely based on Lloyd George and Herbert Asquith) who illustrate the weakness and the failure of men in public life and who are portrayed as objects of satire. The Barnabas brothers, who take a stand for Creative Evolution, assert that, if men cannot do God's work, He will produce a being who can. God proceeds by the method of Trial and Error; and, if man turns out to be one of the errors, he will have to go the way of the mastodon and all the other scrapped experiments.[27]

In Part III ("The Thing Happens"), which takes place in the year A.D. 2170, the nineteenth and twentieth centuries are looked back on as the dark ages.[28] Mrs. Lutestring, the parlormaid of the preceding cycle, is in her third century; and so is the Archbishop of York, identified as Haslam, the rector in the Barnabas cycle. Chinese men and Negro women rule England. There is wide-ranging discussion but little dramatic power in this part.

In Part IV ("The Tragedy of an Elderly Gentleman"—3000 A.D."), the British Commonwealth has moved to the Near East; Bagdad has replaced London as the capital; and the British Isles are the home of the "long-livers" and a famous Oracle. Napoleon appears and confesses to the Oracle that he finds no pleasure in organizing slaughter, but must do it as it is his only talent, his only claim to power and distinction.[29] In a significant passage, Zoo, one of the long-livers, recalls the "War to End War" of a thousand years ago when bombs and gas put an end to "pseudo-Christian civilization."[30]

The final episodes of *Back to Methuselah* are entitled "As Far as Thought Can Reach," and the time is A.D. 31,290. By this date sex, as we know it, has disappeared in Part V; human beings are egg-born and immortal save for accidents. In the egg, they have gone through the phases of infancy and early childhood so that, when they emerge, they are at a stage corresponding to our late teens. They mature in four years to a process approaching the status and attributes of the Ancients, whose lives are largely cerebral. Since they are free of the body and all that is physical or material, the An-cients depend not on love or art, but on pure intellect for pleasure. In the end, Lilith, the first mother, speaks and predicts that Life will never end and that her seed will fill all the million starry man-sions of the future and "master its matter to its uttermost confines." In other words, since the Ancients are on their way to becoming God, Shaw projects a kind of evolutionary Utopia.[31] This last part is an intellectual extravaganza with many overtones of meaning about art and religion; but, because of its rich imaginativeness it is, metaphysically speaking, tantalizingly vague.

Back to Methuselah is altogether too long for the modern theatre, and Shaw must have considered it to be a play for reading rather than staging. When Barry Jackson asked permission to produce it in his Birmingham repertory theatre, Shaw asked him if he had provided for his family; when Lawrence Langer proposed a produc-tion by the Theatre Guild, Shaw called him a lunatic.[32] In the ninety-page preface to *Back to Methuselah*, Shaw expands fully on the theme of Creative Evolution as set forth twenty years before in

Man and Superman. Though recognizing its partial validity, he assails Darwinism as the ultimate explanation of evolution. He refers to Darwin's Theories as "Circumstantial Selection," a process Shaw regards as too materialistic: "If you can turn a pedestrian into a cyclist, and a cyclist into a pianist or violinist, without the intervention of Circumstantial Selection, you can turn an amoeba into a man, or a man into a superman without it." Thus Shaw expresses his belief in the Lamarckian idea of the development of organs and characteristics through will and expectation.[33] He elaborates on his concept of the New Vitalism as opposed to the Old Mechanism in explaining the origin and continuity of life. In this preface, Shaw gives the fullest expression of what he terms his "modern religion."[34]

IV   Saint Joan

Though in form *Back to Methuselah* and Shaw's next play stand in sharp contrast, they are similar in two ways—both reflect the pressures of the war period on their creator and both deal with religious themes. Shaw once said *Saint Joan* would not have been written had he not visualized the subject as relevant to "a world situation in which we see whole peoples perishing and dragging us toward the abyss which has swallowed them, all for want of any grasp of the political forces that move civilization."[35]

Other authors had written of the Maid, among them, Shakespeare, Voltaire, Southey, Schiller, Andrew Lang, Mark Twain, Tom Taylor, Percy MacKaye; but Shaw did not learn much from these predecessors in the field. He felt that Voltaire and Shakespeare did Joan an injustice.[36] Mark Twain's *Personal Recollections of Joan of Arc* Shaw regarded as a romantic creation, "an unimpeachable American school teacher in armor."[37] He learned little, if anything, from Twain's book.[38] The direct source of the play is T. Douglas Murray's *Jeanne D'Arc*, a work which centers on Joan's shrewdness and courage in her trial. On reading it, Mrs. Shaw urged her husband to write a play about the subject, and he readily acceded.[39] It was the second time her direct suggestion bore fruit, the first being *The Doctor's Dilemma*. Shaw not only read Murray's account, he also thoroughly studied the case in Quichert's transcription of the trial in 1431 and the rehabilitation proceeding in 1456.

In its form, *Saint Joan* is a chronicle play like *Caesar and*

Cleopatra, which it resembles also in having as its central figure a character with the attributes of a Superman. Joan exemplifies the strength, the faith, and the wisdom of Shaw's concept of the race that must supersede *homo sapiens* through Creative Evolution if civilization is to be saved. *Saint Joan* is also like *Caesar and Cleopatra* in presenting a main character to whom all the other persons in the play—most of them types—are contributory. Just as Britannus, Rufio, Appollodorus, and even Cleopatra herself are significant chiefly in letting Caesar shine in all his glory and wisdom, so De Baudricourt, Warwick, Dunois, De. Stozomber, Cauchin, the Inquisitor, the Dauphin, and all the others keep the spotlight on Joan.[40] So skillfully does Shaw write, that she is (in Louis L. Martz's words) "the simple cause of every other word and action in the play."[41]

Shaw describes her in the preface as a peasant girl, soldier, "Protestant martyr," yet "a professed and most pious Catholic." She was also "one of the first apostles of nationalism, and the first French practitioner of Napoleonic realism in warfare." "The pioneer of rational dressing for women," Shaw continues, "she refused to accept the specific woman's lot, and dressed and fought and lived as men did."[42] She defied popes and patronized kings. "As her actual condition was pure upstart, there were only two opinions about her. One was that she was miraculous: The other that she was unbearable."[43]

She was a Protestant because she insisted that her religion came from God, not from the Church, as she trusted her inner Voices rather than the traditional dogmas of Catholicism. This left the Church with nothing to do, as Shaw said, "but to burn her or canonize Wycliff and Hus."[44] Shaw had no doubt of her sanity. "Joan must be judged as a sane woman in spite of her voices," he said, "because they never gave her any advice that might not have come to her from her mother wit exactly as gravitation came to Newton."[45] Like Shaw's Caesar, she was a natural, unpretentious person. She spoke in dialect at times and called the future king Lad and Charlie, thereby showing her disregard for titles, officialdom, and worldly station. Her naturalness in speech and behavior (indeed, she talks and acts like a twentieth-century young woman) is part of her charm and appeal.

Though Shaw creates her as a person without sexual attraction or interest, he is careful not to make his Joan a supernatural, self-mortifying saint. Gallant and heroic as she is, she is not the all-perfect protagonist. Charismatic, she has strong power over men "from her uncle to the king, the archbishop, and the military General Staff."[46] She is not without human weaknesses such as stubbornness, conceit; and she has a marked pride in what she conceives to be her God-given capabilities. Shaw portrays her as neither a melodramatic victim nor a romantic heroine.[47]

As there is no conventional heroine in *Saint Joan,* neither are there any villains. In all his dramas Shaw presents his characters, as he saw his contemporaries and historical figures, as mixtures of both good and evil. Accordingly, Joan's judges are not portrayed as incarnations of malice that are bent on sending her to the stake. The Catholic Church is not the villain, and nowhere in the play does Shaw condemn or ridicule the Church, as he sometimes does in his earlier polemical writings.[48] In the trial scene, which is central, Shaw presents both sides of the case, a fact which Eric Bentley praises as adding power to the drama.[49]

Saint Joan is Shaw's nearest approach to tragedy; but it is not tragic in the classical or Shakespearean sense; it is more like the tragicomedies of Ibsen or Chekhov. The controversial epilogue, which brings Joan back to earth for her 1920 canonization, detracts from the tragic effect. Moreover, just as in *Hedda Gabler*, society is to blame for the tragedy of a wasted life; and Shaw makes it clear that the tragedy lies not so much in Joan's fate as in the failure of her society—the establishment of Church and State—to accept and understand her. Indubitably, Joan is one of Shaw's great evocations. "She is," as an astute German critic declares, "the last and most radiant in the long gallery of women that testify to his deep reverence for the high function of the feminine element in life."[50]

This play is the climax of Shaw's career. Though he lived on for more than half a century, nothing that he did afterward is of comparable importance.

CHAPTER 8

The Glimmering Light

T HE year after he launched *Saint Joan*, Shaw received the Nobel Prize for Literature, and he jokingly said that he presumed the prize was given to him to signify the world's relief for his having published nothing in 1925. Though many other honors had been offered to him, this one was the first he accepted.[1] When the King of England had offered him the Order of Merit, he had declined it; and many universities had vainly sought to award him honorary degrees. Relative to the Nobel Prize, Shaw wrote to the Permanent Secretary of the Royal Swedish Academy to say that he had more money than he needed and more renown than was good for his spiritual health. He accepted the prize money (approximately seven thousand pounds), however, to establish a foundation to encourage understanding and intercourse in literature and art between Sweden and the British Isles. One accomplishment of this foundation has been the translation of some of Strindberg's plays for the first time into English.[2]

I A *Group of Lesser Plays*

In the twenty-five years remaining to him, Shaw wrote a dozen plays; and, although none matched his work before 1925, some of them merit our brief mention. One of these, *The Apple Cart*, which is subtitled *A Political Extravaganza in Two Acts and an Interlude*, is a satire on modern democracy and free enterprise. On one side it demonstrates, through King Magnus and his escapades, that a democracy needs a strong leader. On the other side it shows through Breakages Limited that our capitalistic society depends on waste, breakage, and quick obsolescence for its profits and maintenance. The strangest episode in this strange comedy is the famous "wrestling match" in which King Magnus and his mistress Orinthia roll on their boudoir floor when she tries to detain him

134

from returning to his wife. Because this episode is based on more than one actual happening between Shaw and Mrs. Pat Campbell, she was so distressed by the scene that she earnestly insisted upon his deleting it, but he adamantly refused.[3] The most extravagant idea in this play is that of the United States' proposal in Act II to rejoin the British Empire. Though not a great play, it presents some important issues with artistic skill and, as Edmund Wilson insists, with "a music of ideas—or rather, perhaps a music of moralities."[4]

Too True to Be Good (1932) is Shaw's second play in a row to be subtitled *A Political Extravaganza*, but its original, abandoned subtitle was more inclusive and accurate—"A Collection of Stage Sermons by a Fellow of the Royal Society of Literature."[5] It is talk, talk, talk, but much of it is interesting talk about war, the military establishment, democracy, capitalism, the New Science, sex, and the Lost Generation of the 1920s. Hence it is too simplistic to say that the theme of this play is the disillusionment that the pursuit of unlimited riches and pleasures brings, though to show that capitalism is cruel to the rich is the avowed purpose of the play.[6] Actually, *Too True* is a presentation of many ideas, as is true of most of Shaw's dramas. His weapon is not a rifle, but a blunderbuss. As he scatters his fire, he hopes in that way to score more points of truth than with a single shot, however powerful.

A character at the end of Act I announces that "The play is now virtually over; but the characters will discuss it at great length for two acts more. The exit doors are all in order. Goodnight."[7] This speech of the Monster is similar to the dialogue in the non-illusory dramas of such fellow-playwrights as Luigi Pirandello, Thornton Wilder, and Berthold Brecht, whose characters at times speak directly to the audience. Moreover, the seemingly chaotic structure of *Too True to Be Good*, of which Desmond MacCarthy, St. John Ervine, and others have complained is Shaw's way of reflecting the chaos of the postwar era he was depicting.[8] Still another explanation of the play's seeming formlessness is the fact that the story is told as a dream.

II *A Depression Play and Two Others*

On the Rocks (1933) is a play about the Great Depression. At various times he subtitles it *A Political Fantasy in Two Acts*, *A Compendium of Contemporary Politics*, and finally *A Political Comedy*. He did so just as Chekhov described *The Cherry Orchard* and *The Sea Gull* as comedies. There is an implicit hopefulness in the word "comedy" as both playwrights used it.

In *On the Rocks* the protagonist—Ramsey MacDonald is his prototype—is Sir Arthur Chavender, a genial but weak Liberal prime minister who is so upset by the rioting of the unemployed that he is persuaded to enter a sanitarium.[9] While there he reads Karl Marx, and when he returns to No. 10 Downing Street, he announces his advocacy of reforms, including the nationalization of the land. His friends are aghast, and Chavender concludes that the economic re-organization is a task too heavy for him. At the end, the failure of parliamentary democracy is evident. The crowd is singing a hopeful marching song, "England, Arise." As his daughter Hilda rushes out to join the marchers, Sir Arthur understands that she feels what other young people may feel tomorrow.[10]

In a long preface to *On the Rocks*, Shaw argues that the extermination of human lives is in some cases a political necessity. He does not make it clear to some of his critics that liquidations should be done with the strictest care, with painless methods, and without punitive intent. Shaw believed that if anyone becomes untameable and an irretrievable danger to other men, he should be treated as we do the mad dog or the cobra.[11]

The Simpleton of the Unexpected Isles (1934) is one of the strangest plays of his dotage years. Shaw himself called it "openly oriental, hieratic, and insane."[12] Nevertheless, it has a theme worth contemplating: namely, that, as every day is a Day of Judgment, men are on earth to face life as it comes and to make the best of it.[13] On the political side, Shaw envisions the Russian Revolution spreading to England, which withdraws from the British Empire.

Though both plays were written by Shaw during the same ocean voyage, *The Millionairess* (1934 - 35), a comedy that lapses into farce, is a strange contrast to *The Simpleton*. In *The Millionairess* Shaw demonstrates something of his old skill in writing witty dialogue and in presenting farcical situations, but it is far from a major play.[14] Epifania Ognisanti di Parerga, a woman so acquisitive that she is discontented with her "beggarly thirty million pounds," is the last of the forceful women in Shaw's gallery. She is a dynamo, the strongest in the physical sense of all his women. She is also a feminist of feminists, the acme of the independent female. While married to a pugilist whom she accepted for the imagined sexual prowess he did not possess, she leaves him in the care of his commonplace mistress, a Miss Seedystockings (her real name is Smith), and woos an Egyptian doctor who tries to resist her, but cannot.

Epifania is the born female Boss who dominates everyone she meets, and she is also a phenomenally successful moneymaker. The preface is largely concerned with what to do with Bosses, a word Shaw extends to include kings, queens, and dictators. He asks the question still pertinent in these violent days: "What safeguard have the weaponless great against the great who have myrmidons at their call?" Only humane religious or political principles, he believes, can keep Bosses from becoming tyrannical.

III   *A Drama with Three Dictators*

In *Geneva* (1938), his next and last "Political Extravaganza," Shaw, using names that hardly disguised them, presented Hitler (Battler), Mussolini (Bombardone), and Franco (Flanco) as characters; and the scene is the seat of the League of Nations. In Act I, Shaw introduces an actual, but little known, adjunct of the League, the International Committee for Intellectual Co-operation. For lack of money, the committee is in low estate, but it still manages to function. Into its office come a Jew who lodges a complaint against a ruler, another man who wishes to move against the Prime Minister of a Business Government, a widow who seeks a warrant against the President of the Earthly Paradise, an Anglican Bishop who complains about communism in his diocese, and finally a Russian Commissar who protests about a Society for the Propagation of the Bible in Foreign Parts. There is much discussion of war, nationalism, the mixture of races, the League of Nations, and the World Court.

In the fourth act, the three dictators are summoned to Geneva to face charges in the Court; and they all appear and defend themselves. The trials and discussions end, however, as a report comes by telephone that the earth's orbit is "jumping to its next quantum" and is dooming humanity and all other living things to icy destruction. After all the others depart, the Secretary informs the Judge that the dire report is false. Though there are occasional flashes of wit and satire, *Geneva* is, on the whole, a weak play. The characters are mostly mere puppets who voice Shaw's ideas about the League and the Court with some emphasis on man's failure in politics and on the need for his Creator to produce a wiser, abler race. The preface affords Shaw an opportunity to write once more of one of his dominant passions, world peace. Unwilling to give way to pessimism even when writing of the horrible destructiveness of the atom bomb (1945), he muses: "It is conceivable that the next great invention may create an overwhelming interest in pacific civilization and wipe out war. You never can tell."[15]

Without any international or other significant issues is *In Good King Charles's Golden Days* (1939), Shaw's last excursion into history. Its chief claim to attention is that it summons Charles II, Sir Isaac Newton, George Fox (the founder of Quakerism), and the Merry Monarch's friends and mistresses back from the past. They engage in bright and mostly interesting talk. In an unusually short preface, Shaw advocates the Coupled Vote, which would provide that every ballot in every election, to be valid, must be for a man and a woman candidate together in order to assure absolutely equal representation.

After World War II, Shaw wrote *Buoyant Billions: A Comedy of No Manners* (1948), a play which does little more than demonstrate, as did other works of his final years, its author's fall from grace as a playwright. Shaw apologized for the play in the preface, saying that while he lived—he was then eighty-one—he had to write. The most interesting character is the billionaire's seventh son, who is determined to be a World Betterer. Shaw wrote this "trivial play," as he called it, for the Malvern Festival of 1947.

Shakes Versus Shav (1949), a puppet play, written the year before Shaw's death, supports his assertion that nothing could extinguish his interest in Shakespeare.[16] A couplet from this playlet expresses Shaw's hope for his continuing reputation as he moved toward the shadows. Shav pleads with Shakes: "We both are mortal. For a moment suffer / My glimmering light to shine."[17] These lines are the valedictory of his creative genius.

IV   *"Headmaster to the Universe"*[18]

As Shaw moved from the zenith of his career into the declining years of his creative life, he also wrote nonfiction books, a religious tale, and lectures on a wide range of public issues that he presented both on the platform and before the microphone. Although to deal with all of them in detail is beyond the scope of this book, some of them are worthy of note; and one is *An Intelligent Woman's Guide to Socialism and Capitalism*, which he completed and published in 1928. This book, his longest one, contains little more than expatiations and clarification of what he had written in Fabian tracts and in the prefaces to his plays.

Heavily emphasizing equality of income in the opening chapters, he argues that it is the only fair economic arrangement. One great fruit of such equality, he contends, would be the provision of the widest possible freedom in choosing a mate, a freedom which would result in eugenic benefits. Every part of life would improve if all disparity of income were eliminated. (Incidentally, the majority of his fellow-Fabians did not agree with Shaw on equality of income.[19]) In the rest of the book he discourses on taxes, rents, incentives, work, leisure, and scores of other problems of society. He insists on the abolition of poverty, a "crime" which he accuses capitalism of perpetuating, and advocates a gradual, nonviolent movement toward socialism. But how to achieve this revolution without force and bloodshed Shaw does not reveal. Though the *Guide* is somewhat prolix, it is more lucid and more readable than most other economic treatises. Written for his wife's sister, it is partly slanted toward feminist interests and policies, but most of it is relevant to men's problems also. It is a thought-provoking and highly informing book which anyone aspiring to be a liberally educated person should read.

In 1931 Shaw spent ten days in Russia, saw whatever the commissars or their subordinates wished him to see, received honors, and had an audience lasting two hours and ten minutes with Josef Stalin. G B.S.'s enthusiasm was almost unbounded. Ever afterward he saw the Soviet system in roseate hues and often sought to prove to the British and the Americans what they had lost in not following Russia into communism. All in all, Shaw was blind to the weaknesses, failures, and cruelties of the Stalinist regime.[20] This trip caused Shaw to shift his view away from gradualism toward revolutionary change even if it involved violence.

Stranded in Africa five weeks while Mrs. Shaw recuperated from an automobile accident resulting when her husband mistook the accelerator for the brake of their car, Shaw wrote *The Adventures of a Black Girl in Her Search for God* (1933). He conceived of it as a play, but it turned out to be a short story. Though an appealing little fable, it does not add anything of substance to what Shaw said in *Man and Superman, The Shewing-Up of Blanco Posnet, Back to Methuselah* and in their prefaces about the concept of the Creator as well-meaning but not all-powerful—a God developing, like man, through Creative Evolution.

In 1933, in the midst of the Great Depression, Shaw, accompanied by his wife, stopped for twenty-four hours in the United States when on a world tour. It was his only visit to this country. His only lecture on these shores he gave in New York City at the Metropolitan Opera House. The G.B.S. persona got the better of him when he called the Constitution of the United States a "Charter of Anarchism" and declared that the Statue of Liberty should bear on its pedestal Dante's inscription, "All hope abandon, ye who enter here."[21] Nevertheless, he went on to say that, if conditions were right and if the Academy of Political Science, under whose auspices he chose to speak, were to be effective, Americans might yet save civilization.[22] In closing, Shaw paid special tributes to Henry George, his inspiration in the 1880s, and to Archibald Henderson, his biographer-in-chief." Not, on the whole, one of Shaw's better performances, it marked his farewell to the lecture platform.[23]

His last book of nonfiction prose, written when World War II was raging, is entitled *Everybody's Political What's What?* (1944). A work of reference on hundreds of subjects related to war, militarism, education, science, economics, sociology, ethics, and religion—in short, to whatever pertains to human life—it is "full of wise saws and modern instances." Astoundingly, Shaw calls for a revival of the Inquisition, but for one purged of all vengeance, all torture, and all punishment. Composed of a panel of carefully chosen experts, its sole function would be to determine those who are unfit to live in modern civilized society—and quietly, painlessly liquidate them.[24] He continues to praise Russian communism, but World War II leads him more and more to see Hitlerite dictatorships as "insanity." He criticizes democracy as inefficient, a fault ascribable not only to its tendency to depend on talk but also to its failure to find strong leadership. To provide this leadership, he proposes a number of panels for which candidates qualify in competitive examinations.[25]

Though skeptical of churches, Shaw has a great deal to say about the importance of religion and the need to bring the old creeds up to date. "Every church," he declares, "should be a Church of All Saints, and every cathedral a place for the greatest minds of all races, creeds, and colors."[26] This view is all very well for the "greatest minds," but what about the vast majority of people? Shaw fails to recognize the value of churches as places of worship and fellowship and as agencies for social good even though, like all earthly institutions, they fall short of perfection.

Throughout the book he seeks to show that man's political difficulties are not to be attributed to "natural ineradicable villainy," but to simple ignorance.[27] He does not boast that *Everybody's Political What's What* will push back the walls of that ignorance or correct all mistakes. At eighty-eight he concludes the book by saying that he has done only his limited best and adds, "the rest I leave to my betters."[28]

The year before his death Shaw published *Sixteen Self Sketches* (1949), the only autobiographical book he issued in his lifetime. He reveals a great many facts about his infancy, childhood, schooling, his family, his first jobs, his Irish roots, his early struggles as a writer, his religious beliefs, his sexual adventures, his hopes, dreams, triumphs, and frustrations. An important part is entitled "Biographers' Blunders Corrected." Though Dr. Stanley Weintraub's two-volume compilation *Shaw: An Autobiography* largely supersedes it, Shaw's *Sixteen Self Sketches* remains a fascinating and valuable book for anyone curious about its author.

V   *The Magic of the Microphone*

Bidding farewell to the lecture platform in 1933 with his speech at the Metropolitan Opera House in New York City, Shaw came to consider the platform to be obsolete, since the broadcasting microphone had superseded it. "It is foolish," he said, "to talk to a few hundreds when you can talk to millions." As Dan H. Laurence has put it, "He became G.B.S.—World Statesman, often pontificating rather than polemicising, but still striving at ninety as he had at thirty to inculcate in his fellow-men a need to recognize intellect as the greatest of the passions."[29] Over the British Broadcasting Corporation facilities, he talked to inestimably large audiences on both sides of the Atlantic. For example, he harangued America on a shortwave broadcast October 11, 1931, in the midst of the Great Depression. Shaw would have agreed with Thomas Paine's dictum that some people can be reasoned into sense and others must be shocked into it. "Say a bold thing that will stagger them," Paine asserted, "and they will begin to think."[30] Shaw shocked many Americans when he referred to them as "dear old boobs" because of their stand on Russia. He even again defended the Soviet policy of exterminating anyone who cheats in commercial transactions or otherwise shows himself to be a misfit in society. "A well-kept garden must be weeded," Shaw—or was it G.B.S.?—told his audience, adding that he was proud to have been the first to advocate this "necessary reform." At the end of his talk he predicted that the new generation might yet save American civilization.[31] He refused to become at any time an apostle of despair.

Another more significant example of his radio talks as counsellor to the nations is his shortwave broadcast on "This Danger of War" November 2, 1937. Once more he pleaded for the abolition of armed conflict; he had seen more than enough of this moral insanity, often masked as political necessity, in his lifetime. He deplored the loss of young men in war and contended that, if nations had any sense, they would first send old men into the trenches, and sacrifice the young only in the last extremity. The only thing that could prevent war and save civilization was to show, a newer, fairer distribution of wealth, labor, and leisure but this one history lesson was never taught in the schools. "As I see it," he continued, "the social rule must be 'Live and let live,' and people who persistently break this rule must be liquidated."[32] "Live and let live" is the epitome of Bernard Shaw's philosophy.

Shaw summed up his creed for living in an address he made long ago before an audience of students at Brighton: "I am of the opinion that my life belongs to the whole community, and as long as I live it is my privilege to do for it whatsoever I can. I want to be thoroughly used up when I die; for the harder I work the more I live. I rejoice in life for its own sake. Life is 'no brief candle' for me. It is a sort of splendid torch, which I have got hold of for the moment; and I want to make it burn as brightly as possible before handing it on to future generations."[33] The imp called G.B.S. was not looking over his shoulder as Shaw spoke those sentences. They may serve to explain why he won the respect and friendship of such distinguished contemporaries as William Archer, G. K. Chesterton, H. G. Wells, Ellen Terry, the Webbs, the St. John Ervines, and many others who, as we have seen, knew him in his prime.

If the purpose of this book were mainly biographical, certain good friends of his later years would deserve a chapter. There was T. E. Lawrence, "Lawrence of Arabia," who learned much from the Shaws about writing and publishing and who influenced Shaw's concepts of Joan and Private Meek.[34] Dean W. R. Inge, the so-called "Gloomy Dean" of St. Paul's, who was the prototype of Sergeant Fielding in *Too True to Be Good*, was to Shaw what the Reverend Joseph Twichell was to Mark Twain. Inge considered Shaw to be a religious man, "worthy of the Kingdom."[35] Gene Tunney, former heavyweight boxing champion of the world, won Shaw's lasting friendship after expressing doubts about the validity

of the portrayal of the pugilist's life in *The Admirable Bashville*.[36]
Sean and Eileen O'Casey were intimates of the Shaws. In her
memoir entitled *Sean*, Mrs. O'Casey states that Shaw was probably
her husband's best friend, "the man who had stood by him and
befriended him all through his literary life."[37] Lady Gregory, a
leading spirit of the Irish Renaissance, frequently visited the Shaws
at Ayot St. Lawrence; and she dedicated one of her books "To Bernard Shaw, My Kindest Friend."[38]

A most interesting friendship flourished between Shaw and Dame
Laurentia McLachlan, the Abbess of Stanbrook. Though they
differed on religious questions, they found satisfaction in their
relationship; and Shaw expressed thanks for the nuns' holding him
in their prayers.[39] One of the Shaws' closest friends was American-
born Lady Nancy Astor, who accompanied him on the Russian trip,
was a frequent visitor to the Malvern Festival, and was at Shaw's
bedside when the end came on November 2, 1950, at Ayot St.
Lawrence.[40] As she gave the death notice to the reporters who were
waiting at the door, she added to the statement these words: "From
the coffers of his genius he enriched the world."[41]

Shaw left an estate estimated at £367,000 before taxes, the largest
English literary estate in history. The bulk of it he willed to establish a fund for the devising and promoting of a new phonetic
alphabet which he believed would foster understanding among
men. The project proving impracticable, the legatees have succeeded in breaking this part of the will. Shaw bequeathed equal thirds of
his munificent residual estate to the National Gallery of Ireland, the
Royal Academy of Dramatic Art, and the British Museum.[42]

CHAPTER 9

Posthumous Status
and Prospects

FOLLOWING the announcement of Shaw's death, all the lights of Broadway, including the electric signs around Times Square, were dimmed for five minutes—a symbol of the esteem in which the theatrical world held him. Many of his friends and admirers found it hard to believe that he had passed from the scene. It seemed as if his vibrant voice, mind, and personality had been part of the cultural and intellectual life of two continents and beyond since time out of mind.[1]

In truth, Shaw has continued to live through his works. All during the 1950s his plays continued to appear in America, the British Isles, and elsewhere. That decade saw Broadway performances of *The Devil's Disciple, Arms and the Man, Candida, Caesar and Cleopatra, Brassbound's Conversion, Don Juan in Hell, Getting Married, Heartbreak House, Saint Joan,* and *The Apple Cart.*[2] On March 15, 1956, occurred the opening of *My Fair Lady,* a musical comedy based on *Pygmalion,* as we have noted. It has had one of the longest runs in the annals of the American theatre, and it continued to grace the boards in 1976.

But Shaw's recognition in the more than a quarter of a century since his death has been by no means limited to *My Fair Lady.* Probably every week since 1950 one or more of his plays have been presented.[3] In the United States, an estimated fifty licenses have been issued annually, but the number of performances after each license is unknown. Between 1950 and 1975 the repertory licenses granted annually in the United Kingdom averaged fifty, resulting in an estimated one thousand performances each year. Another estimated one thousand productions by amateurs in the United Kingdom were authorized. In the past ten years, six major British productions of Shaw plays have appeared.

Mrs. Warren's Profession was chosen to represent its author at Dublin's Fourth Theatre Festival in 1961. After the festival, the company made an extensive tour of European capitals with the same play.[4] The distinguished Shaw Festival Theatre at Niagara-on-the-Lake, Ontario, Canada, has made a major contribution to Shaw's growing fame. Between 1962 and 1977, it staged more than thirty of Shaw's plays. In 1976 it presented *Mrs. Warren's Profession, Arms and the Man,* and *The Apple Cart,* and in 1977 *Widowers' Houses, The Millionairess,* and *Man and Superman.*[5] Unhappily, the number of Continental European performances is not available, but the Shaw Estate reported its income from European licenses in 1974 approximated that from the United States and Canada. Besides all these stage productions, BBC-TV from 1950 to 1975 presented thirty plays, thirty-seven productions, and fifty-two broadcasts devoted to Shaw. In the same period BBC-Radio gave forty-one plays, ten nondramatic programs, and 189 broadcasts related to Shaw. Three films about him (two of them in German) have been made.

The Shaw Society (London) publishes a journal devoted to its patron saint. Likewise the Shaw Society of America, with headquarters at the State University of Pennsylvania, University Park, issues a quarterly *Shaw Review,* with articles, book reviews, and a highly valuable "Continuing Checklist of Shaviana." To consult this long list is to see evidence of the unceasing interest in Shaw in the later 1970s. Such academic interest in Shaw, one which dates farther back than half a century, shows no signs of abating. Since 1950 one authoritative estimate is that 110 full-length books (in at least six languages) and more than a thousand articles have appeared. The number of doctoral dissertations on Shaw continues to grow year by year.

All these facts have been adduced to support the premise that Shaw has continued to live as an author and to survive in the theatres and on the screens of two continents for more than a quarter of a century since his death.

The future, however, is by no means certain, not for esthetic, but for economic reasons.[6] Ever-increasing labor and other costs, driven to unprecedented heights in a spiraling inflation, will undoubtedly reduce the number of Shaw's plays that will see the light of production. Therefore, the survival of much of his work may depend on the number of persons in the present and future generations who learn to read plays and to enjoy them in "the theatre of the mind."

We have seen that Shaw, because of his difficulty in interesting theatre managers in his early plays, pioneered in writing drama for readers. He continued this practice to the point of composing *Back to Methuselah* with serious doubts that it would be produced at all.

Comedy, particularly the type Shaw wrote, demands a certain kind of reader or playgoer. George Meredith, writing of the comic poet—in which category he might have included Shaw—says that for him "a society of cultivated men and women is required, wherein ideas are current and the perceptions quick, that he may be supplied with matter and audience."[7] Not everyone can or will choose to enjoy the sardonic humor and irony of *The Devil's Disciple, Major Barbara, Heartbreak House,* or a dozen other of Shaw's plays. So far, however, the numbers of his "congregation" have shown no signs of seriously diminishing. But about what the future holds we can only speculate; as our author himself might put it, "You never can tell."

On the negative side, Shaw's penchant for shocking his readers through the G.B.S. persona has repelled many common readers and greatly lessened his influence. When Mark Twain published *Personal Recollections of Joan of Arc,* he was appalled that multitudes of his readers would not take the book seriously. "It is by jingling the bell of the jester," Shaw declared, "that I, like Heine, have made people listen to me. All genuinely intellectual work is humorous."[8] Yes, but many persons turn away from Shaw's significant ideas because they are unable to take him seriously. Paradoxically, Shaw's attention-getting devices have sometimes led potential readers and playgoers to pay little or no attention to him.[9]

On the positive side, Shaw's admirers can point to at least three solid achievements which usually assure permanence for an author. For one thing, he has left a gallery of memorable portraits. In one of his essays John Galsworthy makes the point that "vitality of character creation is the key to such permanence as may attach to the biography, the play, the novel."[10] Among Shaw's characters, Vivie Warren, Lady Cecily Waynflete, Caesar, John Tanner, Dick Dudgeon, Major Barbara, Eliza Doolittle, Saint Joan—to mention merely a few—are likely to take their places alongside the famous and representative characters of Shakespeare, Cervantes, and Dickens.

Another *sine qua non* for durability in literature is an artistic style. Shaw's mastery of language is one of his undeniable accomplishments. In his years of apprenticeship he read the King

James Version of the Bible, Shakespeare, John Bunyan, Swift, Sterne, Dryden, and other books and authors who afforded him models for his writing. He found Samuel Butler, author of *The Way of All Flesh* and *Erewhon*, especially stimulating.[11] As Butler's biographer states, "It is true that Swift and Dr. Johnson had looked forward to the time when people would write in a straightforward way, but at the end of the nineteenth century Butler and Shaw were in fact pioneering the new, natural way of writing which has insensibly asserted itself and is brought to our notice now only when we read the stilted 'styles' of bygone times."[12] The critic Dixon Scott affirms this opinion: "Whatever else Shaw has done, he has hung a glittering new and needed weapon in the armoury of the arts. . . . For rapidity, poignancy, unanimity, promptness, an exquisite timing and adjustment of parts there is no prose to be compared with it in English."[13] There may be some exaggeration in this statement but, at all events, Shaw's style is readable, flexible, and masterful. It is as if he is talking directly and naturally to the reader.[14] T. S. Eliot once wrote, "Our two greatest prose stylists in the drama . . . are, I believe, Congreve and Shaw. A speech by a character of Congreve or Shaw has—however clearly the character may be differentiated—that unmistakable personal rhythm which is the mark of a prose style."[15]

But style, however excellent, is not in itself a passport to survival in literature. To attain, in Milton's phrase, "a life beyond life," an author must have much that is valuable to say about many subjects of universal interest. Throughout this book, we have perceived Shaw as a creator of stimulating ideas and as the explorer of significant themes, often several of them in a single play. Indeed, there is hardly an issue before the world public of today that Shaw's work does not touch upon or encompass. Dealing with timeless as well as timely questions, he is both a philosopher and an artist. Insofar as ideas rule or at least make a difference in the world, Shaw's writings constitute an important contribution. As we have seen, he was a pioneer in the movement for Women's Rights in *Mrs. Warren's Profession* and *Fanny's First Play* as well as in his non-fiction books. Another current and enduring issue, the so-called "generation gap", is noteworthy in *Misalliance, Fanny's First Play*, and *Too Good to Be True*.

Shaw's ruling passion was the advocacy of peace; like John F. Kennedy, he believed that, "Mankind must put an end to war or war will put an end to mankind."[16] The themes of peace and nonviolence permeate such plays as *Man and Superman* (particularly the *Don Juan in Hell* episode), *Caesar and Cleopatra, Captain Brassbound's Conversion, Press Cuttings,* and *Heartbreak House.* It is unnecessary to recall and reiterate the playright's ideas further to make clear why his work and fame, or a large part of them, are still alive more than a quarter of a century after his death. Aldoux Huxley was right when he declared that our world "desperately needs" Shaw's wisdom.[17] No one could sum up Shaw's achievement more aptly than did Thomas Mann, who wrote: "He did his best in redressing the fateful imbalance between truth and reality, in lifting mankind to a higher rung of social maturity. He often pointed a scornful finger at human frailty, but his jests were never at the expense of humanity. He was mankind's friend, and it is in this role that he will live in the hearts and memories of men."[18]

Bernard Shaw has been compared to Plato, Euripides, Aristophanes, Molière, Voltaire, Swift, and Ibsen. Like them, he has added substantially to "the never-concluded Scriptures of Civilization."[19] So long as that civilization endures, there is ample warrant for our believing that he will rank with such immortals.

Notes and References

Preface

Note. Shaw expressed a dislike for the name "George." Accordingly, I shall refer to him as Bernard Shaw except when quoting others.

1. Archibald Henderson, "George Bernard Shaw: Man of the Century," A Lecture at the Library of Congress (Washington, 1957), p. 9.

2. Dan H. Laurence, Introduction, *Bernard Shaw: Collected Letters, 1874 - 1897* (New York, 1965), p. xi.

3. Stanley Weintraub, "Gleanings from the Shaw Archives," *South Atlantic Quarterly*, LXXII, 1 (Winter 1973), 149.

Chapter One

1. Stanley Weintraub, ed., *Shaw: An Autobiography. 1898 - 1950* (New York, 1970), p. 1. Hereafter I refer to this book as Weintraub, *Autobiography*.

2. *Sixteen Self Sketches* (New York, 1949), p. 89.

3. *Three Plays for Puritans* (New York, 1915), Preface, p. xxiv.

4. "Epistle Dedicatory," *Man and Superman* (New York, 1913), p. vi.

5. Holograph note in Shaw Collection, University of North Carolina Library.

6. R. G. Ingersoll, "Shakespeare, A Lecture" (New York, 1900). Dresden Edition, III, 1.

7. Edmund Fuller, *George Bernard Shaw: Critic of the Western Morale* (New York, 1950), p. 8.

8. Archibald Henderson, *George Bernard Shaw: Man of the Century* (New York, 1956), p. 3. For an exhaustive genealogy of the Shaws and allied families, see Henderson, *George Bernard Shaw: His Life and Works* (Cincinnati, 1911), Appendix.

9. Weintraub, *Autobiography*, 1856 - 1898, p. 40.

10. *Sixteen Self Sketches*, pp. 27 - 28.

11. Audrey Williamson, *Bernard Shaw: Man and Writer* (New York, 1963), p. 21.

12. B. C. Rosset, *Shaw of Dublin: The Formative Years* (University Park, Pennsylvania, 1964), pp. 43, 48.

13. *Sixteen Self Sketches*, pp. 30 - 31.

14. Weintraub, *Autobiography*, 1856 - 1898, pp. 20 - 21.

15. *Ibid.*, pp. 24 - 25.

16. Henderson, *Man of the Century*, pp. 18 - 19.

17. *Sixteen Self Sketches*, p. 39.

18. *Ibid.*, pp. 42 - 43.

19. *Ibid.*, p. 43.

20. Henderson, *Man of the Century*, p. 34.

21. Rosset, *Shaw of Dublin*, pp. 219 - 20; *Sixteen Self Sketches*, p. 55.

22. *Sixteen Self Sketches*, pp. 269 - 70.

23. Quoted in Rosset, *op. cit.*, p. 87.

24. *Sixteen Self Sketches*, p. 118.

25. Henderson, *Man of the Century*, pp. 62, 65.

26. *Ibid.*, p. 66.

27. Henderson, *Man of the Century*, pp. 96, 134.

28. Dan H. Laurence, ed., *Collected Letters*, 1856 - 1897 (New York, 1965), p. 18.

29. *Sixteen Self Sketches*, p. 66.

30. Henderson, "Bernard Shaw: Man of the Century," a Lecture at the Library of Congress (Washington, 1957), pp. 8 - 9.

31. *Collected Letters*, 1856 - 1897, p. 403.

32. Henderson, *Man of the Century*, pp. 239 - 40.

33. *Ibid.*, p. 136.

34. Sylvia Bowman, *Edward Bellamy Abroad* (New York, 1962), pp. 105, 114.

35. Henderson, *Man of the Century*, p. 136.

36. *Ibid.*, pp. 136 - 37.

37. Bonamy Dobrée, *Modern Prose Style* (Oxford, 1934), pp. 11 - 13; 211 - 31. Others who write in the new conversational style defined by Dobrée and exemplified by Shaw are Hemingway, Faulkner, Sherwood Anderson, Storm Jameson in fiction; in nonfiction, particularly E. B. White.

38. On Shaw's novels, R. F. Dietrich, *Portrait of the Artist as a Young Superman* (Gainesville, Florida; 1969) is useful.

39. Henderson, *Man of the Century*, p. 110.

40. Preface, *Immaturity* (London, 1930), p. 437.

41. Preface, *The Irrational Knot* (New York, 1911), p. xxv.

42. *Ibid.*, p. 421.

43. *Love Among the Artists* (New York, 1916), "The Author to the Reader," p. 6. This whole prefatory letter is worth reading.

44. *Ibid.*, pp. 6 - 8.

45. Arthur H. Nethercot, *Men and Supermen: The Shavian Portrait Gallery* (Cambridge, 1954), p. 60.

46. *Cashel Byron's Profession* (Carbondale, Illinois, 1968), Introduction by Stanley Weintraub, p. xi.

47. Henderson, *Man of the Century*, p. 103.

48. *Ibid.*, p. 128.

49. Homer E. Woodbridge, *G. B. Shaw: Creative Artist* (Carbondale, Illinois, 1963), p. 4.

50. *Cashel Byron's Profession*, Weintraub Introduction, p. ix.

51. Henderson, *Man of the Century*, p. 108.

52. See *An Unfinished Novel by Bernard Shaw*. Edited with an Introduction by Stanley Weintraub (London, 1958), p. 32 and *passim*.

53. Stanley Weintraub, "The Embryo Playwright in Bernard Shaw's Early Novels," *University of Texas Studies in Literature and Language*, I (1959), 327.

54. *Ibid.*, pp. 333, 338.

55. *Ibid.*, pp. 334 - 35.

56. *Ibid.*, p. 330.

Chapter Two

1. Preface, *Immaturity* (London, 1930), p. xii.

2. Weintraub, ed., *Autobiography*, 1856 - 1897, p. 173.

3. *Sixteen Self Sketches*, p. 82.

4. *Ibid.*, pp. 65 - 66.

5. *Ibid.*, p. 66.

6. Dan H. Laurence, ed., *Collected Letters*, 1856 - 1897, p. 146.

7. William Irvine, *The Universe of G.B.S.* (New York, 1949), pp. 111, 118.

8. Archibald Henderson, *Bernard Shaw: Playboy and Prophet* (New York, 1932), p. 268. I shall refer to this book hereafter as Henderson, *Playboy and Prophet*.

9. Irvine, *op. cit.*, p. 122.

10. Henderson, *George Bernard Shaw: His Life and Works* (Cincinnati, 1911), p. 217.

11. *Ibid.*, pp. 216 - 17.

12. *Ibid.*, p. 219.

13. Irvine, *Universe of G.B.S.*, p. 124.

14. Henderson, *George Bernard Shaw: His Life and Works*, p. 222.

15. *Ibid.*, p. 225.

16. Audrey Williamson, *Bernard Shaw: Man and Writer* (New York, 1963), p. 52.

17. Weintraub, *Autobiography*, 1845 - 1897, p. 190.

18. *Ibid.*, pp. 173 - 202.

19. Williamson, *op. cit.*, pp. 52 - 53.

20. Weintraub, *Autobiography*, 1856 - 1897, p. 220.

21. *The Perfect Wagnerite* (New York, 1911), p. 73.

22. *Ibid.*, p. 75.

23. *Ibid.*, p. 140.

24. *The Quintessence of Ibsenism* (New York, 1914), pp. 140 - 141.

25. Irvine, *Universe of G.B.S.*, p. 137.

26. R. F. Rattray, *Bernard Shaw: A Chronicle* (London, 1952), p. 324.

27. Preface, *Plays Pleasant and Unpleasant* (New York, 1905), p. xxx.

28. Robert E. Rockman, "Dickens and Shaw: Another Parallel," *Shaw Bulletin*, II, 1 (January 1957), 8 - 9.

29. Henderson, *Man of the Century*, p. 104.

30. *Ibid.*, p. 728.

31. *Ibid.*, pp. 725 - 26.

32. *Complete Plays With Prefaces* (New York, 1963), III, xxvii. (To be mentioned hereafter as *Complete Plays*.)

33. Raymond Mander and Joe Michenson, *Theatrical Companion to Shaw* (New York, 1955), p. 21.

34. Laurence, ed., *Collected Letters*, 1874 - 1897, p. 403.

35. Martin Meisel, "Shaw and Revolution," in Norman Rosenblood, ed., *Shaw: Seven Critical Essays* (Toronto, 1971), p. 117.

36. *Complete Plays*, III, 24 - 25.

Chapter Three

1. Don H. Laurence, ed., *Bodley Head Bernard Shaw* (London, 1970), I, p. 371. (To be referred to hereafter as *Bodley Head*.)

2. Viscount Wolseley's article appeared in *The Fortnightly Review* (August 1888), and General Porter's in *The Century Magazine* (June 1888). See Laurence, ed., *Bodley Head*, I, pp. 491 - 95.

3. *Ibid.*, p. 500.

4. E. J. West, ed., *Advice to a Young Critic* (New York, 1955), pp. 8 - 10.

5. Henderson, *Man of the Century*, pp. 429 - 30.

6. J. L. Styan, *The Elements of Drama* (Cambridge, 1963), pp. 170 - 71.

7. Wilde and Shaw began their careers at almost the same time; hence it is difficult to determine who influenced whom. Yet the similarities in tone and dialogue are unmistakable.

8. Henderson, *Man of the Century*, p. 504.

9. *Ibid.*, pp. 540 - 43.

10. Margery M. Morgan, *The Shavian Playground* (London, 1972), fn. p. 65. It may well be that the subtitle *A Mystery* stems not only from the "secret" mentioned in the closing lines of the play, but also from Shaw's presenting in *Candida* moral and religious ideas as medieval mystery plays do. Often Mary, Mother of Jesus, was a character in these plays, and Shaw at first thought of Candida as the Virgin. See *Collected Letters*, 1897 - 1910, p. 623.

11. Martin Meisel, *Shaw and the Nineteenth Century Theatre* (Princeton, 1963), p. 264.

12. *Ibid.*, p. 225.

13. With his sharp tongue and Cockney accent the actor playing Burgess can sometimes "steal the show" as Sir Cedric Hardwicke once did.

14. Dan H. Laurence, ed., *Bodley Head*, I, p. 549. Shaw himself was shy in his first years in London; and, according to Mrs. Charlotte Shaw, he was a shy person all his life.

15. Charles A. Berst, *Bernard Shaw and the Art of Drama* (Urbana, 1973), pp. 39 - 43, 48 - 54, 60 - 62.

16. George A. Riding, "The Candida Secret," *The Spectator*, November 17, 1950. Quoted in Berst, *op. cit.*, pp. 40 - 41.

17. Arthur H. Nethercot, *Men and Supermen: A Shavian Portrait Gallery* (Cambridge, Massachusetts, 1954), p. 11.

18. See "On Shelley and Wagner," in Stephen S. Stanton, ed., *A Casebook on Candida* (New York, 1962), p. 87. Both Nethercot and Berst, cited above, lean toward the Shelleyan theory.

19. Any student of Shaw and/or modern drama may find it interesting to compare and contrast *Candida* to John Anderson's *Tea and Sympathy*. The two plays both deal with a domestic triangle; yet the husbands, except that both are preoccupied with their professional work, are quite different from each other. The two young men are similar in that both are eighteen and each falls in love with an older woman. It is interesting to note that in Act I of *Tea and Sympathy* Tom Lee, the Marchbanks character, and Laura, the Candida, briefly discuss Shaw's play and its outcome.

20. Preface, *Complete Plays*, III, 113.

21. Rattray, *Bernard Shaw: A Chronicle*, p. 107.

22. Meisel, *Shaw and The Nineteenth Century Theatre*, pp. 355 - 56.

23. *Collected Letters*, 1874 - 1898, pp. 546 - 47.

24. Laurence, ed., *Bodley Head*, I, pp. 657 - 59.

25. Preface to *Plays Pleasant and Unpleasant* (Chicago, 1898), p. x.

26. Laurence, ed., *Bodley Head*, I, p. 680.

27. *Theatrical Companion*, p. 49,

28. *Collected Letters*, 1874 - 1897, p. 557.

29. Charles Archer, *William Archer* (New Haven, 1941), pp. 432 - 33.

30. C. B. Purdom, *A Guide to the Plays of Bernard Shaw* (New York, n.d.), p. 137.

31. Stone became associated in his publishing venture with a Harvard classmate, Ingalls Kimball, in 1893; but, by the time Shaw entered the picture, Kimball had departed for New York to enter business leaving Stone the sole proprietor of the firm. See Sidney Kramer, *A History of Stone & Kimball and Herbert S. Stone & Co. With a Bibliography of Their Publications*, 1893 - 1905 (Chicago, 1940), pp. xxi - ii, 98.

32. Kramer, *op. cit.*, pp. 328, 343 - 45.

33. See letters to Grant Richards in *Collected Letters*, 1874 - 1897, pp. 816, 838.

34. In quoting from Shaw, I follow his spelling and punctuation.

35. *Prefaces by Bernard Shaw* (London, 1938), p. 745.

36. *Ibid.*, p. 724.

37. Homer E. Woodbridge, *George Bernard Shaw: Creative Artist* (Carbondale, Illinois, 1963), p. 45.

38. Henderson, *Playboy and Prophet*, p. 486.

39. For an account of Shaw's indebtedness to Dion Boucicault's Irish

melodrama *Arrah-na-Pogue* (1864), see Meisel, *Shaw and the Nineteenth Century Theatre*, pp. 197 - 98.

40. *Complete Plays*, III, xlix.

41. *Ibid.*

42. Henderson, *Playboy and Prophet*, p. 377.

Chapter Four

1. Henderson, *Playboy and Prophet*, p. 349. Also see *The Shaw-Terry Letters: A Correspondence,* edited by Christopher St. John (New York, 1932), p. 88.

2. Laurence, ed., *Collected Letters,* 1874 - 1897, p. 713.

3. *Ibid.*, p. 716.

4. *Ibid.*, p. 718.

5. Christopher St. John, Ed., *Shaw-Terry Letters,* pp. xxvii - viii.

6. *Ibid.*, pp. vii - viii.

7. *Collected Letters,* 1874 - 1897, p. 803.

8. Christopher St. John, ed., *Shaw-Terry Letters,* pp. xxvii - viii.

9. *Ibid.*, p. xxvii.

10. *Collected Letters,* 1874 - 1897, pp. 821 - 23.

11. Janet Dunbar, *Mrs. G.B.S.: A Portrait* (New York, 1963), pp. 145 - 46.

12. *Ibid.*, p. 148.

13. Henderson, *Playboy and Prophet*, p. 350.

14. In *Sixteen Self Sketches*, p. 178, Shaw indicates that the marriage was without sex. Janet Dunbar, Ivor Brown, and Stanley Weintraub all conjecture that the marriage was never consummated. It is a question on which it seems idle to speculate. A full account of the Shaw's home life is in the Dunbar book.

15. John Mason Brown, "Back to Methuselah: A Visit to an Elderly Gentleman in a World of Arms and the Man," *The Saturday Review of Literature*, XXVII, 30 (July 22, 1944), 9.

16. G. K. Chesterton, *George Bernard Shaw* (New York, 1909), p. 51.

17. *Ibid.*, p. 45.

18. Elsie B. Adams, *Bernard Shaw and the Aesthetes* (Columbus, 1971), p. 43.

19. Augustin Hamon, *The Twentieth Century Moliere: Bernard Shaw.* Translated from the French by Eden and Cedar Paul (New York, 1916), pp. 255 - 57.

20. Irvine, *The Universe of G.B.S.*, p. 217.

21. Laurence, ed., *Collected Letters,* 1898 - 1910, p. 48.

22. *Ibid.*, pp. 65, 70.

23. Preface to *Three Plays for Puritans* in *Complete Plays*, III, p. lv.

24. *Ibid.*, pp. lix - lx.

25. Notes, *Caesar and Cleopatra, Collected Plays,* III, 479.

26. *Ibid.*, 480.

27. Irvine, *The Universe of G.B.S.*, p. 230. Irvine's discussion of this play, pp. 230 - 32, is excellent.

28. *Ibid.*

29. Chesterton, *George Bernard Shaw*, p. 151.

30. *The Sanity of Art* (New York, 1908), pp. 5 - 6. Cf. Ralph Waldo Emerson's words in *Self-Reliance*: "To believe your own thought, to believe that what is true for you in your private heart is true for all men—that is genius."

31. *Complete Plays*, III, 361.

32. See Meisel, *Shaw and the Nineteenth Century Theatre*, Chapter 14, especially pp. 359 - 65 and 373 - 75, for a criticism of *Caesar and Cleopatra* as a historical drama.

33. *Complete Plays*, III, 388.

34. *Ibid.*, 412.

35. *Ibid.*, 370.

36. *Ibid.*, 456 - 57.

37. See Woodbridge, *George Bernard Shaw: Creative Artist*, p. 48.

38. Cecil Lewis, Foreword to Donald P. Costello, *The Serpent's Eye: Shaw and the Cinema* (Notre Dame, 1965), pp. 17 - 18.

39. Laurence, ed., *Bodley Head*, II, p. 430.

40. *Ibid.*, p. 418. In the "Notes" following this page Shaw mentions other sources of *Brassbound*.

41. *Collected Letters*, 1898 - 1910, pp. 393 - 94.

42. Roland A. Duerkson, *Shelleyan Ideas in Victorian Literature* (The Hague, 1966), p. 185.

43. S. N. Behrman, *Portrait of Max: An Intimate Memoir of Sir Max Beerbohm* (New York, 1960), p. 23.

44. Christopher St. John, ed., *Shaw-Terry Letters*, pp. 247 - 48.

45. Henderson, *Man of the Century*, pp. 416 - 17.

46. *Collected Letters*, 1898 - 1910, pp. 215 - 16.

47. Audrey Williamson, *Bernard Shaw: Man and Writer*, pp. 46 - 47.

48. E. R. Pease, *The History of the Fabian Society* (London, 1925), p. 135.

49. Irvine, *Universe of G.B.S.*, p. 221.

50. *Ibid.*, p. 222.

51. *Fabianism and the Empire*, p. 38.

Chapter Five

1. Shaw once noted that in Shakespeare likewise it is generally the woman who is the pursuer and the man the pursued; the only exception he could think of was Petruchio in *The Taming of the Shrew*.

2. Charles A. Carpenter, "Sex Play Shaw's Way: *Man and Superman*," *Shaw Review*, XVIII, 2 (May 1975), 73 - 74. See also Louis Crompton, *Shaw the Dramatist* (Lincoln, Nebraska, 1969), pp. 88 - 89.

3. *Complete Plays*, III, 541.

4. *Ibid.*, p. 570. See also Arthur Nethercot, *Men and Supermen*, p. 128.

5. See *supra*, p. 27.

6. *Complete Plays*, III, 506 - 507.

7. Eric Bentley, *Bernard Shaw* (New York, 1957), pp. xxii, 32, 58.

8. *Complete Plays*, III, 587 - 88.

9. *Ibid.*, III, 584, 591.

10. *Ibid.*, 591.

11. An excellent recording of the First Drama Quartet in *Don Juan in Hell* was made by Columbia Records.

12. *Complete Plays*, III, 746.

13. *Ibid.*, 619.

14. *The Perfect Wagnerite* (New York, 1911), p. 77.

15. Thomas Carlyle, *Works* (New York, n.d.), I, 309. Cited by A. M. Gibbs, *Shaw* (Edinburgh, 1965), p. 107.

16. *Complete Plays*, III, 748. Edward Bellamy also believed that such evolution of man to higher forms would lead to the type of socialism, Christian brotherly love, and the Utopian state as he described them in *Looking Backward* (1888). (I am indebted to Dr. Sylvia E. Bowman, the chief authority on Bellamy, for reminding me of this fact.) Shaw probably was influenced somewhat by Bellamy's concept.

17. Laurence, e.d., *Collected Letters*, 1898 - 1910, p. 858.

18. *Complete Plays*, III, 503 - 504.

19. *Ibid.*, 724.

20. Louis Crompton, *Shaw the Dramatist*, p. 104.

21. Henderson, *Man of the Century*, III, p. 595.

22. Mander and Mitchenson, *Theatrical Companion*, p. 84.

23. James M. Salem, "Shaw on Broadway, 1894 - 1965," *Shaw Review*, XI, 1 (January 1968), 31.

24. Mander and Mitchenson, *Theatrical Companion*, p. 87, 331 - 32. For a listing of theatres which have presented *Man and Superman* all over the globe, see Lucile Kelling, "Shaw Around the World" in Archibald Henderson, *George Bernard Shaw: Man of the Century*, Appendix I, pp. 903 - 44.

25. Stanley Winsten, ed., *G.B.S. 90* (New York, 1946), p. 21.

26. "Ireland Eternal and External," *The Atlantic Monthly*, CLXXXIII, 2 (February 1949), 63.

27. *The Matter with Ireland*, edited by Dan H. Laurence and David H. Greene (New York, 1962), p. 81.

28. *Complete Plays*, II, 443. He first entitled it *Rule Britannia*. See *Collected Letters*, II, p. 376.

29. Allan Wade, ed., *The Letters of W. B. Yeats* (New York, 1955), pp. 387, 407. See also *Complete Plays*, II, 433.

30. *Complete Plays*, II, 510.

31. *Ibid.*, 517.

32. Frederick P. W. McDowell, "Politics, Comedy, Character, and Dialectic: The Shavian World of *John Bull's Other Island*," *Publications of the Modern Language Association* LXXXII, (December 1967), 543.

33. *Complete Plays*, II, 585.

34. *Ibid.*, p. 563.

35. Laurence, ed., *Collected Letters*, 1898 - 1910, p. 458.

36. *Complete Plays*, II, 605.

37. *Ibid.*, 555.

38. *Ibid.*, 600 - 601. This speech, as well as others reflecting self-analysis in terms of the national character, is similar to many speeches in Chekhov's plays in which characters talk introspectively of their Russian peculiarities.

39. Frederick P. W. McDowell, *op. cit.*, p. 545.

40. For example, Masha in *The Seagull*, hopelessly in love with Constantin Treplieff, marries Medviedenko, a poor, provincial schoolmaster. Again, in *Uncle Vanya* Sonya's forlorn love for Dr. Astrov matches his love for Helena. *The Cherry Orchard* reveals that Vanya longs for Lopakhin, who has no time for her or any other woman; and Dunyasha is in love with Yasha, not Epikodov, who loves her. In *The Three Sisters*, frustrated love is pervasive.

41. So far as I have been able to find, there is no evidence that Shaw acknowledged Chekhov's influence on the writing of *John Bull's Other Island*.

42. *Complete Plays*, II, 575 - 78.

43. *Ibid.*, 527.

44. *Ibid.*, 606 - 608.

45. Laurence, ed., *Bodley Head*, II, pp. 846 - 47.

46. *Ibid.*, pp. 891 - 92.

47. Henderson, *Man of the Century*, p. 507.

48. In a letter to Siegfried Trebitsche, October 25, 1905, Shaw writes "*John Bull's Other Island* seems to have failed in America." Berg Collection, New York Public Library.

49. *Complete Plays*, V, 763.

50. Letter to Charles Charrington, October 23, 1905. British Museum Shaw Collection.

51. See Claude Bissell, "The Butlerian Inheritance of G. B. Shaw," *Dalhousie Review*, XLI, 2 (Summer 1961), 159 - 73.

52. Laurence, ed., *Collected Letters*, 1898 - 1910, p. 543. The character of Undershaft is based in part on the career of Alfred Nobel, the Swedish inventor and manufacturer of dynamite, who sold munitions to any nation regardless of politics. Louis Crompton (*Shaw the Dramatist*, p. 115) calls him "a Shelleyan radical and humanitarian." He established the Nobel Prizes, including the annual one for peace, which was first awarded in 1901.

53. *Complete Plays*, I, 311 - 12.

54. Irvine, *The Universe of G.B.S.*, p. 164.

55. *Complete Plays*, I, 433.

56. *Ibid.*, 444.

57. Winston Churchill, *Great Contemporaries* (New York, 1937), p. 38.

58. Irvine, *op. cit.*, p. 271. In 1897 Shaw reviewed Henry Arthur Jones's play *The Physician*, in which there is a triangle involving a doctor's passion

in conflict with his professional integrity. Henry James also criticized Jones's play, referring to "the doctor's predicament, his dilemma." See Meisel, *Shaw and the Nineteenth Century Theatre*, pp. 239 - 40.

59. Irvine, *op. cit.*, p. 272.

60. Henderson, *Playboy and Prophet*, p. 616.

61. *Complete Plays*, I, 112.

62. Alfred Turco, "Sir Colenso's White Lie," *Shaw Review*, XIII, 1 (January 1970), 24 - 25.

63. *Complete Plays*, I, 189.

64. Lionel Trilling, *The Experience of Literature* (Garden City, New York; 1967), p. 318.

65. *Ibid.*, p. 319.

66. *Complete Plays*, I, 1.

67. *Shaw on Vivisection* (Chicago, 1951), p. 1.

68. E. J. West, ed., *Shaw on Theatre* (New York, 1958), p. 118.

Chapter Six

1. The foregoing historical summary is based on William Langer, ed., *An Encyclopedia of World History* (Boston, 1948), pp. 619 - 21.

2. Warren Sylvester Smith, ed., *The Religious Speeches of Bernard Shaw* (University Park, 1963), pp. 50, 52.

3. Homer Woodbridge, *G. B. Shaw: Creative Artist*, p. 72.

4. Stanley J. Solomon, "Theme and Structure in *Getting Married*," *Shaw Review*, V, 3 (September 1962), 96.

5. *Complete Plays*, IV, 318.

6. *Ibid.*, 356.

7. *Ibid.*, 391.

8. *Ibid.*, 451. *See* Rodelle Weintraub, ed., *Fabian Feminist*, p. 93.

9. *Ibid.*, 362.

10. *Ibid.*, 374.

11. *Ibid.*, 370.

12. Ivor Brown, *Shaw in His Time* (n.p., 1965), p. 109.

13. *Ibid.*, p. 110.

14. *Complete Plays*, V, 171.

15. Laurence, ed., *Collected Letters*, 1898 - 1910, p. 900.

16. Maurice Valency, *The Cart and the Trumpet* (New York, 1973), p. 290.

17. Laurence, ed., *Collected Letters*, 1898 - 1910, p. 858.

18. *Ibid.*, p. 900.

19. *Complete Plays*, IV, 723.

20. *Ibid.*, 6.

21. *Ibid.*, 7.

22. *Ibid.*, 12.

23. *Ibid.*, 20.

24. *Ibid.*, 31 - 32.

25. *Ibid.*, 87.
26. *Ibid.*, 108.
27. *Complete Plays*, II, 617 - 18.
28. *Sixteen Self Sketches*, pp. 153 - 54.
29. *Complete Plays*, VI, 87.
30. Henderson, *Playboy and Prophet*, pp. 563 - 64 fn.
31. *Complete Plays*, VI, 87.
32. Lillah McCarthy, *Myself and Friends* (London, 1933), p. 136.
33. Henderson, *op. cit.*, p. 617.
34. *Complete Plays*, V, 473 - 74.
35. *Ibid.*, 471.
36. See Rhoda B. Nathan, "Bernard Shaw and the Inner Light," *Shaw Review*, XIV, 3 (September 1971), 110 - 12.
37. *Complete Plays*, V, 323.
38. Roland A. Duerksen, *Shelleyan Ideas in Victorian Literature* (The Hague, 1966), pp. 188 - 89.
39. *Complete Plays*, V, 344. Dr. Duerksen, *op. cit.*, extends the list of parallel passages showing that Shaw clearly followed Shelley's essay.
40. *Complete Plays*, V, 377.
41. *Ibid.*, 381.
42. *Ibid.*, 406.
43. *Ibid.*, 346.
44. *Ibid.*, 491.
45. *Ibid.*, 332 - 33.
46. *Ibid.*, 278.
47. *Bulletin of the New York Public Library*, LXI, 4 (April 1957), 202.
48. For the around-the-world acceptance of *Pygmalion*, consult Henderson, *Man of the Century*, Appendix I, pp. 905 - 44, *passim*.
49. Eric Bentley, *The Theatre of War* (New York, 1972), p. 413.
50. Alan Jay Lerner, "Pygmalion and My Fair Lady," *Shaw Bulletin*, I, 10, (November 1956), 4 - 8.
51. Alan Dent, ed., *Bernard Shaw and Mrs. Patricia Campbell: Their Correspondence* (New York, 1952), pp. 12, 16 - 17.
52. *Ibid.*, p. 189.
53. *Ibid.*, 224.

Chapter Seven

1. *Complete Plays*, I, 486 - 87.
2. Rattray, *Bernard Shaw: A Chronicle*, p. 201.
3. *Complete Plays*, I, 489 - 90.
4. *Ibid.*, 500.
5. *Ibid.*, 575.
6. *Ibid.*, 594.
7. *Ibid.*, 595.
8. Stanley Weintraub, *Journey to Heartbreak* (New York, 1971), p. 334.

160 GEORGE BERNARD SHAW

9. *Heartbreak House* had its world premiere at the Garrick Theatre in
New York City, November 10, 1920, the beginning of Shaw's long associa-
tion with the Theatre Guild. It ran for 125 performances. See Mander and
Mitchenson, *Theatrical Companion*, p. 179.

10. See Weintraub, *Journey to Heartbreak*, "Appendix: Shaw's *Lear*,"
pp. 333 - 34, for a full treatment of the subject.

11. *Complete Plays*, I, 465.

12. Rattray, *op. cit.*, p. 185.

13. *Ibid.*, p. 186.

14. Weintraub, *Journey to Heartbreak*, p. 293.

15. Rattray, *op. cit.*, p. 197.

16. Henderson, *Man of the Century*, p. 295.

17. *What I Really Wrote About the War* (London, 1930), pp. 297 - 98.

18. *Ibid.*, pp. 319 - 20.

19. Alan Chappelow, *Shaw: "The Chucker-Out"* (London, 1969),
p. 359.

20. *Ibid.*, p. 319.

21. *Ibid.*, p. 338.

22. *Ibid.*, pp. 339 - 40.

23. Irvine, *Universe of G. B. S.*, pp. 308 - 309.

24. *Complete Plays*, II, 10.

25. Meisel, *Shaw in the Nineteenth Century Theatre*, p. 60.

26. Weintraub, *Journey to Heartbreak*, p. 291.

27. *Complete Plays*, II, 81 - 82.

28. *Ibid.*, 97.

29. *Ibid.*, 178 - 79.

30. *Ibid.*, 184.

31. Woodbridge, *G. B. Shaw: Creative Artist*, p. 111.

32. Lawrence Langner, *G. B. S. and the Lunatic* (New York, 1963), p. vi.
Also see pp. 30 - 55 for interesting data on *Back to Methuselah*. Other help-
ful sources on it are Meisel, *op. cit.*, pp. 412 - 22, and Margery M. Morgan,
The Shavian Playground, Chapter 13.

33. *Complete Plays*, II, xxiv - v; lxxii - iii, lxxxix.

34. Hesketh Pearson, *G.B.S.: A Full Length Portrait*, (New York, 1942),
p. 257.

35. Langner, *op. cit.*, pp. 70 - 71.

36. *Shaw-Terry Letters*, p. 163.

37. *Complete Plays*, II, 288 - 89.

38. Lennox Robinson, ed., *Lady Gregory's Journals* (New York, 1947),
p. 212.

39. Henderson, *Man of the Century*, p. 599.

40. G. E. Brown, *George Bernard Shaw* (London, 1970), p. 131.

41. Louis L. Martz, "The Saint and the Hero," in R. J. Kaufmann, ed.,
G. B. Shaw: A Collection of Critical Essays (Englewood Cliffs, 1965), p.
149.

42. *Complete Plays*, II, 265.

43. *Ibid.*, 266.

44. Henderson, *Playboy and Prophet*, p. 544.

45. *Complete Plays*, II, 274.

46. *Ibid.*, 306.

47. Louis Crompton, *Shaw the Dramatist*, pp. 196 - 98.

48. Irvine, *The Universe of G.B.S.*, p. 315.

49. Bentley, *Bernard Shaw*, pp. 171 - 72.

50. H. Ludeke, "Some Remarks on Shaw's History Plays," *English Studies* (Amsterdam, 1955), p. 245.

Chapter Eight

1. Later, however, Shaw accepted several honors: the freedom of London in 1935, the honorary freedom of Dublin in 1946, and in the same year the Borough of St. Pancras made him its first honorary freeman.

2. St. John Ervine, *Bernard Shaw: His Life, Work, and Friends* (New York, 1956), p. 505; Henderson, *Playboy and Prophet*, pp. 744 - 45.

3. Christopher St. John, ed., *Shaw-Terry Letters*, pp. 330 - 34.

4. Edmund Wilson, "Bernard Shaw at Eighty," in Louis Kronenberger, ed., *George Bernard Shaw: A Critical Survey* (Cleveland, 1953), pp. 140 - 42.

5. Henderson, *Man of the Century*, p. 632.

6. *Complete Plays*, IV, 609.

7. *Ibid.*, 656.

8. Stanley Weintraub, *Private Shaw and Public Shaw* (New York, 1963), pp. 200 - 201. An interesting sidelight of *Too True to Be Good* is the caricature of the Shaws' close friend, T. E. Lawrence (the famous "Lawrence of Arabia") as Private Napoleon Alexander Trotsky Meek. A full account is in Weintraub, *ibid.*, pp. 201 - 208 and *passim*. Another character, the Elder, is based on Shaw's longtime friend William R. Inge, known as "the Gloomy Dean" of St. Paul's. See Irvine, *Universe of G.B.S.*, p. 371.

9. Henderson, *Man of the Century*, p. 637.

10. *Complete Plays*, V, p. 620.

11. *Ibid.*, pp. 479 - 481. See *Man of the Century*, pp. 638 - 39.

12. St. John Ervine, *op. cit.*, p. 555.

13. *Complete Plays*, VI, p. 538.

14. Dame Edith Evans and Katherine Hepburn have given distinguished performances as Epifania.

15. *Complete Plays*, V, 648.

16. Mander and Mitchenson, *Theatrical Companion*, p. 273.

17. *Complete Plays*, V, 26.

18. This title was originally used by John Mason Brown in *Dramatis Personae* (New York, 1963), p. 101ff.

19. Henderson, *Man of the Century*, p. 281.

20. For a fuller account of Shaw's Russian adventure, see Harry Geduld, Introduction, Bernard Shaw, *The Rationalization of Russia* (Bloomington, Indiana, 1964), pp. 12 - 13. Another source is Shaw's lecture, "The Only Hope of the World," in Dan H. Laurence, ed., *Platform and Pulpit* (New York, 1961), pp. 218 - 26.

21. *The Political Madhouse in America and Nearer Home* (London, 1933), pp. 17, 19.

22. *Ibid.*, pp. 31 - 32.

23. *Platform and Pulpit*, p. xv.

24. *Everybody's Political What's What* (New York, 1944), p. 282.

25. Irvine, *Universe of G.B.S.*, pp. 366 - 67.

26. *Everybody's Political What's What*, p. 363.

27. Beatrice Webb, quoted in *Man of the Century*, p. 387.

28. *Everybody's Political What's What*, p. 366.

29. *Platform and Pulpit*, p. xv.

30. Henry A. Pochman and Gay Wilson Allen, eds., *Introduction to Masters of American Literature* (Carbondale, Illinois, 1969), pp. 24 - 25.

31. *Platform and Pulpit*, pp. 233 - 34.

32. *Ibid.*, pp. 282 - 86. To Shaw the axiom applies not only to man but also to all living creatures, particularly the vertebrates. His vegetarianism was motivated partly by his revulsion toward the slaughterhouse.

33. Quoted by Archibald Henderson in *George Bernard Shaw: His Life and Work*, p. 152. It is also found in Henderson's lecture, "George Bernard Shaw: Man of the Century," published by the Library of Congress, 1957. The excerpt is from Shaw's address at the Municipal Technical College and School of Art, Brighton, England, March 6, 1907.

34. For a full account of Lawrence and the Shaws, see Stanley Weintraub, *Private Shaw and Public Shaw* (New York, 1963), *passim*.

35. Henderson, *Man of the Century*, pp. 875 - 76.

36. See "G. B. Shaw's Letters to Gene Tunney," *Collier's* CXXVII (June 23, 1951), 16 - 17, 51 - 53.

37. Eileen O'Casey, *Sean* (New York, 1972), p. 210.

38. Lady Isabella Augusta Gregory, *Lady Gregory's Journals*, 1916 - 1930, edited by L. Robinson (London, 1946), pp. 199 - 216.

39. See "The Nun and the Dramatist," Correspondence of Shaw and Dame Laurentia McLachlan, *The Atlantic Monthly*, CXCVIII, 1 (July 1956), 27 - 34, and *ibid.*, 2 (August 1956), 27 - 34.

40. Henderson, *Man of the Century*, p. 474.

41. Elizabeth Langhorne, *Lady Astor and Her Friends* (New York, 1974), p. 255.

42. Dan H. Laurence. *Shaw, Books, and Libraries.* (Austin: University of Texas, 1976) pp. 26 - 28. See also St. John Ervine, *Bernard Shaw*, p. 596.

Chapter Nine

1. Shaw's ashes and those of Charlotte, who died in 1943, were mingled and scattered among the flowers and shrubs of "Shaw's Corner." In his will, he said that he preferred the garden to the cloister.

2. Anon., *New York Theatre Critics' Reviews*, XI - XXI (1950 - 1959), *passim.*

3. For the statistics supporting this statement and for other facts set forth in this chapter we are indebted to Warren S. Smith and the editor of *The Shaw Review* for Dr. Smith's article, "Some Vital Statistics on G.B.S.—Twenty-five Years After, 1950 - 1975," *Shaw Review*, XVIII, (September 1975), 90.

4. Anon., "Dublin's Fourth Theatre Festival," *Modern Drama*, V, 1 (May 1962), 22.

5. Brochure supplied by the Shaw Festival Theatre.

6. On economics and the theater, see Norris Houghton, *The Exploding Stage*, (New York, 1971), pp. 242 - 47.

7. George Meredith, *An Essay on Comedy and the Uses of the Comic Spirit* (New York, 1910), p. 2.

8. *Man of the Century*, p. 893.

9. See Arthur H. Nethercot, "The Schizophrenia of Bernard Shaw," *The American Scholar*, XXI (1952), 455ff.

10. John Galsworthy, "The Creation of Character in Literature," *Candelabra* (New York, 1933), p. 291.

11. Henderson, *Playboy and Prophet*, p. 263.

12. R. F. Rattray, *Samuel Butler: A Chronicle and an Introduction* (London, 1935), p. 24.

13. Dixon Scott, *Men of Letters* (London, 1923), pp. 18, 22.

14. Notably Mark Twain, Ernest Hemingway, and E. B. White are among those who also have achieved this heightened colloquial style of writing.

15. T. S. Eliot, *On Poetry and Poets*, (New York, 1957), p. 76

16. John F. Kennedy, Address to the United Nations General Assembly, September 25, 1961.

17. Aldous Huxley, "A Birthday Wish," in S. Winsten, ed., *G.B.S. 90: Aspects of Bernard Shaw's Life and Work* (New York, 1946), p. 271.

18. Quoted in Edgar Rosenberg, "The Shaw / Dickens File: 1885 to 1950. Two Checklists," *The Shaw Review*, XX, 3 (September 1977), 148.

19. This phrase is from a brilliant address by Ernest Bernbaum, "The Unsought Springs of Civilization," *PMLA*, LXII, 2 (1947) Proceedings, Supplement, Part 2, p. 1202.

Selected Bibliography

The chief depositories of Shaw's manuscripts, original letters, documents, and other rare data, published and unpublished, are the British Museum, the New York Public Library (the Berg Collection), and the libraries of Cornell University (Barnard F. Burgunder Collection), University of North Carolina (the Archibald Henderson Collection), the University of Texas in Austin (the Hanley Collection), and Yale University.

PRIMARY SOURCES

1. Correspondence

Collected Letters, 1897 - 1975. Edited by Dan H. Laurence. New York: Dodd, Mead, 1965; London: Reinhart, 1965.

Collected Letters, 1898 - 1910. Edited by Dan H. Laurence. New York: Dodd, 1972. (The third volume is in progress. Professor Laurence has resigned as editor, and his successor is to be appointed in 1978).

Advice to a Young Critic and Other Letters. Notes and Introduction by E. J. West. New York: Crown Publishers, 1955.

Bernard Shaw's Letters to Granville Barker. Edited by C. B. Purdom. New York: Theatre Arts Books, 1957.

Bernard Shaw and Mrs. Patrick Campbell: Their Correspondence. Edited by Alan Dent. New York: Knopf, 1962.

Ellen Terry and Bernard Shaw: A Correspondence. Edited by Christopher St. John. New York: G. P. Putnam's Sons, 1932.

Florence Farr, Bernard Shaw, W. B. Yeats. Letters edited by Clifford Box. New York: Dodd, Mead, 1942.

"G. B. Shaw's Letters to Gene Tunney," *Collier's,* CXXVII (June 23, 1951), 16 - 17, 51 - 53.

"The Nun and the Dramatist," the correspondence of Shaw and Dame Laurentia McLachlan, the Abbess of Stanbrook. Edited by the Nuns of Stanbrook. *The Atlantic Monthly,* CXCVIII, No. 1 (July 1956), 27 - 34. *Ibid.,* No. 2 (August 1956), 27 - 34.

"Some Unpublished Letters of George Bernard Shaw." Edited by Julian Park. *University of Buffalo Studies,* Volume 16, No. 3, 1939.

To a Young Actress: The Letters of Bernard Shaw to Molly Tompkins. (The correspondence between Shaw and an American actress from 1921 through 1949.) Edited with an Introduction by Peter Tompkins. New York: C. N. Potter, 1960.

2. Sets of Shaw's Works

The Bodley Head Bernard Shaw. Collected Plays with Their Prefaces. Edited by Dan H. Laurence. London: Max Reinhardt, The Bodley Head, 1970 - 1974. 7 Volumes. Index to the Entire Edition (compiled by A. C. Ward) at end of Volume 7. Contains all the known plays and much previously uncollected material, including Shaw's program notes, self-interviews, and some fugitive playlets, such as Shaw's first dramatic venture, the 1878 *Passion Play,* never before published.

Shaw, Complete Plays, with Prefaces. New York: Dodd, Mead, 1962. 6 Volumes. (Now superseded by the Bodley Head edition.)

The Works of Bernard Shaw. London: Constable, 1930 - 34. 31 Volumes. Contains the five completed novels, the short stories, plays, and the major critical essays, including *The Quintessence of Ibsenism, The Perfect Wagnerite, The Sanity of Art, The Intelligent Woman's Guide to Socialism and Capitalism, What I Really Wrote About the War, Doctors' Delusions, Crude Criminology, Sham Education, Our Theatres in the Nineties, Music in London, Pen Portraits and Reviews,* and *Essays in Fabian Socialism.*

3. Fiction

Cashel Byron's Profession Newly Revised, with Several Prefaces and an Essay on Prizefighting. Also, The Admirable Bashville, or Constancy Unrewarded, Being the Novel of Cashel Byron's Profession Done into a Stage Play in Three Acts and in Blank Verse. Chicago: Herbert S. Stone, 1901.

Cashel Byron's Profession. Preface by Harry T. Moore. Introduction by Stanley Weintraub. Carbondale and Edwardsville: Southern Illinois University Press, 1968.

Immaturity. London: Constable, 1931.

The Irrational Knot. New York: Brentano's, 1926.

Love Among the Artists. New York: Brentano's, 1916.

Short Stories, Scraps and Shavings. New York: Dodd, Mead, 1934.

An Unsocial Socialist. New York: Brentano's, 1905.

An Unfinished Novel. Edited with an Introduction and Notes by Stanley Weintraub. London: Constable; New York: Dodd, Mead, 1958.

4. Drama

Androcles and the Lion, Overruled, Pygmalion. New York: Brentano's, 1916.

Androcles and the Lion, An Old Fable Renovated. With a parallel text in Shaw's alphabet, to be read in conjunction with showing its economies in writing and reading. Harmondsworth, Middlesex, and Baltimore: Penguin Books, [1962].

The Apple Cart: A Political Extravaganza. London: Constable & Co., 1930.

Back to Methuselah: A Metabiological Pentateuch. New York: Brentano's, 1921.

Buoyant Billions, Farfetched Fables, and *Shakes versus Shav.* New York: Dodd, Mead, 1951.

Candida. A Pleasant Play. New York: Brentano's, 1918.

Candida: A Mystery. Edited with an Introduction and Notes by Raymond S. Nelson. Indianapolis: Bobbs-Merrill, [1973].

A Casebook on Candida. Edited by Stephen S. Stanton. New York: Crowell, 1962. Paperback.

The Doctor's Dilemma, Getting Married, and *The Shewing-Up of Blanco Posnet.* New York: Brentano's, 1911.

Don Juan in Hell. From *Man and Superman.* Illustrated with photographs from the Paul Gregory Production. Introduction by John Mason Brown. Foreword by Charles Laughton. New York: Dodd, Mead, 1951.

Geneva, Cymbeline Refinished, and *Good King Charles.* New York: Dodd, Mead, 1947.

Geneva. Edited by Gerard Anthony Pilecki. A critical study of the evolution of the text in relation to Shaw's political thought and dramatic practice. The Hague: Mouton, 1965. Bibliography.

Heartbreak House, Great Catherine, and *Playlets of the War.* New York: Brentano's, 1919.

In Good King Charles's Golden Days: A History Lesson. London: Constable & Co., 1939.

John Bull's Other Island and *Major Barbara.* New York: Brentano's, 1907.

Man and Superman: A Comedy and a Philosophy. New York: Brentano's, 1904.

Man and Superman. Edited by Alan William England. Oxford: Blackwell, 1969. Notes and Bibliography.

Misalliance, The Dark Lady of the Sonnets, and *Fanny's First Play: With a Treatise of Parents and Children.* New York: Brentano's, 1914.

Plays: Pleasant and Unpleasant: I, Unpleasant. New York: Brentano's, 1910. (*Widowers' Houses, The Philanderer, Mrs. Warren's Profession.*)

Plays: Pleasant and Unpleasant: II, Pleasant. New York: Brentano's, 1910. (*You Never Can Tell, Arms and the Man, Candida,* and *The Man of Destiny.*)

Saint Joan: A Chronicle Play in Six Scenes and an Epilogue. New York: Brentano's, 1924.

Saint Joan, Major Barbara, and *Androcles and the Lion.* With Prefaces. New York: Random House, [1941; 1952].

Saint Joan. Edited by Stanley Weintraub. New York: Bobbs-Merrill, 1971. Bibliography.

Saint Joan Fifty Years After. Edited by Stanley Weintraub. Baton Rouge: Louisiana State University Press, 1973. Bibliography.

Seven Plays. With Prefaces and Notes. New York: Dodd, Mead, 1951. (*Mrs. Warren's Profession, Arms and the Man, Candida, The Devil's Disciple, Caesar and Cleopatra, Man and Superman,* and *Saint Joan.*)

168 GEORGE BERNARD SHAW

The Simpleton, The Six, The Millionairess. New York: Dodd, Mead & Company, 1936.
Three Plays for Puritans. New York: Brentano's, 1915. (*The Devil's Disciple, Caesar and Cleopatra,* and *Captain Brassbound's Conversion.*)
Too True to Be Good, Village Wooing, and *On the Rocks.* New York: Brentano's, 1934.
Translations and Tomfooleries. London: Constable, 1926. Contents: *Jitta's Atonement, The Admirable Bashville, Press Cuttings,* and four other minor plays.
You Never Can Tell. A Pleasant Play. Introduction by S. N. Berhrman. Lincoln: University of Nebraska Press, 1961.

5. Nonfiction, Nondramatic Writings by Shaw
Bernard Shaw's Nondramatic Literary Criticism. Edited by Stanley Weintraub. Lincoln: University of Nebraska Press, 1972. (A valuable anthology of Shaw's writings on novelists, poets, memoirists, sociologists, sex, and greatness in literature. The introduction deals with Shaw "the social critic as literary critic.")
Bernard Shaw: A Prose Anthology. Selected by H. M. Burton. London: Longmans, Green and Co., 1959. (A rich collection of Shaw's writings on himself, education, music, theatre, religion, philosophy, social, political, and economic subjects.)
Bernard Shaw's Ready-Reckoner: A Guide to Civilization. Edited by N. H. Leigh-Taylor. New York: Random House, 1965. (Extracts from Shaw's writings on poverty, Christianity, crime and punishment, democracy, capitalism, socialism, human relations, and education.)
Collected Music Criticism of George Bernard Shaw. London Music in 1888 - 89 and Music in London 1890 - 94. 4 Volumes. New York: Vienna House, Inc., 1974.
The Crime of Imprisonment. Illustrated by William Gropper. New York: Philosophical Library, 1946. First written as preface to Sidney and Beatrice Webb's *English Prisons Under Local Government.* Also issued as *Imprisonment* by the Department of Christian Social Service of the National Council of the Protestant Episcopal Church. New York: Brentano's, 1924.
Dramatic Opinions and Essays. 2 Volumes. London: Constable, 1907.
Everybody's Political What's What? New York: Dodd, Mead, 1944.
(Editor) *Fabian Essays in Socialism.* London: George Allen & Unwin, 1931.
Fabianism and the Empire. A Manifesto by the Fabian Society. London: Grant Richardson, 1900. (Mostly written by Shaw.)
The Fabian Society: Its Early History. Fabian Tract No. 41. London: Fabian Society, 1892.
How to Become a Musical Critic. Edited by Dan H. Laurence. New York: Hill and Wang, 1961. (Hitherto uncollected writings of Shaw about music and musicians, including composers, from his "ghost apprentice" days in 1876 to his comments on "Music Today" in 1950.)

How to Settle the Irish Question. London: Constable, 1917.

The Impossibilities of Anarchism. Fabian Tract No. 45. London: Fabian Society, 1895.

The Intelligent Woman's Guide to Socialism and Capitalism. New York: Brentano's, 1928.

London Music in 1888 - 89, as heard by Corno di Bassetto (Later known as Bernard Shaw) with some further autobiographical particulars. London: Constable, 1937.

The Matter with Ireland. Edited by Dan H. Laurence and David H. Greene. New York: Hill and Wang, 1962. (Brings together many of Shaw's copious writings on Ireland and Irish problems, reflecting his love for his native land and his pride in it.)

Music in London, 1890 - 94. 3 Volumes. London: Constable, 1932.

My Dear Dorothea. A practical system of moral education for females, embodied in a letter to a young person of that sex. Illustrated by Clare Winsten. With a Note by Stephen Winsten. New York: Vanguard Press, 1957.

On Language. Edited with an introduction and notes by Abraham Lauber. Foreword by James Pitman. New York: Philosophical Library, 1963.

Pen Portraits and Reviews. London: Constable, 1932.

The Perfect Wagnerite. A Commentary on "The Ring of the Niblungs." London: Grant Richards, 1898.

Platform and Pulpit. By Bernard Shaw. Edited with an Introduction by Dan H. Laurence. New York: Hill and Wang, 1961. (Of Shaw's estimated 2,000 speeches this book presents thirty-seven in chronological order from 1885 to 1946. A good selection, well edited.)

Plays and Players. Essays on the Theatre. Selected with an Introduction by A. C. Ward. London: Oxford University Press, 1952. (A selection of Shaw's writings on Shakespeare, Beaumont and Fletcher, Ibsen, Pinero, Barrie, and G.B.S. himself.)

The Political Madhouse in America and Nearer Home. London: Constable, 1933. A printing of Shaw's lecture "The Future of Political Science in the United States," delivered at the Metropolitan Opera House, New York City, April 11, 1933. Also published as *The Future of Political Science in the United States.* New York: Dodd, Mead, 1933.

Preface to *Three Plays by Brieux* with English Versions by Mrs. Bernard Shaw, St. John Hankin, and John Pollock. New York: Brentano's, 1914.

The Quintessence of G.B.S. Edited by Stephen Winsten. New York: Creative Age Press, 1949. (An anthology of "the wit and wisdom" of Shaw on a wide variety of subjects personal and philosophic.)

The Quintessence of Ibsenism. London: Walter Scott, 1891; completed up to the death of Ibsen, with new Preface. London: Constable, 1913.

The Religious Speeches of Bernard Shaw. Edited by Warren S. Smith. Foreword by Arthur H. Nethercot. University Park: The Pennsylvania State University Press, 1963. (Eleven addresses dating from 1906 to 1937 supplement the spiritual themes of Shaw's plays.)

The Road to Equality: Ten Unpublished Lectures and Essays, 1884 - 1918.
   By Bernard Shaw. Edited with an Introduction by Louis Crompton.
   Boston: Beacon Press, 1971. (Reveals new light on Shaw's long
   struggle for economic and social justice.)
The Sanity of Art. New York: Benjamin R. Tucker, 1908.
Selected Non-Dramatic Writings of Bernard Shaw. Edited by Dan H.
   Laurence. Boston: Houghton, Mifflin, 1965. (Contains *An Unsocial
   Socialist, The Quintessence of Ibsenism,* essays, and reviews.)
Shaw: An Autobiography, 1856 - 1898. Selected from His Writings by
   Stanley Weintraub. New York: Weybright and Talley, 1969. *Ibid.,*
   1898 - 1950. The Playwright Years. New York: Weybright and Talley,
   1970.
Shaw on Music. A Selection from the Music Criticism of Bernard Shaw.
   Edited by Eric Bentley. Garden City, New York: Doubleday, 1955.
Shaw on Religion. Edited by Warren Sylvester Smith. New York: Dodd,
   Mead, 1967. (Excerpts from Shaw's works related to religious subjects.)
*Shaw on Shakespeare. An Anthology of Bernard Shaw's Writings on the
   Plays and Production of Shakespeare.* Edited, and with an Introduc-
   tion by Edwin Wilson. New York: E. P. Dutton and Company, 1961.
Shaw on the Theatre. Edited by E. J. West. New York: Hill and Wang,
   1958. (Contains forty-nine essays, letters, and articles collected for the
   first time in book form.)
Sixteen Self Sketches. New York: Dodd, Mead, 1949.
William Morris as I Knew Him. New York: Dodd, Mead, 1936. Also in
   Morris, May. *William Morris, Artist, Writer, Socialist.* New York:
   Russell and Russell, 1966. Volume II.

SECONDARY SOURCES

1. Concordance, Special Bibliographies, and Guides
The most important source of books and articles about Shaw from 1951 to
   the present is the "Continuing Checklist of Shaviana," in each issue of
   The Shaw Review (formerly *The Shaw Bulletin*), a quarterly published
   by the Shaw Society at the University of Pennsylvania, University
   Park, Pennsylvania. Edited by Stanley Weintraub. Included are works
   by Shaw, books and pamphlets about Shaw, and periodical articles and
   doctoral dissertations based entirely or partly on Shaw. Most of the
   items are annotated.
BROAD, C. LEWIS and VIOLET M. *Dictionary to the Plays and Novels of Bernard Shaw.* New York: The Macmillan Company, 1929. Useful book,
   but outdated. Contains synopses of Shaw's novels and major plays with
   bibliography of writings abut him to 1927.
A Concordance to the Plays and Prefaces of Bernard Shaw. Compiled by E.
   Dean Bevan. Detroit: Gale Research Company, 1971. 10 Volumes.
   (The Constable Standard Edition [1930 - 1938] of the works of Bernard
   Shaw is used throughout the Concordance.)

Drama Criticism. A Checklist of Interpretation Since 1940 of English and American Plays. By Arthur Coleman and Gary R. Tyler. Denver: Alan Swallow, 1966. 2 Volumes. Shaw, Vol. I, pp. 186 - 95.

Dramatic Criticism Index. A Bibliography of Commentaries on Playwrights from Ibsen to the Avant-Guard. Compiled and edited by Paul F. Breed and Florence M. Sniderman. Detroit: Gale Research Company, 1972. Shaw, pp. 605 - 56.

George Bernard Shaw: A Selected Bibliography (1945 - 1955) *(Part One: Books.* Compiled by Earl Farley and Marvin Carlson. *Modern Drama,* II, 2, September 1959, pp. 188 - 202. *Ibid.,* Part II: *Periodicals. Modern Drama,* II, 3, December, 1959, pp. 295 - 325.

HARDWICK, MICHAEL AND MOLLIE. *The Bernard Shaw Companion.* New York: St. Martin's Press, 1974. Except for a "Sampler of Quotations," it adds little to its predecessors in the field.

HENDERSON, LUCILE KELLING. "Shaw and Women: A Bibliographical Checklist" *Shaw Review,* XVII, 1 (January 1974), 60 - 66. Valuable contribution.

MANDER, RAYMOND, AND MITCHENSON, JOE. *The Theatrical Companion to the Plays of Shaw.* New York: Pitman Publishing Company, 1955. Indispensable for its reliable information about the places and dates of the staging of Shaw's plays.

Modern Drama. A Checklist of Critical Literature on 20th Century Plays. By Irving Adelman and Rita Dworkin. Metuchen, New Jersey: The Scarecrow Press, 1967. Shaw, pp. 264 - 89.

PFEIFFER, JOHN R. "A Shaw / Science Fiction Checklist." *Shaw Review,* XVI, 2 (May, 1973). Boon for enthusiasts about this subject.

PURDOM, C. B. *A Guide to the Plays of Bernard Shaw.* New York: Thomas Y. Crowell, 1963. (Apollo Edition, 1965.) An authoritative handbook. Particularly valuable is its "Notes on Production" for each of the plays.

RADAR, SHIRLEY. "Cumulative Index to *The Shaw Review,* vols. I - XVIII (1950 - 1975)." *Shaw Review,* XVIII, 3 (September 1975), 110 - 24. Highly valuable to the scholar, student, and any Shavian.

RODENBECK, JOHN. "A Shaw/Shakespeare Checklist." *Shaw Review,* XIV, 2 (May 1971), 95 - 99. Includes Shaw's writings on Shakespeare and works by others about Shaw and Shakespeare.

WAGENKNECHT, EDWARD. *A Guide to Bernard Shaw.* New York: D. Appleton and Company, 1929. Expository rather than critical. Wagenknecht looks upon Shaw as "a journalist-prophet." Brief and mostly out of date.

2. Biographies and Memoirs

CHAPPELOW, ALLAN. *Shaw "The Chucker-Out": A Biographical Exposition and Critique.* Illustrated. Foreword by Vera Brittain. London: George Allen & Unwin, 1969. Rich potpourri of memorabilia, including Shaw's utterances on many subjects from the alphabet to war and peace.

————. *Shaw the Villager and Human Being. A Biographical Symposium*. Illustrated. Foreword by Dame Sybil Thorndike. New York: Macmillan, 1962. Reflects Shaw's great affability and concern for his fellow-townsmen as his chauffeur, postmistress, housekeeper, apiarist, gardener, physician, chemist, and many others record their memories and impressions.

CHESTERTON, GILBERT K. *George Bernard Shaw*. New York: John Lane Company, 1909. One of the earliest and frankest studies of Shaw—it antedates Archibald Henderson's first book—this biography by a friend, critic, and Roman Catholic still has value.

COSTELLO, DONALD P. *The Serpent's Eye: Shaw and the Cinema*. Notre Dame, Indiana: University of Notre Dame Press, 1965. Narrates Shaw's long fascination with the movies, his early refusals to have his plays filmed, and his later capitulation to Gabriel Pascal.

DU CANN, C. G. L. *The Loves of George Bernard Shaw*. New York: Funk and Wagnalls Co., Inc., 1963. Undocumented, sensational, and often inaccurate account of Shaw's relations with women from Alice Lockett to Molly Tompkins.

DUNBAR, JANET. *Mrs. G.B.S.: A Portrait*. New York: Harper and Row, 1963. Highly competent account of Shaw's courtship and marriage as well as of Charlotte Shaw's private life.

ERVINE, St. JOHN GREER. *Bernard Shaw: His Life, Work and Friends*. New York: William Morrow and Company, Inc., 1956. Based on more than forty years of friendship, this book by a fellow-Irishman, though critically biased in Shaw's favor and undocumented, affords many insights.

HARRIS, FRANK. *Bernard Shaw: An Unauthorized Biography. Based on First Hand Information, with a Postscript by Mr. Shaw*. New York: Simon and Schuster, 1931. Not a dependable source. Harris is obsessed with Shaw's sexual power or lack of it. (See Shaw's *Sixteen Self Sketches*, pp. 175 - 207.)

HENDERSON, ARCHIBALD. *Bernard Shaw: Playboy and Prophet*. New York: D. Appleton and Company, 1932. Though this author's *Bernard Shaw: Man of the Century* largely supersedes it, this book still possesses value for the student. It is more readable than the other two volumes by Shaw's "authorized" biographer.

————. *George Bernard Shaw: His Life and Works*. London: Hurst and Blackett. 1911; also Cincinnati: Stewart and Kidd, 1911. Official biographer's first book on Shaw; valuable on the background and early achievements.

————. *George Bernard Shaw: Man of the Century*. New York; Appleton-Century-Crofts, 1956. Final, culminating book of a firsthand study of Shaw extending over fifty years. A monumental work packed with detailed information which no worthy biographer of Shaw can ignore. Incorporates much of Henderson's previous works.

_____. *Table-Talk of G.B.S. Conversations Between Bernard Shaw and His Biographer.* London: Chapman and Hall, 1925. Five dialogues on "Things in General; the Drama, the Theatre, and the Films; England and America; Literature and Science; the Great War and the Aftermath."

IRVINE, WILLIAM. *The Universe of G.B.S.* New York: McGraw-Hill Book Company, 1949. Best book on Shaw's economic, social, and religious ideas as they affected his plays and other writings.

LANGNER, LAWRENCE. *G.B.S. and the Lunatic.* New York: Atheneum, 1963. Illustrated with forty pages of photographs and eight pages of documents. An account of Shaw's thirty-year "partnership" with the Theatre Guild, which produced twenty-five of his plays, including world premieres of *Caesar and Cleopatra, Pygmalion, Heartbreak House,* and *Saint Joan.*

MINNEY, R. J. *Recollections of George Bernard Shaw.* Englewood Cliffs, New Jersey: Prentice-Hall, 1969. A "mosaic of impressions" based mainly on the author's conversations about Shaw with Bertrand Russell, H. G. Wells, Sir Cedric Hardwicke, Rex Harrison, Dame Sybil Thorndike, Wendy Hiller, Dame Edith Evans, Mrs. Alice Laden (his housekeeper), and many others.

PATCH, BLANCHE. *Thirty Years With G.B.S.* London: Victor Gollancz, Ltd., 1951. His faithful secretary for the last third of his life presents Shaw as a terrifically industrious human being who loved animals, birds, and most people, including children. Anecdotal.

PEARSON, HESKETH. *G.B.S.: A Full-Length Portrait.* New York: Garden City, 1946. English edition entitled *Bernard Shaw: His Life and Personality.* London: Reprint Society, 1948. Based on personal acquaintance with Shaw. Lively in style.

_____. *G.B.S.: A Postscript.* New York: Harper, 1950; London: Collins, 1951. Brings Shaw's life to its end. Published with preceding book. New York: Harper, 1952.

RATTRAY, R. F. *Bernard Shaw: A Chronicle.* New York: Roy Publications, 1951. Year-by-year account of Shaw's writing, speaking, and other activities with a great many quotations from letters, prefaces, essays, and sometimes rare sources.

ROSSET, B. C. *Shaw of Dublin: The Formative Years.* University Park, Pennsylvania: The Pennsylvania State University Press, 1964. Most authentic work so far on the life of Shaw up to his early London years. Presents evidence on many issues, including the relationship of Shaw's mother and the mysterious George John Vandaleur Lee.

WEINTRAUB, STANLEY. *Private Shaw and Public Shaw. A Dual Portrait of Lawrence of Arabia and G.B.S.* New York: George Braziller, 1963. Biographical study of a fruitful friendship. Throws light on *Saint Joan, Too Good to Be True,* and *Seven Pillars of Wisdom.*

WILLIAMSON, AUDREY. *Bernard Shaw: Man and Writer.* New York: The

Crowell-Collier Press, 1963. Full of interesting data; pedestrian in style.

WINSTEN, STEPHEN. *Days With Bernard Shaw.* New York: The Vanguard Press, 1949. An Ayot neighbor's and fellow-writer's richly anecdotal book of reminiscences.

3. Critical Books and Articles

It is not practicable to include here more than a carefully chosen sampling of the stupendous number of articles and books about Shaw. Many others than those listed will be found in the Notes and References.

ABBOTT, ANTHONY S. *Shaw and Christianity.* New York: The Seabury Press, 1965. Best book on Shaw's religious thinking. Well documented.

ADAMS, ELSIE B. *Bernard Shaw and the Aesthetes.* Columbus: The Ohio State University Press, 1971. Expounds Shaw's concept of art and his relation to the movement led by Wilde, Swinburne, Whistler, and Pater. Scholarly book for scholars.

BARR, ALAN P. *Victorian Stage Pulpiteer: Bernard Shaw's Crusade.* Athens: The University of Georgia Press, 1973. Unmasks the G.B.S. persona; presents Shaw as a serious social critic and religious thinker.

BENTLEY, ERIC. *Bernard Shaw.* New York: New Directions Books, 1957. Though it is not adulatory, Shaw regarded this as the best book written about himself as a dramatist. No student of Shaw should overlook it.

———. *The Playwright as Thinker.* New York: Reynal and Hitchcock, 1946. Includes, among other things, a highly valuable interpretation of Shaw's ideas. Bentley disagrees with Edmund Wilson's assertion that Shaw was "confused" and unable to integrate his art, politics, and philosophy.

BERST, CHARLES A. *Bernard Shaw and the Art of Drama.* Urbana: University of Illinois Press, 1973. Perceptive critiques of ten major plays from *Mrs. Warren's Profession* to *Saint Joan.*

BOXHILL, ROGER. *Shaw and the Doctors.* New York: Basic Books, Inc., 1969. Perceptive, thorough account of Shaw's views on physicians, the medical profession, and medical science. Should be required reading for medical-school students.

BROWN, G. E. *George Bernard Shaw.* London: Evans Brothers Limited, 1970. Small book with large value. Concise and penetrating survey of Shaw as critic, dramatist, and thinker.

BROWN, IVOR. *Shaw: In His Time.* Great Britain: Thomas Nelson and Sons Ltd., 1965. Places Shaw in his milieu. Contains an excellent brief account of the Shaws' marriage.

CARPENTER, CHARLES A. *Bernard Shaw and the Art of Destroying Ideals: The Early Plays.* Madison: University of Wisconsin Press, 1969. Analyzes *Unpleasant Plays, Pleasant Plays,* and *Three Plays for Puritans* along with parts of *The Quintessence of Ibsenism.*

CRAWFORD, FRED D. "Journals to Stella." *Shaw Review*, XVIII, 3 (September 1975), 93 - 110. Compares Shaw and Swift in their relationship to women. Quotes excerpts from letters of the two authors. Both Ellen Terry and Mrs. Pat Campbell are included. Interesting.

CROMPTON, LOUIS. *Shaw the Dramatist*. Lincoln: University of Nebraska Press, 1969. Criticizes Shaw's major dramas with the exception of *John Bull's Other Island*. Avoiding formalistic analysis, he deals with Shaw's work ideologically, emphasizing the ethical ideas in the plays.

DIETRICH, R. F. *Portrait of the Artist as a Young Superman: A Study of Shaw's Novels*. Gainesville: University of Florida Press, 1969. The only book-length study of Shaw's five unsuccessful works of fiction.

DOHERTY, BRIAN. *Not Bloody Likely: The Shaw's Festival: 1962 - 1973*. N.p., Canada: J. M. Dent & Sons, 1974. Fullest, most authoritative account of the Shaw Festival Theatre at Niagara-on-the-Lake. Reflects a sense of Shaw's place in modern drama.

DUERKSEN, ROLAND A. *Shelleyan Ideas in Victorian Literature*. The Hague: Mouton, 1966. Sound, comprehensive account of Shelley's influence on Shaw.

ELLMAN, RICHARD, ed. *Edwardians and Late Victorians*. English Institute Essays, 1959. Gerald Weales' essay on "The Edwardian Theatre and the Shadow of Shaw" explains Shaw's dominance of English drama in the first ten years of the twentieth century as overshadowing other playwrights of the era.

EVANS, T. F., ed. *Shaw: The Critical Heritage*. London: Routledge & Kegan Paul, 1976. Rich, useful collection of articles in books, periodicals, and newspapers concerning Shaw's plays, but not his novels or, to any extent, his nonfiction.

FISKE, IRVING. *Bernard Shaw's Debt to William Blake*. Foreword and Notes by Bernard Shaw. London: The Shaw Society (Shavian Tract No. 2), 1951. Uses parallel passages to show the great influence of the poet on the work of Shaw, who held Fiske's little book in high esteem.

GASSNER, JOHN. *Ideas in the Drama*. New York: Columbia University Press, 1964. Shaw's relation to Ibsen and the drama of ideas constitute Gassner's subject in this compilation.

GEDULD, H. M. "Bernard Shaw and Adolf Hitler." *Shaw Review*, IV, (January 1961), 11 - 20. Declares that Shaw's "comic-strip analysis of Hitler" stemmed from the pro-Soviet sympathies of a tired old man, who saw the German dictator "through the injustices of the Versailles Treaty and unfortunately saw no further."

GILMARTIN, ANDRINA. "Mr. Shaw's Many Mothers." *Shaw Review*, VIII, 3 (September 1965), 93 - 103. Interesting survey with valuable insights into Shaw's portrayals of some of his women.

HUGGETT, RICHARD. *The Truth About 'Pygmalion.'* London: William Heinemann Ltd., 1969. Based on three years of research into the play and its performances. Mrs. Patrick Campbell is predominant.

KAUFMANN, R. J., ed. *G. B. Shaw: A Collection of Critical Essays.* Englewood Cliffs, New Jersey: Prentice-Hall, Inc., 1965. A book in the Twentieth Century Views series, this collection includes writings by Eric Bentley, Robert Brustein, Louis Crompton, G. Wilson Knight, and Margery M. Morgan. Outstanding is a contribution by Berthold Brecht, showing Shaw's influence on his work.

KAYE, JULIAN B. *Bernard Shaw and the Nineteenth-Century Tradition.* Norman: University of Oklahoma Press, 1955. Relates the work of Shaw to Ibsen, to the French dramatists of "well-made" plays, and to his British compeers of the Victorian Era.

KRABBE, HENNING. *Bernard Shaw on Shakespeare and English Shakespearean Acting.* Copenhag: Ejnar Munksgaard, 1955. A study of Shaw's dealings with Shakespeare over a period of more than sixty years, based on an intimate knowledge of the plays. Presents Shaw as an exacting critic of the actor, though keenly appreciative of all original talent.

KRONENBERGER, LOUIS, ed. *George Bernard Shaw: A Critical Survey.* New York: The World Publishing Company, 1953. Re-prints twenty-two essays by critics of varying statures, including Max Beerbohm, James Huneker, G. K. Chesterton, W. H. Auden, Eric Bentley, and Thomas Mann.

LAURENCE, DAN H. *Shaw, Books and Libraries.* Austin: Humanities Research Center, University of Texas at Austin, 1977. Bibliographical Monographs, No. 9. Fascinating account of Shaw's relation to the British Museum and other libraries. Presents fresh data about Shaw's estate.

LORICHS, SONJA. *The Unwomanly Woman in Bernard Shaw's Drama and Her Social and Political Background.* Uppsala, Sweden: University of Uppsala Studies in English, No. 15, 1973. Valuable on *Mrs. Warren's Profession, Major Barbara, Getting Married, Fanny's First Play, Pygmalion,* and *Saint Joan.*

MACCARTHY, DESMOND. *Shaw.* London: MacGibbon and Kee, 1951. A contemporary theatre critic and acquaintance of the playwright reviews almost all of the Shaw canon. Comments on the players' skill, or lack of it, in their roles.

MEISEL, MARTIN. *Shaw and the Nineteenth-Century Theater.* Princeton, New Jersey: Princeton University Press, 1963. Scholarly book on Shaw's relationship to the popular theatre of his predecessors, including W. S. Gilbert, Pinero, Robertson, Tom Taylor, Jones, and Boucicault. Has a useful bibliography.

MENCKEN, HENRY L. *George Bernard Shaw: His Plays.* Boston: John W. Luce and Co., 1905. Journalistic exposition of fifteen plays; describes "their plots, characters, and general plans simply and calmly without reading into them anything invisible to the naked eye." In 1905, doubted that Shaw would ever be popular.

MORGAN, MARGERY. *The Shavian Playground. An Exploration of the Art of George Bernard Shaw.* London: Methuen, 1972. Stresses the dramatic function of ideas in Shaw; sees the plays as art forms rather than merely channels for his doctrines.

NETHERCOT, ARTHUR H. *Men and Supermen: The Shavian Portrait Gallery.* Cambridge: Harvard University Press, 1954. One of the solid achievements of Shavian criticism despite a tendency to be dogmatic at times. Interprets the main characters in all the plays.

————. "The Schizophrenia of Bernard Shaw." *American Scholar,* XXI (1952), 455 - 67. Without suggesting Shaw was psychotic, the author asserts that the later plays give particular evidence of Shaw's shaping some of his ideas to gain acceptance.

NORWOOD, GILBERT. *Euripedes and Shaw, With Other Essays.* London: Methuen, 1921. Compares the two dramatists as civic-minded artists who opposed war.

OHMANN, RICHARD M. *Shaw: The Style and the Man.* Middletown, Connecticut: Wesleyan University Press, 1962. Explores the various facets of Shaw's mastery of his medium, especially his achievement as a talker-writer guided by his commitment to "applicability to human conduct."

QUINN, MARTIN, guest ed. "Shaw and Dickens: A Special Issue," *The Shaw Review,* XX, 3, (September 1977). Important source of information on Shaw's deep interest in and immense indebtedness to Charles Dickens.

ROY, R. N. *George Bernard Shaw's Historical Plays.* Delhi: The Macmillan Company of India Limited, 1976. An Indian scholar's interpretation of *The Man of Destiny, Caesar and Cleopatra, Saint Joan* and *In Good King Charles's Golden Days.* Asserts that Shaw used history as a means of promoting his idea of Creative Evolution.

SMITH, PERCY J. *The Unrepentant Pilgrim. A Study of the Development of Bernard Shaw.* Boston: Houghton Mifflin Co., 1965. Traces Shaw's early development through his critical writings, novels, and plays. Stresses the religious thinking as evolved in the 1890s.

TURCO, ALFRED, JR. *Shaw's Moral Vision: The Self and Salvation.* Cornell University Press: Ithaca and London, 1976. Book by a scholar for scholars. Critical analysis of fourteen of Shaw's plays.

VALENCY, MAURICE. *The Cart and the Trumpet. The Plays of George Bernard Shaw.* New York: Oxford University Press, 1973. Relying mainly on letters, the plays and other primary sources, interprets Shaw's work from the beginning through *Saint Joan,* with attention to the dramatist's roots.

WALL, VINCENT. *Bernard Shaw: Pygmalion to Many Players.* Ann Arbor: The University of Michigan Press, 1973. Recounts how from the time of his earliest success as a dramatist Shaw formed friendships with important actors and actresses (especially the latter) and advised them assiduously on the interpretation of his plays.

178

WEINTRAUB, RODELLE, ed. *Fabian Feminist*. University Park: The Pennsylvania State University Press, 1977. Collection of twenty-five essays on Shaw and women's rights. Nine of the essays—Shaw's own contribution—are inaccessible elsewhere.

WEINTRAUB, STANLEY. *Journey to Heartbreak. The Crucible Years of Bernard Shaw, 1914 - 18*. New York: Weybright and Talley, 1971. Major contribution to Shavian criticism, it interprets a climactic segment of Shaw's drama written immediately before, during, and after World War I. Emphasizes the lasting effects of war on the playwright's work and thought.

———, ed. *The Portable Shaw*. New York: Viking-Penguin, 1977. Excellent introduction and authentic annotations. Contents include *Adventures of the Black Girl in Her Search for God, Devil's Disciple, Don Juan in Hell, Pygmalion,* and *Heartbreak House*.

———. "Shaw Around the World: A Special Issue," *The Shaw Review*, XX, I, January 1977. Articles on Shaw in Scandanavia, the Netherlands, France, Portugal, and Japan.

WEST, ALICK. *George Bernard Shaw: "A Good Man Fallen Among Fabians."* New York: International Publishers, 1950. Traces the conflict of Fabianism and Shaw's dramatic vision in the novels, the early plays, and particularly in *Major Barbara*.

WHITMAN, ROBERT F. *Shaw and the Play of Ideas*. Cornell University Press: Ithaca and London, 1977. "Unashamed attempt to spread the gospel according to George Bernard Shaw 'which' attempts to proselytize as well as to serve scholarship." Emphasizes Hegel's influence on Shaw.

WILSON, COLIN. *Bernard Shaw: A Reassessment*. New York: Atheneum, 1969. Book of hero-worship with some tempering. Rejects the idea that Shaw was a "late Victorian," but sees him as a Romantic who, like Pirandello, did not present his plays as representational.

WILSON, EDMUND. *The Triple Thinkers*. New York: Harcourt, Brace, 1938. Writing of "Bernard Shaw at Eighty," the critic sees both his weaknesses and his merits. Compares him to Plato, but argues that Shaw failed to integrate his art, politics, and metaphysics.

WINSTEN, STEPHEN, ed. *G.B.S. 90: Aspects of Bernard Shaw's Life and Work*. New York: Dodd, Mead, 1946. Contributors include Gilbert Murray, John Masefield, Sidney Webb, C. E. M. Joad, H. G. Wells, Lord Dunsany, Dean W. R. Inge, Gabriel Pascal, and Aldous Huxley.

WOODBRIDGE, HOMER E. *George Bernard Shaw: Creative Artist*. Carbondale: Southern Illinois University Press, 1963. Presents insights that come from a long, thoughtful study of Shaw's plays. Scantily documented.

ZIMBARDO, ROSE A. *Twentieth Century Interpretations of Major Barbara. A Collection of Critical Essays*. Englewood Cliffs, New Jersey: Prentice-Hall, 1970. Selections range from mediocre to excellent.

Index

179